THE BOURBON DRINKER'S COMPANION

A Guide to American Distilleries

THE BOURBON DRINKER'S COMPANION

XXX

A GUIDE TO AMERICAN DISTILLERIES

WITH TRAVEL ADVICE, FOLKLORE, AND TASTING NOTES

XXX

BY COLIN SPOELMAN

CO-FOUNDER & DISTILLER, KINGS COUNTY DISTILLERY

ABRAMS IMAGE
NEW YORK

Editor: Michael Sand
Designer: Zach Bokhour
Design Manager: Danielle Youngsmith
Managing Editor: Lisa Silverman
Production Manager: Denise LaCongo

Library of Congress Control Number: 2023945945

ISBN: 978-1-4197-6609-1
eISBN: 978-1-64700-906-9

Text copyright © 2024 Colin Spoelman
Illustrations copyright © 2024 Andrew Joyce, except pp. 22, 34–35, 38, 41, 46–47, 130
by Colin Spoelman; pp. 30–31 by Sebit Min; and p. 136 by Danielle Youngsmith
All photography by the author, except: p. 9, Dronegenuity; p. 12, Wally Dyer/scotchnsniff.com;
p. 15, Cornett for visitlex.com; p. 20, AP/Bardstown Fire Department; pp. 23, 59, 65, 124 (top),
University of Louisville Lin Caufield Archive; p. 43, Benjamin Norman/New York Times;
p. 77, OverflightStock; p. 100, Evans/Hutton Archive via Getty Images; p. 109, 110, Uncle
Nearest; p. 120, Brandon Buza/Buza Photography LLC; pp. 122, 123 (third from top), Buffalo Trace
Distillery; p. 124 (center), Lucky 8/History Channel; p. 125 (top), Alamy, (center), Bulleit/Diageo,
(bottom) Library of Congress; p. 143, the Chuck Cowdery Blog; pp. 146, 184, Valery Rizzo;
p. 147, NY Distilling Co.; p. 152, Hudson Whiskey/Whisky Advocate; p. 154, Tony Cenicola/New
York Times, p. 166, Wigle Whiskey; p. 171, Emilio Pabon Photography; p. 187, Koval Distillery;
p. 190, New Holland Brewing; p. 193, Hiram Walker & Sons Limited; pp. 195, 196, Cedar Ridge;
p. 199, Rodney White/USA TODAY Network; p. 269, Jamie Boudreau/Canon

Cover © 2024 Abrams

Printed and bound in China
1 3 5 7 9 10 8 6 4 2

The insights and observations in this book are the opinions
of the author based on his professional experience.

Abrams Image books are available at special discounts when purchased in
quantity for premiums and promotions as well as fundraising or educational use.
Special editions can also be created to specification. For details, contact
specialsales@abramsbooks.com or the address below.

Abrams Image® is a registered trademark of Harry N. Abrams, Inc.

ABRAMS The Art of Books
195 Broadway, New York, NY 10007
abramsbooks.com

CONTENTS

PROLOGUE

There's a little two-lane road that meanders from Lebanon Junction to Boston, Kentucky. It dips and rises along the contours of the land. Cross over a roiling river named Wilson Creek and in a few minutes the forest gives way to a broad meadow. In the middle, an emerald city of corrugated metal, stainless-steel tanks and silos, and great multistory sheds with tiny windows out of scale with human beings stands sentinel in the sun. The buildings are covered in what appears to be black soot, though it is actually a fungus that thrives on alcohol. A railroad track leads across the road into the belly of the facility. Despite the scale of this factory, there is an eerie quiet, though wisps of steam emanate all around, the only clue there is life inside.

As you cross the tracks, a waft of cooking corn curdled with a sweet smell of fermentation arrives, with the sharp tang of something slightly more potent. Steam billows from a series of valves on enormous silver tubes that travel over and around buildings like a lazy pipe organ. Follow the gentle curve in the road and a few more rickhouses stand out in the Kentucky sun, and then the forest begins again and it is gone.

This is one of Kentucky's many bourbon distilleries, the Jim Beam Booker Noe plant. It isn't open to the public, which makes it all the more enchanting and mysterious, though what goes on in the factory is perfectly routine. Distilleries do the alchemical work of taking something prosaic, like corn, wheat, rye, or barley, and rendering it into a marvelous, complex elixir that with a single sip can recalibrate the fortunes of the hard work of a day.

As a drinker, I love whiskey, but I became a distiller to try to understand the black magic involved in making the stuff. After nearly two decades in this endeavor, I'm still wrapping my mind around it. But I also have found kinship with other distillers, and have stood in awe of their machinery, from the labored-over wooden vats of fermenting mash, hand-stirred by paddles, to the gleaming steel lakes of commercial distillers, often built in rooms so enormous that humans meander on catwalks around the rims of tanks taller than apartment buildings.

I came to understand whiskey by its people and its processes, its factories and their surrounds, whether that was farmlands or urban industrial corridors. Liquor-store shelves of whiskey held great stories, but also so many false promises and half-truths, and the only way to get to the bottom of it—all of it—was to get out on the road and see for my own eyes what was behind each label, brand, and bottle.

That journey and those stories are what you will find in this book.

The Jim Beam Booker Noe Plant in Boston, Kentucky, isn't open to the public. Many of the distillers around the country are open to the public, making those that aren't all the more intriguing.

HOW TO USE THIS BOOK

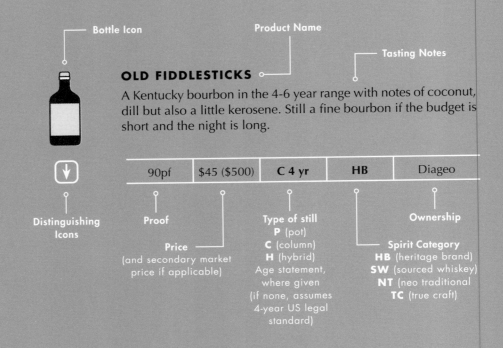

Bottle Icon

Product Name

Tasting Notes

OLD FIDDLESTICKS

A Kentucky bourbon in the 4-6 year range with notes of coconut, dill but also a little kerosene. Still a fine bourbon if the budget is short and the night is long.

90pf	$45 ($500)	**C 4 yr**	**HB**	Diageo

Distinguishing Icons

Proof

Price
(and secondary market price if applicable)

Type of still
P (pot)
C (column)
H (hybrid)
Age statement, where given
(if none, assumes 4-year US legal standard)

Ownership

Spirit Category
HB (heritage brand)
SW (sourced whiskey)
NT (neo traditional)
TC (true craft)

ABOUT THE SELECTION

The tasting notes in this book cover 182 whiskeys from prominent distillers. I included whiskeys that the average person can usually find on most retail shelves. I included a few whiskeys that are hard to find, but only a handful. And most are priced below $100 on most shelves. This is meant to be a walk through the world of bourbon as it is now, a decade and a half into the bourbon boom, for the average traveled consumer who can afford to buy a few bottles in the $100 range. This is not a guide to bourbon values for collectors looking to resell whiskeys. I focused on distillers and their direct products with a methodical approach. There are surely worthy bottles that aren't discussed here, but ultimately, these are simply my own subjective, idiosyncratic, personal favorites from extensive travels in whiskey—and my hope is that, by my sharing them, you may find new favorites too.

CODEX TO ICONS

 CLASSIC: An all-around solid whiskey for its type.

 HONEST: An honest product; a badge of honor for transparency & authenticity.

 SUPERLATIVE: An outstanding whiskey, worth savoring on the most special occasions.

 ORGANIC: Certified organic under USDA guidelines.

 GOOD VALUE: Drinks above its price, a growing rarity in American whiskey.

 OVERRATED: A good but typically overrated whiskey not worth the price or the hype.

 HIDDEN GEM: A terrific whiskey not well known to most drinkers.

 VARIABLE: An uneven presentation due to single barrel or deliberately batched.

 UNUSUAL: An unusual but excellent whiskey, for the adventurous drinker seeking novelty.

 CAVEAT EMPTOR: Some whiskeys are hard for me to evaluate objectively. Consider the source.

NO RATINGS?

Numerical ratings reduce a lot of complex information to a single data point, are predictable (see Chapter 8) and often easy to manipulate. I'd rather respect people's subjectivity and speak to their own preferences. I have only included whiskeys that are 4 or 5 star whiskeys in this book, and what further differentiates them is multifaceted and impossible to fairly distill to a number grade.

American whiskey has nearly doubled in size over the past decade, growing from 300 to 2,300 licensed distillers and sales of nearly fifty million cases. Bourbon, once nearly exclusive to Kentucky, is now made in all fifty states, even Hawaii.

1

SUPERLATIVE

The perfect whiskey.

It's a concept that beguiles the drinker from their first savoring sip. This is nice, but what am I missing? What is out there that I can't afford? What is out there that I can't find? Even if I could find that great whiskey, what if I don't have the palate to discern and appreciate it? These are the nagging questions that have fueled a boom in American whiskey not seen since the end of Prohibition. The internet has served as an accelerant, sending hordes of would-be connoisseurs on a feverish search for limited bottles, without much connection to the whiskey itself.

These hunters are sometimes drinkers, sometimes hoarders, sometimes flippers, but always buyers, roaming through liquor stores, rarely interacting with the sales staff, checking a phone for some perceived intelligence from an online group as to the resale value of a particular bottle. Collectively, these consumers are fomenting an illegal online market, where whiskey bottles bought at retail might sell at several times the original offered price. Scotch has become so coveted that certain bottles are often sold through the kinds of auction houses that handle rare historic treasures or fine art. Even Japanese whisky, once a novelty, is now so sought after that common brands from five to ten years ago are impossible to find, despite murky rules that offer no guarantee that the whisky inside is anything other than rebottled Scotch whisky—but don't tell the enthusiasts and collectors.

These prices may have very little correlation to objective quality, and it can be hard to know if the price drives the hype or the hype drives the price. For those not able to buy these whiskeys, the internet affords visibility without accessibility, easily feeding into ready-made mythologies. Still, American whiskey has seen the most change in the last decade, and laws of supply and demand have been pitted against an industry that has to anticipate trends five to seven years in advance. And lately, those predictions have come up direly short.

The stories of this rise are remarkable. Dixon Dedman, whose family ran a small inn in Danville, Kentucky, created a brand of whiskey to revive a label initiated by his ancient relatives named Kentucky Owl. That first run of a few thousand bottles became so desirable that liquor giant Stoli bought the brand outright in a rumored eight-figure deal. And if that weren't enough, the company is building a $150 million bourbon park designed by Pritzker Prize–winning starchitect Shigeru Ban, with aging pyramids, a convention center, a "vintage dinner train" around a limestone quarry—all on the promise of a few thousand cases and in spite of the fact that the particular batch of coveted bourbon is long gone and will be impossible to replicate.

For the majority who enjoy American whiskey, most believe the best whiskey is in fact something accessible but rare. A pearl hiding in plain sight for the believer with a good palate, maybe a rare "dusty" find at a liquor store on a forgotten shelf—something the average drinker might discover if only they have the adventurous spirit and discerning taste to appreciate it. Maybe it's an old unopened bottle found at an estate sale, the kind of whiskey from a bygone era they don't make anymore. Maybe it's a one-of-a-kind barrel pick, an increasingly common practice for stores and whiskey clubs alike. Maybe a special bottling only available at the distillery itself? A craft whiskey that has come of age? There are even whiskeys purportedly synthesized in a lab environment by engineers who claim to have replicated the chemical signatures of old, lost whiskeys. Maybe there is truth to their claims, and the best whiskey is the one stripped of all the romance and rarity that age dictates?

As a distiller, I happen to have a slightly different view on the topic of the world's best whiskey, and it will probably surprise no one when I tell you that the answer is easily revealed and given away freely, without sifting through a poorly coded website's listicle or enduring the Reddit trolls—or even reading to the end of this book: There is no best whiskey in the world. Sorry to disappoint. Taste is subjective. But that is hardly

Bourbon hunting requires its own camouflage (really an ad campaign for the tourism board of Lexington, Kentucky).

quiet comfort to the bourbon hunters, who clearly have their eyes set on the illusion of perfection.

Yet there are great whiskeys. There are whiskeys that to my palate stand out from their peers and within their type, weird whiskeys that cross boundaries and stretch the idea of whiskey, classic drams that remind me of the perfection of an old Kentucky bourbon or a peaty single malt. There are robust whiskeys and delicate whiskeys; hot whiskeys and smooth whiskeys; whiskey made for sipping and shooting and even putting into a cocktail. I'm interested less in the obvious winners, the twenty-five-year-old Scotches, and the Van Winkles of the world, and more into the multiplicity of whiskey: cheap whiskeys, funky whiskeys, odd whiskeys. These would have been hard to find just ten years ago, but whiskey has become more heterogeneous, rich with novelty and in the precarious position of having perhaps too much of everything. It is tulip mania in Whiskeytown, and the warehouses are full to bursting—so much so that two enormous warehouses in Kentucky have already collapsed under the weight of their own whiskey, waiting for an audience that may be soon be saturated with whiskey galore.

There's never been a better time to go looking for great whiskey, as there are examples of it all over the place, still hiding in plain sight, despite all the din and clamor from online masses, who tend to have predictable preferences and follow a surprisingly small and unadventurous group of tastemakers. And even more heartening is that price often has very little correlation with quality, so that anyone with a few bucks and a good palate can sip beautiful whiskey day in and day out without ever feeling the nag of missing out.

XXX

Why whiskey? Over the last half-century, beer, wine, and other spirits have had their day. Within distilled spirits, vodka has been the clear category leader for decades, though whiskey is growing much faster now and vodka is slowing. That might be because vodka branding is about image and identity, whereas whiskey's storytelling is more about authenticity, transparency, and credibility. Look no further than Tito's, an explosively growing vodka brand that bested staid competitors like Absolut, Grey Goose, and Stoli merely by making a vodka bottle that looks like a whiskey bottle with a false story about being handmade (Tito's has defended its packaging as legally permissible exaggeration).

I like whiskey, but I can also step outside my preference and look at it from a wider vantage. There are other spirits that are just as strong, but they are often designed to be mixed or diluted. Whiskey generally requires drinkers to slow down, its potency something to sip softly and savor, not just a time capsule made long ago but a place capsule too—the record of a field of grain, the rain that watered it, a forest from somewhere else. It is elemental: earth, water, air, and fire all play a role in whiskey's craft.

Sales of alcohol are up and have accelerated during pandemic lockdowns, when people first stocked up on inexpensive staples, then gravitated to higher-end spirits as boredom took over and newly relaxed rules allowed for different avenues to purchase (mostly online). And indeed, the sad alone-drinking of quarantine has also prompted a backlash to the increase in alcohol consumption, as media returns to a favorite topic of temperance: the benefits of periodic sobriety rituals, cannabis-based alternatives, and scary medical advice (from the CDC!) that warns any amount of alcohol consumption is deleterious to health (as if you thought otherwise).

I might be old-fashioned in thinking that the destabilizing effects of potent alcohol can be useful, even productive, if used cautiously and respectfully. In the dozen or so years I have been making whiskey, the world has seen less openness, less humility, less curiosity, even as we hear over and over how much more connected we are. The connection I get from sharing a glass of whiskey always feels truer than so many other forms of connection. When I look at whiskey this way, I know that for all the twenty million barrels of whiskey aging in the United States, it doesn't seem like nearly enough.

Whiskey transcends class, culture, and politics. Unlike food, it is a deliberate pleasure, a nonessential indulgence that is meant to be taken cautiously and conscientiously. Whiskey tasting is convivial, but it is also drinking, and we should be careful not to pretend it is anything more, or abuse its cathartic effects with excessive indulgence, as real harm can come from one night of overconsumption as much as dependence on alcohol over time. Whiskey works best when it is a slightly rarefied pleasure.

But it has been a great pleasure for me and has brought me close to people all over the world, and perhaps this is why the subject of great whiskey endures as a contrivance. The line between opinions and beliefs has all but disintegrated in a polarized world. Being curious or unsure of something is perceived as a shortcoming for so many topics. Whiskey remains a safe discussion, one that may start some fights, but they are frivolous arguments in a world of consequential ones. Finding commonality is a very human desire, and whiskey is a perfect vehicle for that basic and present yearning.

XXX

I got interested in whiskey only after leaving Kentucky. I grew up in the eastern, Appalachian, part of the state, the coalfields that are more known for moonshine, company towns, and union disputes than horse racing, bourbon, and bluegrass. The moonshine and bourbon parts of Kentucky are related, of course, by blood and geology, but in Kentucky it is a great big deal which side of the state you come from. Once you leave, it becomes a meaningless distinction. Kentucky is Colonel Sanders, Derby Day, and bourbon whiskey to anyone elsewhere, and I came to understand this was my cultural inheritance, regardless of how accurate those cultural touchstones might have been to my own experience.

My hometown, Harlan, sits at the headwaters of the Cumberland River in Kentucky coal country, in a mostly dry county that still had bootleggers when I reached the age of curiosity around alcohol—fourteen in my case. These were not people up in the woods making moonshine; they were people who would drive to Virginia, where it was legal, or Richmond— almost to Lexington—where it was cheap, and resell it marked up by half to high school kids and alcoholics. You could get moonshine, but that wasn't what we were after. Zima, Icehouse, Red Dog, and Mad Dog 20/20 were all beverages that I recall purchasing from a bootlegger. They followed the trends of the day—they were businesspeople, after all.

After moving to New York, I'd get asked about which bourbon was best, and for a while, I'd just shrug. They don't teach it in schools in Kentucky, contrary to what people seem to expect. I tried to explain that I grew up in the moonshine part of the state, and I'd watch people's eyes go wide and they would incredulously ask, "You can get moonshine?" I could, and on a trip back to Kentucky, I solicited a plastic milk jug full of the finest I could find brokered by the drummer from my high school band. By sharing that Kentucky moonshine with friends, I grew interested in distilling, and eventually, with the help of a still purchased off the internet, began doing so in my apartment.

That is, of course, illegal, and the particulars of that topic are covered in another book (*The Kings County Distillery Guide to Urban Moonshining*), but I laid a foundation of distilling experience that gave me the confidence to open Kings County in 2009 with my college friend David Haskell and began legally distilling there in 2010. It just so happened that our timing couldn't have been better. While other startup distillers were making gin and vodka, our business was whiskey-centric from the beginning. We began with a moonshine, or what we might call today a "white whiskey," but regardless, it is the whiskey maker's purest artform: unaged distillate, rarely intended for sipping, but arguably ripe for rediscovery next to silver tequila, mezcal, grappa, and other pot-distilled, flavor-forward spirits.

Moonshine was having a resurgence of popularity, fed by a profusion of hobby distillers who had discovered through the internet that they could trade information anonymously and even purchase equipment to distill "essential oils" online, with a knowing wink to the government comparable to buying a water pipe for "tobacco use only." Craft distillers were educating a much wider and larger audience than would ever visit Kentucky's bourbon trail, which was also surging with curious visitors. And a television show on Discovery purported to document illegal distillation, all of which fascinated a public that still clung to the idea, stoked nearly a century ago by government propaganda, that illicit distillation was dangerous—even though toxic alcohol is usually knowingly adulterated with industrial chemicals rather than haplessly formed by a novice distiller working with grain, sugar, or fruit.

We had a hunch the real lasting interest was in aged whiskey and started laying down barrels of it early on. But we couldn't have anticipated just how much whiskey was about to boom. While we were filling half of a five-gallon barrel out of our one-room distillery, the rest of the bourbon industry was cranking up their stills to meet a rapidly growing demand.

And then everything exploded.

A barrel warehouse collapsed at the Barton 1792 Distillery in June 2018. A collapse at O. Z. Tyler and a fire at a Jim Beam warehouse near Frankfort, Kentucky, the following summer highlight the challenges of storing enough whiskey to fuel the surging bourbon boom.

2

BOOM!

In the 1980s, there were only a dozen distilleries in the United States making whiskey, and they are the ones we all know from airport bar bottles: Jack Daniel's, Jim Beam, Maker's Mark, and a few others. Some of those distillers were adding high-end offerings to their classic lines, small batch or older age-statement bottles that were designed as stand-alone brands. Few realized that these specialty whiskeys were made at the same distilleries as the more well-known value brands, and few cared that much to know that Blanton's wasn't distilled at the Blanton's Distilling Company, as the label claims, but at the Buffalo Trace Distillery along with many other brands, on the world's largest bourbon still.

The multiplicity of labels touting small production at small distilleries created the illusion of a diverse industry when, in fact, the whiskey business had become fairly homogeneous, with only a few corporate owners operating a handful of distilleries that all made whiskey more or less in the same style. Specialty offerings did taste different, in the sense that they were older and more robust (and often higher proof) than the flagship whiskeys, but the only things really differentiating them were potency and age, since they were drawn from the same lots as the others. Good whiskey, to be sure, but running a little short on credibility for an industry whose billboard advertising depended entirely on its made-by-hand, "small batch" image. Which left the curious and skeptical drinker wondering how small batch it could really be if they were advertising it on a billboard?

Furthermore, the idea of the independent or family-owned distillery, one that answered to no board of directors or marketing agency's mandate but only to tradition and excellence, proved to be a fanciful fiction. The old Pennsylvania rye that thrived in the Monongahela valley

WHERE IS AMERICAN WHISKEY MADE?

There are many brands, but only a dozen or so distilleries that produce in any volume. Even within that group, four companies produce nearly 75% of American whiskey: Brown-Forman (Jack Daniel's), Beam Suntory, Sazerac, and Heaven Hill. This is an estimate from 2015, but the general thrust is still valid.

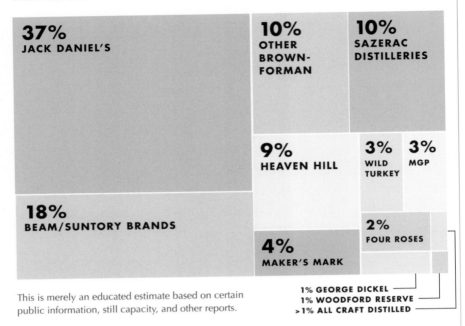

37%
JACK DANIEL'S

10%
OTHER BROWN-FORMAN

10%
SAZERAC DISTILLERIES

9%
HEAVEN HILL

3%
WILD TURKEY

3%
MGP

18%
BEAM/SUNTORY BRANDS

4%
MAKER'S MARK

2%
FOUR ROSES

This is merely an educated estimate based on certain public information, still capacity, and other reports.

1% GEORGE DICKEL
1% WOODFORD RESERVE
>1% ALL CRAFT DISTILLED

was all gone; the remaining big rye brands moved to Kentucky bourbon factories, the smaller brands discontinued. Even the master distiller, once a factory manager, got put out to pasture signing bottles in the gift shop, making internet videos, and flogging the latest flavored whiskey brand extension.

Still, the classic American whiskey tasted just fine, and once one got over the initial insult of being gently misled about who and where things were made, most carried on with the process of tasting through the field of commercial whiskey. Twelve- to eighteen-year-old bottles were easily found at good prices. It was all happy hunting, since good whiskey was sitting out pretty much everywhere. Bourbon at the time was the bison of the Old West, slow-moving, easily found, and rewarding for all. But then things started to change.

Pappy Van Winkle in uniform

By this point, nearly everyone has heard of "Pappy," the mytholog-ical bourbon that appears on shelves once a year, if it appears there at all, and commands secondary market pricing of $1,500 to $10,000 or more per bottle for the three Pappy products in the Van Winkle line. An allocation strategy has made it slightly more available in bars, but only the very committed or very rich have coughed up the inflated prices for a pour or a bottle.

What is this rare whiskey and why did it change the bourbon business forever? The story begins with Julian Proctor Van Winkle, a Louisville distillery owner who ran one of the smaller, family-owned distilleries that shuttered as bourbon popularity began to dwindle after the 1960s. Van Winkle owned and ran the Stitzel-Weller distillery in Louisville, and after his death, the Van Winkle children sold the distillery in 1972, including all but the family-named whiskeys. Soon the grandchildren inherited the Rip Van Winkle name—a trademark that dates to the 1850s and a brand that was popular before Prohibition, even before it was connected to the family with the same last name.

The Van Winkle grandchildren weren't great at selling whiskey until their stock, some of it pulled from defunct and forgotten distilleries, started to age into its twenties. The whiskey, which was overaged by any distiller's palate of the day, was a novelty in the bourbon world, which again, had become very homogeneous. Even some of the older whiskeys on the market were pale in comparison to the extra-aged Van Winkle.

This happened alongside a broader food trend, where consumers had been gravitating to more-intense flavors: sriracha instead of ketchup, heavy IPAs instead of pale lagers, and peaty, Islay Scotches rather than milder highland malts. Consumers liked the robust, richer, woodier, intense flavors of older bourbons. The Van Winkle line was superaged bourbon when there simply wasn't much other superaged bourbon around, and it was sourced from smaller distillers of a sort that didn't survive the bourbon crash in the 1980s, including Stitzel-Weller, the family distillery that finally stopped production in the early 1990s. It did taste different from the other bourbons, most of which didn't even carry an age statement, or if they did, only a few were more than a decade old. Van Winkle bottled flavorful bourbon, even rule-bendingly overaged bourbon, and drinkers used to the sameness of the market responded with enthusiasm. It also helped that it had an age statement like a fine Scotch; bourbon makers and drinkers alike have always suffered an inferiority complex as it relates to their longer-aged, more expensive peers across the pond. Van Winkle's whiskeys satisfied the American desire for universally perceived superiority in the whiskey space.

Still, what was once in the bottles that launched a revolution is long gone, and anyone drinking Van Winkle today is drinking fine whiskey, but whiskey that tastes not very much like those early bottles, if there was much consistency in the first place. Jimmy Russell, the legendary distiller at Wild Turkey, once quipped to me about Van Winkle, "With those bottles, you never know what you're going to get." It was clear to me that Russell, as a meticulous and lifelong distiller, begrudged the hype of a bottler pulling from so many uneven sources.

That conversation was some years ago, and these days you have a pretty clear idea of what you are going to get: Buffalo Trace's wheated bourbon recipe, since the distillery has been the contract distiller for the Van Winkle whiskeys since the early 2000s. The scarcity of Van Winkle led fans to Weller 12 Year, once a widely available mid-to-bottom-shelf wheated bourbon from Buffalo Trace, but that too became scarce, along with lesser varieties of Weller, Antique and Special Reserve. Blanton's, a full-flavored single-barrel offering, became hard to find on shelves. Then E. H. Taylor, Elmer T. Lee, and Rock Hill Farms followed—all Buffalo Trace–distilled products (some more deserving of attention than others). Buffalo Trace has been distilling for almost two centuries and it runs a behemoth still. The Van Winkle label might have been rare, but its distiller made a steady river of adjacent whiskeys, and proximity was close enough for many bourbon sleuths to snatch up other bottles made on-site as a "find," which over time became a self-fulfilling prophecy as those bottles eventually grew truly scarce.

Willett, too, was experiencing the same kind of obsession with rare bottles. Long an independent bottler, Willett gained some notoriety for Black Maple Hill and some ridiculously aged offerings of their Family Estate label, including a 25-year rye. Willett rebuilt their long-dormant distillery, and in 2012 and began laying down their own whiskey. The

The Willett Distillery brought the idea of a small, family-run distillery back to Kentucky bourbon. It had a long history as an independent bottler, sitting on a good inventory of well-aged whiskeys at the start of the bourbon boom.

youth of Willett's leadership and charm of the tours at their well-situated Bardstown distillery helped establish the brand as the premier small player in Kentucky, essentially filling the family-run small heritage distillery idea that Stitzel-Weller once embodied.

As the pace of whiskey sales accelerated, many brands like Knob Creek, Ancient Age, and Barton began dropping age statements. Others, like Elijah Craig, increased their age statement and increased prices dramatically before dropping an age statement altogether. Even Maker's Mark, faced with a shortage, announced a drop in proof, opting to literally dilute the whiskey in order to make more bottles, a decision they quickly walked back after consumers revolted. Media proclaimed a whiskey shortage, a slightly misleading statement since there was plenty of bourbon on shelves, but mostly the mainstream variety. Age-statement whiskey from heritage producers and well-made mid-shelf brands started to be hard to find.

Whiskey, unlike nearly every other consumer product, can't legally be bought and sold online.* It must be physically purchased in a licensed liquor store, creating a shopping experience somewhat similar to antiquing or thrifting: sifting through lots of predictable things to find something beautiful and rare. Bourbon hunters traded notes on *honey holes* (good retailers that didn't know what they had) and scoffed at *taters* (newbies who couldn't distinguish good bottles from hyped bottles).

Food and cocktail culture were changing too. The craft cocktail movement, which didn't derive its name from craft spirits so much as its antipathy toward the culture of rapid consumption of vodka-based, sugary nightclub drinks, focused on smaller, higher proof, more flavorful drinks that showed the bartender's hand in its creation. Bartenders embraced whiskey as an antidote to the colorful multi-tinis that were popular in the 1990s and 2000s. The farm-to-table movement became interested in sourcing ingredients from small farmers and local growers, which set the conditions for an interest in local spirits.

---

* While many websites provide online purchase, they must be routed through a legally licensed brick-and-mortar liquor store, still a relative rarity in spirits commerce.

Small distilleries started to open, first on the West Coast and then around the US all at once. The number of distilleries jumped from fewer than a hundred to three hundred by the time Kings County opened in 2010, then doubled and doubled again. Of more than 2,300 new distilleries, an estimated 1,500 are producing whiskey, a considerable surge from the thirteen legacy distillers in Kentucky that were operating in the 1980s.

As so many distillers have started to release aged spirits, craft whiskey has become a buzzword, but the tricky thing is, no one knows exactly what it is. Unlike craft beer, which provided a flavor alternative to commercial watery lagers, even the best craft whiskey tasted different from though not necessarily better than the middle-grade commercial distiller whiskey, which was at least four years old, made from a handful of ingredients with no artificial additives, and had time, tradition, and price on their side.

There was plenty that was different about the small distillers that were popping up in terms of process and philosophy, even if their young whiskeys weren't an obvious improvement over commercial whiskeys, if an improvement at all. They capitalized on years of marketing from the big companies, who had been explaining that small and handmade were better, even if they didn't exactly embody the marketing they disseminated. So, when actual small producers started to come around, their methods and storytelling resonated with an audience eager for an artisan whiskey, serving a slightly different audience than the mainstream bourbon hunters, but not without some important overlap.

Craft was easy to dismiss as young, but young whiskey can be good whiskey, and early players like Hudson, Balcones, Garrison Brothers, FEW, and Koval found audiences for whiskeys that held up in blind tasting. Even now, some of these are still polarizing, with traditionalists dismissing them, but regardless, they did chart a course for success in craft distilling as a business that has diversified American whiskey and created both local and independently owned alternatives to the mainstream.

In those early days of craft, there wasn't a lot of confusion as to which was which. The good craft distillers were making better distillate that hadn't aged very long. The commercial distillers were making cheap distillate

New traditional distillers are column-distilled whiskey producers that can deliver serious volume but often rely on conventional recipes and don't deviate from the standards set by Kentucky bourbon. These distillers, like Firestone & Robertson in Fort Worth, seen here, are traditional in the sense of replicating the mainstream style of contemporary bourbon as it has been for the past century, but not necessarily pre-Prohibition techniques and processes.

that they aged very well. They were simply two different approaches to the same ends.

Complicating everything, though, was the amount of sourced whiskey that ended up dominating the market, since the commercial distillers couldn't adjust their brands fast enough to sate the appetite of the market for novelty, and the craft distillers couldn't produce nearly enough. "Sourced" whiskey simply refers to a distiller buying barrels of aged whiskey from the bigger, heritage distillers through brokers. Brands like High West, Angel's Envy, Widow Jane, WhistlePig, Smooth Ambler, and Templeton filled a void in the market by creating new brands using the same whiskey the commercial distillers were using. The best of these, like High West and Angel's Envy, did this openly and added creativity in their blending and finishing. Others merely pretended they were actually making the whiskey through marketing sleight of hand. Templeton promoted its small batch nature on labels, and a "Prohibition-era recipe," when in fact its whiskey was being distilled at the old Seagram plant in Indiana now known as MGP* that makes millions of cases of generic whiskey for private brands to bottle as their own. Templeton and several other brands were hit with lawsuits challenging their *handmade* or *small-batch* marketing. (Templeton settled with consumers and changed its labels.) Purists turned away, but Templeton and most other brands kept growing unabated.

These whiskeys may have been perceived as craft by some folks but were not made at a small scale by independent distillers. They were manufactured at a mass scale and then tweaked by independent bottlers. That may be a small distinction, but it created plenty of confusion in the marketplace, where grain-to-glass craft distillers jockeyed for sales with seemingly local brands built from whiskey sourced from Kentucky or Indiana.

Some sourced whiskeys, like Kentucky Owl, Blue Run, and Mic Drop, became cult favorites, but had trouble maintaining hype in subsequent releases. Others, like Barrell bourbon, continued to release excellent whiskeys year over year. It is a difficult business—only three of the heritage distilleries were offering any volume of sourced whiskey to bottlers, and the best of that got picked over very quickly, so unless someone had a continuous contract with the distiller, these cult releases were nearly impossible to sustain, since they relied on older stock that was soon depleted. A handful transitioned to their own production facilities, though very few have fully migrated to their own house-made supply.

For me, as a distiller, I define "craft" by the distillery. If it was made outside the heritage distillers, it's a craft whiskey. Who are the heritage distillers? They are, in order from largest to smallest: Jack Daniel's, Jim Beam, Heaven Hill, Buffalo Trace, Brown-Forman, Barton, Four Roses, Maker's Mark, Wild Turkey, MGP, and George Dickel. That's it. That's

---

* A recent rechristening to Ross & Squibb hasn't stuck; most consumers still call it MGP, and I've used that in the book for clarity.

AN AMERICAN WHISKEY FAMILY TREE, AS OF 2012

This chart, which first appeared in *The Kings County Distillery Guide to Urban Moonshining* (and later on GQ.com), charted the world of commercial bourbon at the time, which was dominated by a dozen distillers and even fewer corporate owners. It showed the relative simplicity and homogeneity of bourbon recipes and brands, but was also a guide for new consumers. If you wanted to try Pappy, maybe Weller was the next best thing?

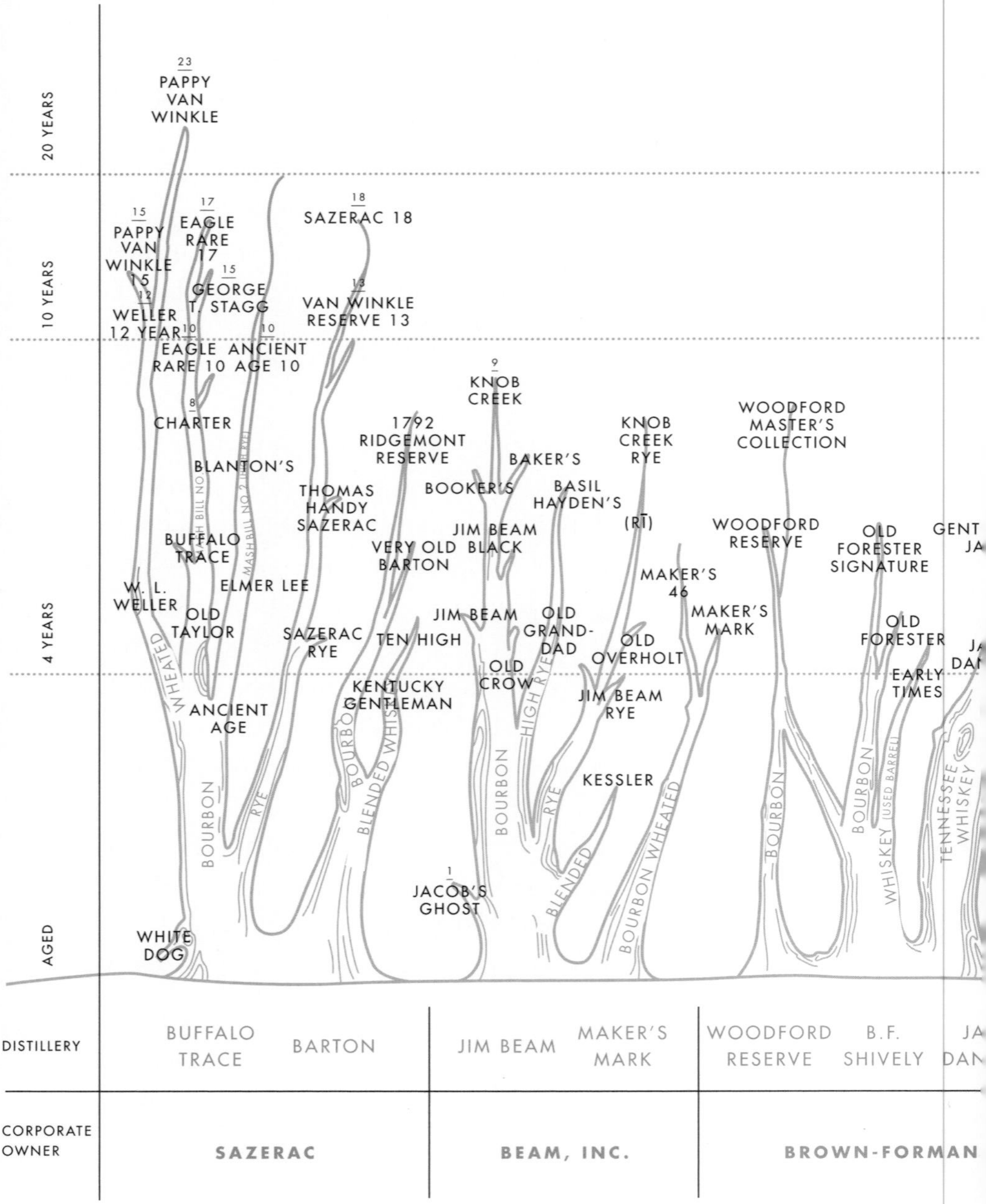

Vertical axis: 20 YEARS · 10 YEARS · 4 YEARS · AGED

23 PAPPY VAN WINKLE

15 PAPPY VAN WINKLE 15
17 EAGLE RARE 17
18 SAZERAC 18

12 WELLER 12 YEAR
15 GEORGE T STAGG
13 VAN WINKLE RESERVE 13

10 EAGLE RARE 10
10 ANCIENT AGE 10

9 KNOB CREEK

8 CHARTER

1792 RIDGEMONT RESERVE

KNOB CREEK RYE

WOODFORD MASTER'S COLLECTION

BLANTON'S

THOMAS HANDY SAZERAC

BOOKER'S
BAKER'S
BASIL HAYDEN'S
(RT)

BUFFALO TRACE
VERY OLD BARTON
JIM BEAM BLACK

WOODFORD RESERVE

OLD FORESTER SIGNATURE

GENT JA

W. L. WELLER
ELMER LEE

MAKER'S 46

OLD TAYLOR
SAZERAC RYE
TEN HIGH
JIM BEAM
OLD GRAND-DAD
OLD OVERHOLT
MAKER'S MARK

OLD FORESTER

JA
DAN

KENTUCKY GENTLEMAN
OLD CROW
JIM BEAM RYE

EARLY TIMES

ANCIENT AGE

KESSLER

JACOB'S GHOST 1

WHITE DOG

Stem labels: BOURBON · RYE · MASH BILL NO. 2 · MASH BILL NO. 1 · WHEATED · BOURBON · BLENDED WHISKEY · BOURBON · HIGH RYE · RYE · BLENDED · BOURBON WHEATED · BOURBON · BOURBON (USED BARREL) · TENNESSEE WHISKEY

DISTILLERY								
BUFFALO TRACE	BARTON		JIM BEAM	MAKER'S MARK		WOODFORD RESERVE	B.F. SHIVELY	JA DAN

CORPORATE OWNER				
SAZERAC		BEAM, INC.		BROWN-FORMAN

It would be impossible to update this chart for today, as many brands have new ownership, significant new distillers have opened, brands have reformulated, older age statements were depleted, and many smaller distillers were omitted—this was intended to show the world of commercial or heritage distillers at the time and represents the last time the world of bourbon could be drawn so plainly. A field of upstart blades of grass could have represented the hundreds of new smaller distillers in and beyond Kentucky that were changing the landscape forever and today would be entwined with these larger branches an impenetrable thicket of distilleries, brands, and expressions.

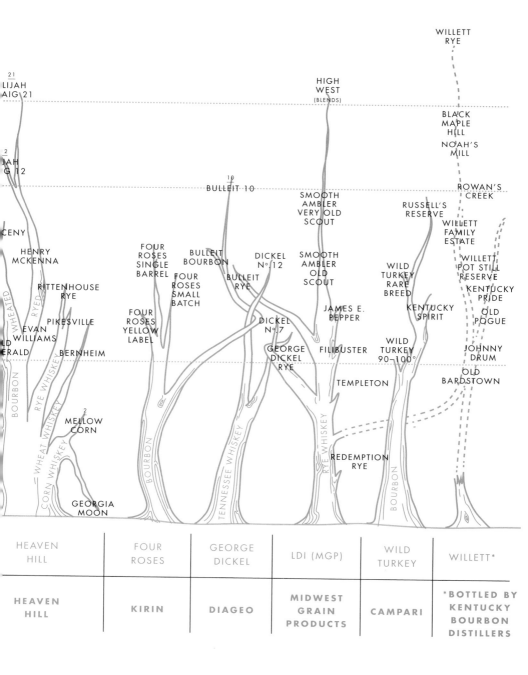

the entire landscape of commercial American whiskey distillation. I call them the commercial, heritage, or legacy distillers, and by my estimate, they account for 99 percent of all whiskey sold in America today. If it is sourced from one of these distillers, I don't consider it to be craft whiskey; I consider it to be sourced whiskey. However, I should point out that while at the beginning of the craft boom, there was clear distinction between craft and commercial distillers, the line is getting hazy.

There is now a new category of distillers, like Castle & Key, Wilderness Trail, and Bardstown Bourbon Company, that are actually larger than some of the legacy players. Others, like New Riff, Angel's Envy, Firestone & Robertson, and Tennessee Distilling, are large enough that calling them craft is almost silly, since they are clearly in a different league than the guy in a garage with a pot still, which describes even some of the more well-known craft players. For now, I'm calling them new traditional distillers, since they are mostly in the South and make fairly standard mash bill* bourbon and rye in column stills.

Even if these new traditional distilleries are huge compared to other well-known craft distillers, the market is still dominated by whiskeys from the legacy distillers, since those remain the only whiskeys that are mature in quantity. Federal whiskey production records show American whiskey production doubled from 2011 to 2017, but sales have gone up only by 44 percent. Much of that whiskey is still too young to release, but it fore-shadows a future where there is more supply than demand, which hasn't slowed the steady stream of announcements for new multimillion-dollar distilleries or expansion projects.

Another way to think about the future of whiskey is to track the pinch points of the bourbon boom. First the contracts for new distillate dried up or were curtailed, suggesting that distillation was maxed out in 2012. Then there was a barrel shortage due to an unusual growing season and high demand at cooperages in the two years that followed. Now there is

---

* A mash bill, or mashbill, is a recipe of grains that go into a whiskey recipe, usually listed by percentage. Bourbon, for instance, must have a mash bill that includes 51 percent corn or more. Most mash bills include a malted grain, usually barley, for starch conversion, but enzymes can be added separately.

a shortage in the industry of warehouse space as more whiskey barrels pile up. But a flood of two-year whiskey in 2024 foreshadows a deluge of mature whiskey starting in 2027, and it is anybody's guess how that will play out in a fickle market. In an era when consumers are abandoning beer for spiked seltzer, will whiskey give way back to vodka? Will the next generation even drink alcohol?

All of this merely bolsters my claim that we are in a golden era for whiskey. The 2020 pandemic created more access to whiskey by removing some barriers to shipping and e-commerce that made specialty bottles easier to find (and quicker to sell out). And though media reports warned that small distillers were in danger of closing, we didn't see that happen. Most distillers found ways to pivot; some even sold hand sanitizer by distilling beer that was going stale at closed restaurants into high-proof alcohol, showing creativity and resilience.

Still, even more disruptive to whiskey than the pandemic will be the mere fact of having more whiskey than there is demand. We haven't yet seen a culling of the herd, and when we do, some great,

The cooperage shop at Stitzel-Weller distillery, a holy site for American whiskey, and a peaceful interlude on my travels

THE RELATIVE SIZE OF COLUMN-STILL DISTILLERS

Most American whiskey is made at two dozen column-still distilleries located throughout the Ohio River Valley, mostly in Kentucky. This graphic shows every distiller with a 24-inch column or greater, and the relative capacity of established distillers and ambitious newcomers. American whiskey is expanding rapidly, and this overview will quickly be outdated as distillers race to expand their

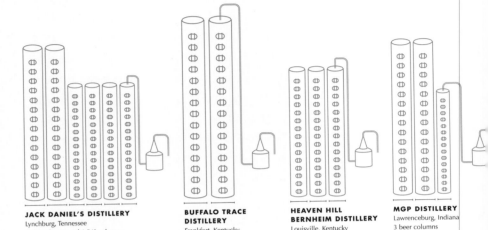

JACK DANIEL'S DISTILLERY
Lynchburg, Tennessee
2 72" columns and 4 54" columns

BUFFALO TRACE DISTILLERY
Frankfort, Kentucky
2 84" columns

HEAVEN HILL BERNHEIM DISTILLERY
Louisville, Kentucky
3 60" columns

MGP DISTILLERY
Lawrenceburg, Indiana
3 beer columns
Size approximate

DIAGEO DISTILLERY
Lebanon, Kentucky
Configuration unknown
Based on 10M proof gallon
annual output

MAKER'S MARK DISTILLERY
Loretto, Kentucky
3 36" columns

BARDSTOWN BOURBON CO.
Bardstown, Kentucky
3 36" columns
under construction

WILD TURKEY DISTILLERY
Tyrone, Kentucky
60" column

HEAVEN HILL SPRINGS
Bardstown, Kentucky
60" column
under construction

GREEN RIVER DISTILLERY
Owensboro, Kent
54" column

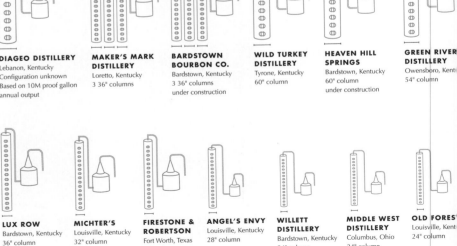

LUX ROW
Bardstown, Kentucky
36" column

MICHTER'S
Louisville, Kentucky
32" column

FIRESTONE & ROBERTSON
Fort Worth, Texas
32" column

ANGEL'S ENVY
Louisville, Kentucky
28" column

WILLETT DISTILLERY
Bardstown, Kentucky
24" column

MIDDLE WEST DISTILLERY
Columbus, Ohio
24" column

OLD FORES
Louisville, Kent
24" column

capacity. But it also gives a sense of scale. A distiller's capacity is determined by the diameter (not the height) of their stills, and this give us a sense for who is making 98 to 99% of American whiskey.

For a sense of further scale, the largest distiller, Jack Daniel's, makes about 2,400 barrels a day. Wilderness Trail, a midsize newcomer, makes about 240.

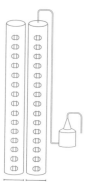

JIM BEAM BOOKER NOE
Boston, Kentucky
2 72" columns

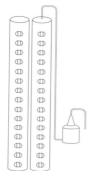

FOUR ROSES DISTILLERY
Lawrenceburg, Kentucky
2 72" columns

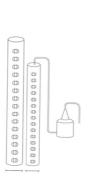

BROWN-FORMAN DISTILLERY
Louisville, Kentucky
48" and 60" columns

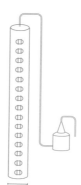

JIM BEAM DISTILLERY
Clermont, Kentucky
72" column

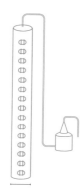

BARTON 1792
Bardstown, Kentucky
72" column

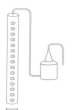

CASCADE HOLLOW DISTILLERY (DICKEL)
Tullahoma, Tennessee
42" column

BULLEIT DISTILLERY
Shelbyville, Kentucky
42" column

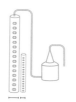

WILDERNESS TRAIL
Danville, Kentucky
36" and 18" columns

CASTLE & KEY
Millville, Kentucky
32" and 24" columns

TENNESSEE DISTILLING
Robertson, Tennessee
36" column

SOUTHERN DISTILLING
Louisville, Kentucky
18" column

FINGER LAKES DISTILLING
Burdett, New York
18" column

PEEERLESS DISTILLERY
Louisville, Kentucky
14" column

JEPTHA CREED DISITLLERY
Shelbyville, Kentucky
12" column

JAMES PEPPER DISTILLERY
Lexington, Kentucky
12" column

SAZERAC OF TENNESSEE
Murfreesboro, Tennessee
24" column

SAGAMORE SPIRITS
Baltimore, Maryland
24" column

NEW RIFF DISTILLERY
Newport, Kentucky
24" column

RABBIT HOLE DISTILLERY
Louisville, Kentucky
24" column

BLACK DIRT DISTILLERY
Warwick, New York
24" column

WHAT IS AMERICAN WHISKEY?

Many are looking for authenticity in whiskey. There are four kinds of commercial whiskey: heritage, neo-traditional, sourced, and craft.

HERITAGE BRANDS

Distilled at large distilleries in the Ohio River watershed and typically make up the majority of commercial whiskey.

EXAMPLES: Barton, Buffalo Trace, Four Roses, George Dickel, Heaven Hill, Jack Daniel's, Jim Beam, Maker's Mark, Old Forester, Wild Turkey, Woodford Reserve

SOURCED WHISKEYS

Brands that don't typically distill the majority of whiskeys that go into their brands, even if they operate a token still on-site. Innovation is usually in blending and finishing.

EXAMPLES: Barrell Bourbon, High West, Kentucky Owl, Lost Lantern, Milam & Greene, Pinhook, Uncle Nearest, WhistlePig

NEO-TRADITIONAL WHISKEYS

Distilled at newer, 24" or larger column-still setups, generally in the South, at distilleries opened after 2005.

EXAMPLES: Angel's Envy, Bardstown Bourbon Co., Castle & Key, Firestone & Robertson, New Riff, Sagamore Spirits, Taconic, Tennessee Distilling, Wilderness Trail, Willett

TRUE-CRAFT WHISKEYS

Made on smaller equipment columns smaller than 24," pot stills, or hybrid stills and focus on ingredients, recipes, and creativity.

EXAMPLES: Balcones, Coppersea, Corsair, Few, Garrison Brothers, Hudson Whiskey, Kings County, Koval, Leopold Brothers, Peerless, Westland, Westward, Woodinville

underfinanced whiskeys will be lost. Those that survive will do so because they can make a good product and a clear argument for what defines their whiskey. The best distilleries outside of Kentucky aren't trying to replicate Kentucky bourbon, and the best new distillers in Kentucky are trying to reclaim authenticity from bigger players that had gotten a little lost. What to make of this new landscape of whiskey? How will we understand the variety and complexity of whiskey that is flooding the country that bears little resemblance to the past fifty years of production?

I set off to travel around the country to answer these questions with an open mind, a thirsty palate, and a curious heart, setting aside my own preconceptions from marketing and branding. I started visiting distillers, the places and people who make whiskey, and tasting their bottles in some cases for the first time, in others starting from scratch with a fresh perspective, in search of truly great whiskey.

The Old Forester Distillery on Main Street is an architectural masterpiece and a remarkable adaptation to a historic site. But despite being a decent-sized operational distillery, most of the whiskey in Old Forester bottles is made at a distillery elsewhere in Louisville.

THE WHISKY MAP OF SCOTLAND

The heritage of Scotch whisky can be traced to several regions that have been articulated in slightly different ways over the years, but as an organizing principle seem to endure.

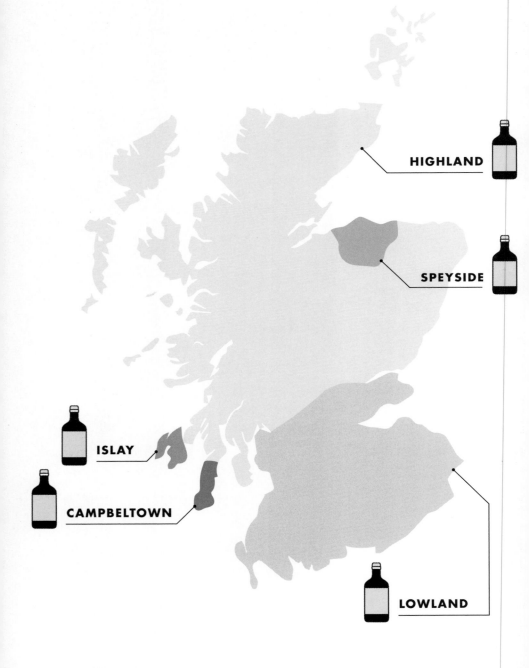

3

CARTOGRAPHY

Any well-planned trip begins with a map. While there are maps of wine regions all over the world, whiskey has yet to be subjected to much mapping. Scotland is an exception, and there is a well-known map that identifies the regions of Scotch whisky. Its origins go back at least a hundred years. As the distilling business has shifted geographically, so have the regions recognized by the Scotch Whisky Association (SWA), the trade organization representing Scotch distillers.

Theoretically, the regions suggest flavor differences that carry from distiller to distiller in a particular region. This is only nominally true, and the idea of terroir in whiskey is a hotly debated topic. *Terroir*, a French word meant to encompass all of the environmental factors that affect winemaking, like climate and soil composition, certainly plays a role in whiskey-making, but so do the talent and agenda of the distiller and the tools they have to work with, as well as tradition and economic or commercial imperatives.

If anything, delineating regions in whiskey feels very arbitrary for modern Scotch (in truth, winemakers aren't quite sure of geographical regions either, or of *terroir*). But as an organizing principle, it has outlasted many others, perhaps because it is absolute and simple. In fact, all world whiskeys are first divided by geography, with Scotland, the United States, Canada, Ireland, and Japan being most known for whiskeys. But if countries were regions, these too would be problematic: Japanese whiskey isn't all that different from Scotch in style and flavor, and Irish and Canadian whiskeys have loose rules that don't always indicate strong flavor differentiation.

The spirits writer David Wondrich has proposed another taxonomy for whiskey that puts culture and production techniques over geography.

His categories are pot still* whiskey for Scotch, Japanese, and Irish whiskeys distilled from barley in pot stills. He proposes mash bill whiskey for column-distilled⁺ whiskeys roughly in the American and Canadian model. A third type is grain whiskey for more neutral whiskeys distilled to a higher proof in column stills. A final, catch-all type is blended whiskeys, which covers any mix of the above.

If Wondrich's categories are clear and logical to the distiller, most consumers don't really care that much about mechanism of distillation, or whether a whiskey has been blended (straight whiskey typically mixed with more neutral spirit) or mingled (a blend of straight whiskeys). Consumers are interested in knowing the where and when of a whiskey, and even the why. And that brings us back to geography and regionalization.

XXX

In 2015, a group of new distillers gathered at the American Craft Spirits Association, in Denver. New York whiskey makers had done very well in the competition, with several picking up medals. Nicole Austin from Kings County, Christopher Williams of Coppersea, and a few others got together and proposed the idea of a New York–style rye whiskey. The rough parameters were set as a whiskey distilled in New York State from at least 75 percent New York–grown rye that meets the criteria for straight rye whiskey from the federal government (there is also a requirement for

* Pot stills are crude devices that vaporize a liquid on one side of the still and condense the vapor back to liquid, the most fundamental process of distillation. The simplest pot still will often resemble a copper pot over a fire, with a tube running to a coil of pipe in a bath of cold water. This most basic still type, also called an alembic, is used for spirits that retain a lot of character from the fermented liquid inside them. Pot stills are common to traditional Scotch whisky, Cognacs and fruit brandies, traditional tequila, and some rums—and often require two separate distillations to achieve a desired strength and flavor (though some Irish whiskeys are triple-distilled). Pot stills are run by batch, and give the distiller latitude over flavor in each batch.
† Column stills were invented in the early 1800s and can continuously distill a steady feed of fermented liquid into alcohol. Formed by a vertical pipe with various plates or baffles, steam is fed into the bottom of the still to heat the cascading beer, and the still is tuned so only alcohol vapor emerges. Column stills are generally used for more-neutral spirits, but often do a first pass in North American whiskeys, followed by a second distillation in a doubler or thumper, which more closely resembles a pot still. The flavor merits of pot and column stills are hotly debated, but column stills are unquestionably more efficient and used for the production of nearly all commercial American whiskey.

WHISKEY MAP OF AMERICA, ca. 2000

America has two distinctive whiskey regions: Kentucky, making bourbon and rye; and Tennessee, which makes bourbon with a minor process tweak called Tennessee whiskey.

low barrel-entry proof,* and a scrapped idea about distilling seasons). If a New York whiskey satisfies those rules, you could call your whiskey "Empire Rye" and get a little logo from the newly convened trade organization on the label.

A group of seven distillers led the pilot program and began to lay down inventory. As many craft producers were asking themselves how to differentiate their whiskey from Kentucky rye, Empire Rye became a clear answer to the high-corn, column-distilled ryes coming from the heritage distillers and, more importantly, an answer to the question of how small, new distillers might carve a place for themselves in the face of a persistent penchant to categorize whiskey by geography.

---

* The proof at which a spirit is entered into a barrel. For bourbon and rye whiskey made in the US, this is 125 proof or less. Some distillers argue a lower entry proof makes a more approachable spirit, but there are cost advantages to higher entry proof, as the barrel is the most expensive ingredient in whiskey-making, and more alcohol in the barrel means fewer barrels and less physical warehouse space.

Rye whiskey was America's first whiskey; it proliferated in New York, Pennsylvania, Maryland, and in other parts of the Northeast from colonial times through the Gilded Age. It was not until 1885 that corn surpassed rye as the primary grain in American whiskey, though both were used heavily until Prohibition. Within rye there were Monongahela rye (a high-rye straight whiskey) and Maryland rye, which had a higher corn content. Some newspaper advertisements point to an "Onandago" rye, a style (or perhaps a brand) that once existed in western New York before Prohibition. As whiskey popularity dwindled in the 1960s and '70s, the great old rye distilleries that were left (Schenley, Overholt, and Michter's, to name a few) were shuttered and the brands moved to bourbon distilleries in Kentucky or Indiana. Rye whiskey completely died out in the region for which it was known, only to be resuscitated by small distillers in the 2000s like Dad's Hat, Wigle, and Hudson.

Could modern-day New York distillers create a rye whiskey that would stand out as a legitimate alternative to rye made elsewhere? Personally, I thought the idea sounded kind of ill-conceived. Making a high-rye rye whiskey in New York wasn't enough to differentiate it from any other rye, and consumers would perceive it as marketing noise, but I played along, and we put down about twenty barrels in the first year and kept the project going. Rye is a difficult grain to work with and yields much less per pound of grain, making our costs much higher for the whiskey. Furthermore, the market wanted bourbon by a factor of 50:1, and I wasn't sure a Kings County rye would have customers, especially for an expensive rye differentiated only by the state of distillation rather than a significant recipe or process tweak.

Two years passed. Nicole left for Tullamore D.E.W. in Ireland as commissioning engineer for their column still, and we continued to make small amounts of rye after the harvest in October each year, but the project languished. In 2017, Christopher sent around an email reminding everyone that it was time to crack open at least a few of those first barrels. I immediately wished we had laid down four (or forty) times what we did.

For one thing, our rye was very good, and as someone who has never liked rye very much, I quickly realized that I had never really had rye as

The founding distillers of Empire Rye, here posing in 2017 for a *New York Times* article by Clay Risen

it could be made: rich and pungent with Christmas spice on the finish. I also hadn't realized that provenance alone could make Empire Rye unique. On top of that, there was the collective nature of the project, which ended up resonating with all our customer accounts. I spent more time with other New York distillers in the month around the Empire Rye launch than I had in years. Together, we made something that was greater than our own whiskeys, and for that reason, I was proud to promote the whole as much as our contribution to it. And since bourbon has long been seen as Kentucky's cultural property, Empire Rye proved a viable whiskey that didn't tread on anyone else's territory.

Empire Rye might be seen as an early example of craft distillers bringing regionality back to American whiskey, something that was cut off at the knees with Prohibition, and finally destroyed with the industry consolidation of the 1960s and '70s and with the rise of vodka in the 1980s.

OLD ROANOKE WHISKEY.

Rectified whiskey, thirty-five gallons; honey, three gallons; decoction of strong tea, one quart; of bitter almonds, bruised, eight ounces (the almonds should not be rancid, as they leave an unpleasant taste on

TUSCALOOSA WHISKEY.

Starch filtered rectified whiskey, one hundred gal lons; pale ale, four gallons; Jamaica rum, three gal lons. This should be colored very slightly, as the spirit used may contain sufficient coloring for the whole. This whiskey usually comes in half barrels, and stands deservedly high with consumers; as yet it only has a local reputation.

Old newspaper advertisements and blending manuals for rectifiers point to a whiskey past that has been lost to time, but offer clues as to what that whiskey landscape might have been like—and how contemporary distillers might find inspiration in the past.

Old newspapers and blending manuals provide some clues as to what whiskey used to be in this country. No one knows what Onandago Rye tasted like, or Tuscaloosa whiskey, or Old Roanoke, for that matter—though blending manuals offer a vague sense. Is the craft movement an opportunity to bring back some of these lost styles, or to invent new ones? American whiskey has been 97 percent bourbon (or Tennessee whiskey) and 3 percent rye for a long time. What else might there be? The whiskey map of America from the year 2000 would show the "regions" of Kentucky and Tennessee. What will the whiskey map of America look like in 2050?

Fortunately, craft distillers are already providing clues. Like craft beer, craft distillers concentrate in population centers, offering a receptive local audience. Even now, a national map of craft distillers allows for some generalizations that might point to future regional styles and the future of American whiskey.

For instance, just as with brewers, the distillers of the Northeast are geeky and process-oriented; so too are its whiskeys, with rye and alt bourbons being popular. Will the New England IPA have its corollary in whiskey? Empire Rye might be an answer.

Texas has made a name for its whiskeys, which age quickly in a dry desert climate, with notes of leather and barbecue. Brewer-derived single malts populate the Pacific Northwest and are as a group more robust than their international counterparts. Unaged whiskeys, or moonshines, might be frowned on by whiskey geeks, but have a healthy audience in the Appalachian highlands, where distilling tradition runs even deeper than the bluegrass.

These regional trends may point to a future of whiskey with as much stylistic variety as the wines of France, and future maps may delineate regions of American whiskey, just as the regions of Scotland are now bending to include new distillers and whiskeys.

WHISKEY MAP OF AMERICA 2050

Will the US evolve distinctive whiskey regions, as can be found in Scotland? It's happening already. Here are some ideas about what the future of regionality in American whiskey will look like in twenty-five years.

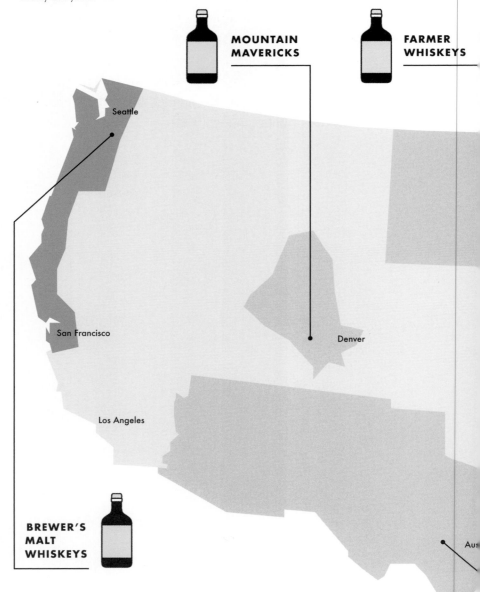

MOUNTAIN MAVERICKS

FARMER WHISKEYS

Seattle

San Francisco

Denver

Los Angeles

BREWER'S MALT WHISKEYS

Aus

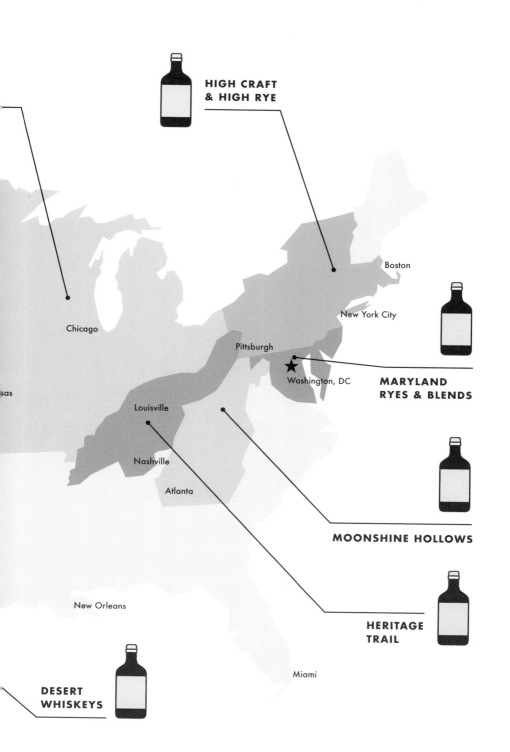

HIGH CRAFT & HIGH RYE

Boston

New York City

Chicago

Pittsburgh

Washington, DC

MARYLAND RYES & BLENDS

sas

Louisville

Nashville

Atlanta

MOONSHINE HOLLOWS

New Orleans

HERITAGE TRAIL

Miami

DESERT WHISKEYS

The inside of a Kentucky rickhouse or rackhouse, this one located at the Barton 1792 Distillery in Bardstown.

4

HERITAGE TRAIL

A book about American whiskey could begin in Staten Island, where the first commercial distillery was established in 1640. It could begin at Berkeley Plantation in Virginia a few years prior, when George Thorpe was known to be experimenting with fermented beverages and may have made use of a small copper still he owned, though evidence suggests he got only as far as a corn beer. Or in the Massachusetts Colony in 1648, where Lucy Downing wrote to her brother John Winthrop of the potential for distillate from rye, but lamented that the crop was eaten up before the more plentiful corn crop came in—the first recorded mention of corn and distillation in the same thought. If whiskey began on the Atlantic coast, it unquestionably flourished in the Ohio River valley after the Civil War and especially in Kentucky, where it is nearly synonymous with bourbon whiskey—so much so that many still assume bourbon can only be made in Kentucky, even though it is now made in every state in the union.

Kentucky is a complicated place for me. I grew up here, but my ancestry is elsewhere—I came from practical, religious, and thrifty Dutch people who congregated in western Michigan. My parents relocated to eastern Kentucky a year before I was born. So, I have always been an outsider in terms of ancestry, but I had never known any other place growing up. My dad pastored three small churches in the southeastern coalfields, where the valleys are long and convoluted, shadows linger into mid-morning, and evening falls long before sunset. Cross one mountain and you're in Virginia; cross another and you're in Tennessee.

At first look, that Appalachian part of Kentucky has very little connection to the bourbon part of Kentucky, but if you remove the highbrow associations with fine whiskey and horse racing, you have substance abuse and gambling, which feels pretty square with my part of Kentucky, along with prescription and garden-variety drug abuse, chronic boredom, and a certain mischievousness that comes from the sum of all the previous parts. This very much forged my sense of self as a young person, and I owe a lot of my relationship to vice (and virtue) from being raised in Kentucky.

Kentucky was always home, for me, but paradoxically, it was also a home I was glad to leave when the time came, though holidays and vacations brought me back over the years and my fondness grew in proportion to my adult freedom. When my dad died in 2015, I stopped having a strong reason to go back.

I felt a sense of loss not just for my dad, but for so much more than that also: the two-lane highways, the kudzu, the dilapidated church buildings, and a rich culture still singular in an increasingly homogeneous American experience. I felt a part of myself at risk of losing something very important and inexplicable. Not just because I was becoming an urban person, or a northern person, but because Kentucky reminds me of who I was before so much changed—in myself and in the world. Before smartphones, social media, and financial responsibilities. When I had so much time, I could waste it sitting on a vine-covered riverbank under a railroad trestle watching an afternoon drip away with friends.

Something about Kentucky is still from a pre-digital era. Hit the seek button on the radio outside of the cities and you'll hear one or two stations and a lot of static. You can't rely on Ubers, as they often don't exist. Airbnbs aren't generally charming. The geotags are all empty. It's not that you are off the grid here, though that is a part of the feeling, but the grid simply doesn't belong to this place. Which is the appeal for me, and I suspect for a lot of others who are drawn to bourbon because of the way it forces a reckoning with time itself. To return to an era before we all became victims of immediacy.

XXX

Flying to Kentucky will take you to one of three major airports: Lexington, Louisville, or, for the more advanced, the Cincinnati airport, which is in northern Kentucky and maybe a little busier and less expensive than the other

Barrels roll to the warehouse at Woodford Reserve, in Versailles, Kentucky.

two. Since Louisville has become a bourbon mecca with many bourbon sites within just a few blocks, I would recommend it as a starting place.

All the hotels in Louisville cater to bourbon tourism, but the most storied are the Brown and the Seelbach. Both are lovely, but the Brown retains maybe a little more of its old glory. If you stay at the Brown, I feel obliged to suggest you try the Hot Brown, an open-faced turkey sandwich soaked in Mornay sauce topped with bacon. It is meant, perhaps, to sop up indecency after a night of uncareful consumption. Many swear by it, and I have now done my duty by passing along the suggestion.

My preferred place to stay is the 21c, a more contemporary hotel with an art gallery on the ground floor (there is one in Lexington too). This concept might seem gimmicky or pretentious, but it doesn't end up that way somehow, though the real benefit is the restaurant, Proof on Main, which itself is a bourbon destination and does a highbrow version of Kentucky's cuisine of simple staples like cornbread, biscuits, chicken, ham, and green beans. A lot of the middle part of Kentucky is fast food or comfort food, so enjoy the fine dining in Louisville while you are here. Proof on Main is a good place to start.

Many distilleries have developed visitor centers with miniature distilleries on Main Street. The first, the Evan Williams Bourbon Experience, is a little bit of an amusement park ride with a bourbon tasting, but the result has a good amount of humor and fun. Other Main Street attractions are the Michter's Fort Hamilton Distillery and the Old Forester Distillery, both of which are notable for fitting working distilleries into old buildings ill-suited for the program. Old Forester is the more architectural space and the more credible brand. Old Forester was the first whiskey to be bottled, according to lore, and until recently was quite thin, with notes of bubble gum and candy corn, but they have invested in a brand overhaul and have come out with a number of specialty bottlings, often drawing inspiration from different eras in whiskey history. (The 1920 bottle is especially good.) Present-day Michter's has no connection to the historic Michter's brand of Pennsylvania aside from an abandoned trademark, so it's a little hard to get enthusiastic about this history, since it feels opportunistic and disingenuous.

Yet the best distiller on Main Street is Peerless Distilling. In contrast to most other distillers on Main Street, Peerless is an independent, small distillery and all its products are made here. The brand has a familiar story (for Kentucky at least) about an old family brand being resuscitated, but their distillery is built around a remarkable 14-inch diameter Vendome* column that emulates a working macrodistillery in miniature. Peerless is most known for a young rye that launched at a then-shocking price of $120 for a 750ml bottle, a rich price for many, but the liquid was good and backed the price, instantly raising the threshold for new craft brands. A bourbon followed a few years later, which was less impressive, but distinctive.

While on the west end of Main Street, be sure to look out for the Louisville Slugger Museum (it's hard to miss, since there is a giant baseball bat by the entrance), and the Louisville Science Center is a nice place to send the kids while bourbon tasting.

Head east past downtown on Main Street and you will come to Angel's Envy Distillery, which is not just a visitor center but the main production plant and home of the brand. Angel's Envy is a label mostly known for sourced bourbon and rye whiskeys that have been finished in other barrels (port, rum, etc.), more of a Scotch tradition than was popular for American whiskeys. This has been adopted by other American brands (mostly non-distilling producers, as Angel's Envy was until 2016, when it began operating at this site). Lincoln Henderson, a Brown-Forman executive, created the brand, though his son Wes took over after he passed away in 2014. Wes is a bourbon booster in the old model: generous, jovial, and enthusiastic—I enjoy watching him talk whiskey with anyone. He's a bit on the outside (Angel's Envy was an upstart until Bacardi bought the brand in 2015), but as such, he is comfortable with any audience. If there is anyone today who has inherited the performance artistry of personifying a bourbon brand the way that Booker Noe, Jimmy Russell, and Pappy Van Winkle all embodied, it's Wes.

On the east side of town, you'll find Copper & Kings, a distiller hoping to bring American brandy to prominence by using the home of bourbon

---

* Vendome Copper & Brass Works is a Louisville-based manufacturer of distillation equipment, having served the distillation business for more than a century.

MAP OF
LOUISVILLE, KENTUCKY
FEATURING DISTILLERIES AND OTHER POINTS OF INTEREST

64

1 **2**

KENTUCKY SCIENCE CENTER

3

LOUISVILLE SLUGGER MUSEUM

264

4

OHIO RIVER

6

5

CHURCHILL DOWNS

1. PEERLESS DISTILLING CO.
Craft distiller off Main Street using miniature column distillery setup; great rye and other whiskeys.

2. MICHTER'S FORT HAMILTON
Visitor Center for Michter's brand.

5. STITZEL-WELLER
The original Van Winkle distillery, now run as a Diageo gift shop, with no active distilling.

3. 21C HOTEL
Contemporary hotel with a fine bourbon selection and great food at Proof on Main.

4. HEAVEN HILL'S BERNHEIM DISTILLERY
Massive 3-column distillery for Heaven Hill brands.

6. BROWN-FORMAN'S SHIVELY PLANT
Makes Old Forester, Early Times, Coopers Craft and some of what goes in Woodford Reserve.

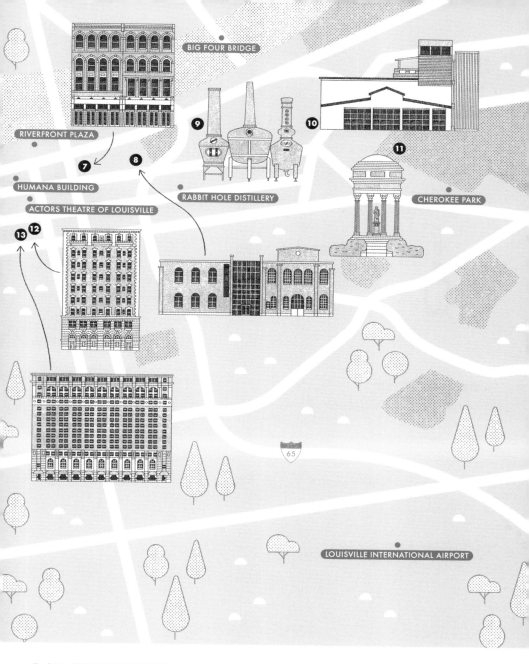

BIG FOUR BRIDGE

RIVERFRONT PLAZA

7

8

9

10

11

HUMANA BUILDING

RABBIT HOLE DISTILLERY

CHEROKEE PARK

ACTORS THEATRE OF LOUISVILLE

13 **12**

65

LOUISVILLE INTERNATIONAL AIRPORT

7. OLD FORESTER DISTILLERY
Mini distillery for Old Forester on a historic site.

8. ANGEL'S ENVY DISTILLERY
Home to barrel-finished bourbons in a newly built facility.

9. VENDOME COPPER & BRASS
Makes most of the equipment for American distilleries.

10. COPPER & KINGS
Brandy distillery worth a stop if you are tired of bourbon.

11. CAVE HILL CEMETERY
Visit the final resting place of George Garvin Brown, Pappy Van Winkle, Col Sanders, and Muhammad Ali.

12. THE SEELBACH HOTEL
F. Scott Fitzgerald was a patron and may have based Gatsby on George Remus, another guest.

13. THE BROWN HOTEL
Get the hot brown if you must, but talk bourbon with the bartenders, who know everything.

LOUISVILLE URBAN BOURBON

PEERLESS RYE

A spot-on rye whiskey full of cinnamon and caramel, just the right amount of barrel spice. This isn't quite the funky rye of Pennsylvania or New York, but a balanced rye for a bourbon drinker.

107.6pf (variable)	$120	C 2 yr	TC	Independent

OLD FORESTER 1920

Big, classic barrel-forward profile and high proof make this a perfect whiskey for many bourbon fans, and it's easily found and great whiskey. Holiday spice cake, caramelized bananas, rich toffee.

115pf	$55	C	HB	Brown-Forman

OLD FORESTER

Entry-level Old Forester as it's been reimagined in recent years is priced well as a mid-tier whiskey, with notes of butterscotch and raisin, but there are better whiskeys in this price range (and brand).

86pf	$25	C	HB	Brown-Forman

as a geographical starting point. The idea of American brandy is a good one, but there are other producers that do it more authentically and interestingly. The distillery has an impressive modern design that manages to be more of an event space than a working factory but is still worth a stop

ANGEL'S ENVY BOURBON FINISHED IN PORT BARRELS

Angel's Envy should be credited with starting the barrel finishing craze in American whiskey. Angel's Envy bourbon is sweet on the palate, but bright and juicy. If you like sweeter whiskey, this is one for you.

86.6pf	$45	C	NT	Bacardi

ANGEL'S ENVY RYE FINISHED IN RUM CASKS

In some cases, barrel finishes feel like a cheap trick. Angel's Envy Rye is a little heavy-handed on the rum finish, without much of the rye grain showing. Lots of flavor, but doesn't always feel like it all comes together.

100pf	$70	C	NT	Bacardi

BLADE & BOW

A middling whiskey posing as a top-shelf entry, I include it because it is inspired by old Stitzel-Weller marketing. As whiskey it's fine, cinnamon and brown sugar, nice dry finish. But with this profile, there are better options.

91pf	$50	C	HB	Diageo

COPPER & KINGS AMERICAN CRAFT BRANDY

Not a whiskey but an interesting bourbon-country brandy. The Butchertown Brandy is the house-made juice, though the mostly sourced-American brandy label is a solid, brawny brandy that's a good price and good for cocktails. There are so many good craft brandies, it's hard to recommend this over less orchestrated offerings, but it's a nice change of pace in bourbon country.

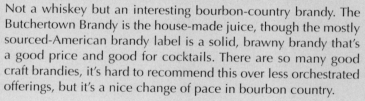

90pf	$30	C+P	SW	Constellation

as a counterpoint to bourbon. Butchertown Grocery Bakery, nearby, is recommend for casual fare.

There are two other sites of interest east of downtown Louisville. Vendome Copper & Brass Works is a manufacturer of stills and distilling equipment for nearly all the major distillers in the country and about half of the craft distillers. They aren't open to the public, but sometimes they have the gates open, and you can catch a glimpse of the columns and doublers being fabricated in their vast shop. Cave Hill Cemetery is a historic rural cemetery where you can find the graves of many great bourbon figures: George Garvin Brown, J. T. S. Brown, Paul Jones, W. L. Weller, Louis Stitzel, and Julian Proctor Van Winkle (Pappy). Colonel Sanders (Jim Morrison of Kentucky) and Muhammad Ali are also here, so make time to visit the great and greatest of many disciplines.

Southwest of downtown is where the real distilleries are. Brown-Forman's Shively plant and Heaven Hill's Bernheim distillery both produce a substantial percentage of the bourbon sold in the United States, but neither is open for tours. Michter's has a production distillery, and the old Stitzel-Weller distillery, run from the end of Prohibition until 1972 by the Van Winkle family, is now owned by corporate giant Diageo. Diageo had little taste for American whiskey until very recently, selling off or (arguably) mismanaging most of its American whiskey brands, but in the last decade it has played catch-up with Bulleit, a brand mostly born of a creative agency's imagination and with little genuine tie to any legitimate bourbon history. The Van Winkle story is slipped into some buildings here, along with a more contemporary boondoggle in Blade & Bow, but for any true bourbon fan, this is a place of history, curiosity, and sadness—of fickle corporate giants, an independent distiller run aground in the 1970s, when bourbon collapsed and gave way to lighter spirits—a holy site neglected.

XXX

To truly appreciate bourbon country, you must leave the city, take the highway south or east, and then, as soon as time allows, get off the interstate. Kentucky is backroads, winding hollows and rivers, two-lane roads that follow the gentle topography of the bluegrass. Limestone is often mentioned on bourbon tours as improving whiskey by filtering impurities and softening water. This is definitely fuzzy science (whiskey is distilled, which is the very act of separating it from water and any mineral content that water might have), but one that has a visible basis in the landscape.

Stitzel-Weller, seen here around 1960 when it was still operational

Kentucky is also known for its caves (also a product of limestone), and according to one distillery tour, the calcium in limestone is what makes racehorse bones so strong. Regardless of the credibility of any of this, the limestone is here, often a chalky layer of a roadcut under a sandstone cap.

Kentucky is also older than its neighbors. The area that today is known as bourbon country is the oldest part of the United States west of the Appalachian Mountains, settled before people moved into other parts of the South and Midwest. Look at a population map of the late 1700s and there will be a little bubble around bourbon country and emptiness all around. There are odd reminders of this history in the architecture: A dilapidated Federal-style brick house on a hill will stand in a completely different time continuum from a ranch house closer to the road, with cars up on concrete blocks. Mortarless stone fences line the lanes around Lexington, and horse farms and their white wood fences run though a lot of central Kentucky. Nature is an unstoppable force here. In the summer, much is overgrown and succumbing to the natural world, which buzzes with insect song at dusk in humid air.

MAP OF
BLUEGRASS KENTUCKY
FEATURING DISTILLERIES AND OTHER POINTS OF INTEREST

8

71

JEPTHA CREED

LOUISVILLE

BULLIET

FORT KNOX

FRANKFORT

64

150

127

65

7

1

6

WILD TURKEY

5

BARDSTOWN

LUX ROW DISTILLERS

2

3

HEAVEN HILL
VISITOR CENTER

INDIANA

31E

4

MAMMOTH CAVE   BOOKER NOE PLANT

LIMESTONE BRANCH

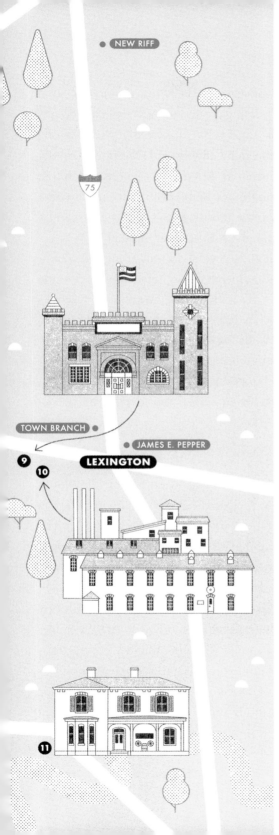

1. JIM BEAM
Largest bourbon brand's main distillery is oriented to lowbrow tourism, but with legitimate bourbon credibility and a nice location.

2. BARTON 1792
A workhorse distillery often overlooked, currently owned by Sazerac. A nice tour and home to a few well-regarded brands.

3. WILLETT
Long-standing family-run distillery making a range of cult favorite brands. Straddles old bourbon royalty and current mania.

4. MAKER'S MARK
Home of the first craft bourbon, an outlier brand started in the 1950s as a premium bourbon before such things existed. Still a worthy bottle & stop.

5. FOUR ROSES
Once under the radar, Four Roses is a cult favorite among bartenders and enthusiasts. Its gift shop is especially great.

6. WILD TURKEY
Now owned by Campari, a storied sourced brand from Brooklyn now has a host of great whiskeys on a beautiful site.

7. BUFFALO TRACE
Storied heritage distiller of Blanton's, Weller, Pappy Van Winkle, and other coveted bourbons in a beautiful setting on the Kentucky River.

8. NEELEY FAMILY DISTILLERY
Visit this creative, authentic moonshine & whiskey distillery run in a family tradition, besting much larger distillers.

9. CASTLE & KEY
Long abandoned, this distiller was given new life in 2015 and stands as a testament to the rebirth of bourbon popularity.

10. WOODFORD RESERVE
Historic distilling site completely revamped in the 1990s to emulate a Scotch distillery with pot stills for show. Still, a good tour spot.

11. WILDERNESS TRAIL
Off the beaten path, this microbiologist PhD's brand-new distillery grew to become one of the largest and most loved distillers in the state.

Another thing you will notice in Kentucky is water. Rivers, creeks, lakes, and streams carve up the landscape. Water drew the animals that made Kentucky such an attractive hunting ground to the American Indians who likely gave the state its name, and water drew early settlers along Daniel Boone's Wilderness Road through Cumberland Gap from Virginia. Much of Kentucky has become farmland, but there is just as much that remains wild and forested. This quality of being both wild and ancient sets a mood when you leave town, an almost-eerie serenity that can be very beautiful at dawn or dusk but can seem stark at midday.

The Bourbon Trail, as it is called, isn't really a trail at all, but a constellation of sites roughly bounded by Interstate 64, Interstate 65, and the Bluegrass Parkway. It is the invention of a trade group, the Kentucky Distillers Association, and not all distilleries pay to be members, so do not mistake its literature as a definitive, objective listing of bourbon sites. The Bourbon Trail isn't so much a road with a beginning and end with stops along the way as a series of follies in a vast English garden, some easily found, some in a deep, untraveled corner, but each its own reward to the adventurous seeker.

Leaving Louisville, you have a choice to go east or south. We'll go east.

XXX

If you haven't left the highway by the time you reach Shelbyville, this is a good place to get off. Exit I-64 at Taylorsville Road and head to Jeptha Creed Distillery, a fine stop to begin a tour of bourbon country. Joyce Nethery is matriarch of the family and leads the distillery with her daughter. Jeptha Creed takes its name from Jeptha Knob, the highest point in Bluegrass Kentucky, the geologic remnants of an ancient meteor crater. Their most popular spirit is a four-grain bourbon made with 'Bloody Butcher' corn, but I gravitated to their pawpaw brandy, a spirit truly unlike any other in the United States. The family has some military connections and does a lot of programming around veterans and service members.

Head north on Taylorsville Road into Shelbyville, turn toward Frankfort on Benson Pike, and you'll pass the brand-new Bulleit Distillery, built arguably as a concession to the din of voices that were complaining, loudly and publicly, that Bulleit had no distillery. Note that even at current

CAPITAL SPIRITS

JEPTHA CREED FOUR GRAIN BOURBON

An unusual bourbon from a small, but traditional distillery that emphasizes farm-to-bottle production. This bourbon has some of the peppery notes I associate with heirloom corn, and is aged nicely—but may be too distinct from other Kentucky bourbons for traditionalists.

98pf	$53	C	TC	Independent

JEPTHA CREED PAWPAW BRANDY

What a strange spirit, distilled from fermented pawpaws, a fleshy fruit found in the Kentucky woodlands! More like a rum than a brandy, but neither quite describes this local delicacy.

85pf	$50/375ml	C	TC	Independent

BULLEIT FRONTIER WHISKEY

Bulleit is a middle-of-the-road bourbon that is as good as most in the price range. The brand has seen flavor drift upward in quality. Still, it's a bourbon that most traveled drinkers have long since moved past.

90pf	$40	C	HB	Diageo

BULLEIT RYE

Bulleit rye is the easiest to recommend from Bulleit. It has a lot of oak and complex earthy flavors that suit a well-aged rye whiskey when price-range peers taste thin. There's a reason almost half of the rye whiskey sold in the United States is Bulleit.

90pf	$40	C	HB	Diageo

BULLEIT 10 YEAR

It can be hard to find a ten-year bourbon at mainstream pricing, but Bulleit is softer than peers (I like Russell's Reserve in this age range). Toffee, cinnamon, and clove define this whiskey.

91.2pf	$55	C 10 yr	HB	Diageo

Jeptha Creed, just off the highway near Shelbyville, is a good jumping-off place for the bourbon trail.

capacity, the distillery won't support the size the brand is now, but a second Diageo distillery, in Lebanon, which is not public facing, will eventually make up some of the difference.

Bulleit began as a whim of some executives back in the Seagram days, as a Wild West–themed "frontier whiskey." The brand was to be called Bullet, but there was a hang-up in that a similar brand existed in the market already, mostly an export brand of sourced whiskey, run by a Lexington lawyer, Tom Bulleit. Seagram acquired the brand in 1997, then the Seagram empire famously fell apart due to mismanagement, shunting its brands to conglomerate giants Diageo and Pernod Ricard.

Bulleit began as its concept suggested: cheap bourbon in novel packaging at a time when there wasn't a lot of novelty in bourbon positioning. Sourced from Four Roses, the whiskey wasn't special, but it has improved substantially (and its price has gone up accordingly) since I first tried it in

One of the original doublers at Stitzel-Weller, which was refurbished by Vendome and used in the Bulleit Distillery in Shelbyville, built in 2017 and opened to the public in 2019

2008, performing especially well in the cocktail community in progressive places like San Francisco and Brooklyn. However, the brand has lately been plagued with high-level scandals (see p. 125) and insiders with a window behind the scenes will find sympathy with those who worked hard to build this brand only to be undermined by its corporate parent, tarnishing its progressive veneer. With so many choices in American whiskey, there are plenty of skeletons in the Bulleit closet that are disqualifying for this consumer.

One small note of interest at the Shelbyville facility is that the doubler* in the distillery is actually the refurbished doubler for the old Stitzel-Weller distillery in Louisville, whose plant Diageo inherited and serves as a visitor center today.

Continue east on Benson Pike and you'll arrive in Frankfort. Head north on Highway 421 and you'll arrive at Buffalo Trace, cathedral of American whiskey and one of the oldest sites in American distilling.

---

* In heritage bourbon production, a doubler is a copper chamber that performs a second distillation after a beer column, mimicking a pot-still finish.

Buffalo Trace Distillery, seen from the Kentucky River, has the best claim as the oldest operating distillery in the US.

If you are new to American whiskey, you might be forgiven for not knowing Buffalo Trace. After all, its flagship is a well-regarded but newer brand introduced in 1999. But Buffalo Trace makes the most sought-after whiskeys in the United States, and that is due almost entirely to a deal struck in 2003 with Julian Van Winkle III, Pappy's grandson.

Julian's grandfather rode a great wave of fortune as a bourbon distiller in Louisville, from working the streets as a salesman for W. L. Weller, through the dark days to Prohibition, to the excitement and promise that boomed through bourbon's heyday in the 1950s, until his death in 1965 at the age of ninety-one. The few leftover dusty bottles of Stitzel-Weller–made whiskey are an obsession for hunters, but so far as I can tell the bulk of whiskey was mostly middle-of-the-road bourbon that played to specific audiences: Old Fitzgerald, the flagship (Irish Americans), Cabin Still (old-timers), Rebel Yell (Lost Causers). By the early 1970s, the distillery was limping along, but many stakeholders wanted to sell, and so Julian Jr. reluctantly agreed, though he retained the Rip Van Winkle brand in the deal.

FIVE FROM BUFFALO TRACE

BUFFALO TRACE BOURBON

As an everyday bourbon, Buffalo Trace has it all: It can be found most of the time, and it's a nice balance of oak, heat, baking spice, and everything you want in a bourbon. Keep one always.

90pf	$35	C	HB	Sazerac

W. L. WELLER 12-YEAR

A lighter-bodied, older whiskey, which makes this such a winner. Dry and rich with toffee and leather, this is a whiskey that avoids the sweetness and heat of its younger brothers (special reserve and antique) while presenting a near-perfect whiskey.

90pf	$85 ($300)	C 12 yr	HB	Sazerac

BLANTON'S SINGLE BARREL BOURBON

Blanton's is fine bourbon, but not worth the hype around the bottle. It's such a mainstream flavor profile (heavy oak, corn syrup, nutmeg), I'll steer you toward easily found peers like Knob Creek and Russell's Reserve that out-drink it.

93pf	$85 ($250)	C	HB	Sazerac

STAGG (JR)

While George T. Stagg from the Antique Collection is nearly impossible to find (and the rare bourbon often worth secondary pricing), non-antique Stagg (once known as Stagg Jr.) is hardly a downgrade, is easier found, and is delicious.

129.5pf (variable)	$55 ($300)	C	HB	Sazerac

PAPPY VAN WINKLE 15-YEAR BOURBON

The hype around Pappy is generally disqualifying—no whiskey is worth the hysteria. But Pappy 15 is oak-forward, rich and decadent, and a very fine whiskey, if we could simply leave it at that.

95pf	$129 ($2,200)	C 15 yr	HB	Sazerac

Julian III, Pappy's grandson, spent most of his career trying to rebuild the brand, selling bourbon in ceramic decanters and buying odd lots of whiskey from dying distilleries when bourbon was essentially worthless. Julian bought a decaying distillery in Lawrenceburg to warehouse and bottle his whiskeys, but even as he struggled to sell whiskey, contracts for aged whiskey started to become scarce.

Around the same time, according to family legend, a bottle of the Van Winkle Family Reserve earned the previously unmatched rating of 99 from the Beverage Testing Institute, which seems to have been a big deal at the time. I don't know the Beverage Testing Institute to have any particular relevance (or reverence) today, but I'm relying largely on Julian's well-worn narrative.

With a superlative review and the momentum of a long-dormant whiskey market growing again, Julian forged a partnership with Buffalo Trace to distill the Van Winkle line of whiskeys, and the stage was set for a revolution in American whiskey that would percolate for about a decade and then come to a rolling boil—at Buffalo Trace.

Since Pappy fever took hold around 2011, it has never relented, with bottles on the secondary market creeping up in price each year. Aspirants sought out alternatives in the form of the W. L. Weller lineup of wheated bourbon. Soon Blanton's, a single-barrel bourbon, found an audience with an ornate bottle loosely based on Chambord's globus crucifer, with a series of running-horse pewter stoppers in place of a cross, each with one of the letters of Blanton's by its feet (collect 'em all!). Blanton's disappeared from shelves. Soon Eagle Rare and E. H. Taylor disappeared. One could almost simply look at the list of brands distilled at Buffalo Trace and buy them assuming that they would become sought after, no matter how middling the whiskey, as Elmer T. Lee and Rock Hill Farms proved as they too soon vanished from the market.

I remember visiting a Liquor Barn in Louisville and the whole Buffalo Trace aisle (they have several bourbon aisles in Kentucky) had been cleared out like a great blizzard or snowstorm was about to arrive, which is simply a warning that one shouldn't visit Kentucky with the expectation of finding rare whiskeys, since savvy locals have already picked over the shelves.

The irony behind all of this is that Buffalo Trace is the world's largest bourbon distillery, with twin 84-inch columns,* each capable of producing more bourbon than any other still in the United States. Sazerac, which owns Buffalo Trace, has been dramatically increasing its distillation and warehousing capacity both in Frankfort and at other locations.

Buffalo Trace is overseen by Harlen Wheatley, a distiller who has the bearing of a football coach running afternoon detention, a cranky perfectionist hewing to tradition. To his credit, Buffalo Trace is continually investing in projects that bend tradition, including Warehouse X, which studies climatic impacts on whiskey during aging, and a newer project to keep American whiskey at a cool, steady temperature to prolong aging and force higher age statements comparable to Scotch whisky.

There is a strong argument from many whiskey makers that the sweet spot for bourbon is seven to twelve years, and anything beyond that is overaged. I appreciate and certainly share the view that older is not necessarily better (our first seven-year whiskey barrel wasn't necessarily as good as our standard four-year). But I like the idea of old American whiskey and think that if anyone can make a 35-year-old American whiskey taste decent, it's Harlen Wheatley and Buffalo Trace. I like that extremes should exist, and Harlen is one of the few people in a position to push American whiskey to its absolute limit.

For me, the best product coming out of Buffalo Trace is the flagship whiskey, which is most easily found and reasonably priced. For the dollar, it's the best value in American whiskey, and doubling your budget might only get you only marginally better whiskey. Blanton's and E. H. Taylor are solid finds at suggested retail price, but not beyond. George T. Stagg is a remarkable whiskey, if you can ever find it. Their other whiskeys are so inflated in price that it's best to avoid them, as there are dozens of more interesting whiskeys that can be had for so much less, without the baggage of conspicuous consumption.

Sazerac's top-selling whiskey isn't exactly a whiskey at all, but a cinnamon liqueur with a Canadian whiskey base. Fireball sold twenty-eight

---

* Column diameter is a rough measure of the capacity of a distillery. The bore size of the column determines the maximum number of proof gallons in a 24-hour period, a figure the federal government uses to keep track of the taxable potential of a distiller.

The Old Taylor Distillery, long a site for urban explorers, was once the first tourism-oriented distillery, with its own train station, rose garden, and complimentary bottle for visitors. It's been gently restored and rebranded as Castle & Key by the new owners, who have preserved much of the original beauty from 1887.

times the flagship bourbon from Buffalo Trace in 2019 and is the top-selling liqueur in the US, above Jägermeister. It's so popular, a lawsuit alleges that Sazerac ran out of whiskey to produce it. Sazerac has started making Fireball that is no longer labeled as whiskey, but regardless, Fireball has been a cash cow for Sazerac and has given them the enviable market position of having the single most highbrow, expensive American whiskey on the market as well as the most lowbrow, most ubiquitous, cheap flavored whiskey at the same time.

XXX

Heading south out of Frankfort on Glenns Creek Road will take you to three important distilleries of the past, inhabited by three very different distilleries of today.

The first is Glenns Creek Distilling, a tiny craft producer occupying one of the outbuildings of the Old Crow Distillery, a plant famed for the nineteenth century's best-known brand, and a pot-still whiskey long after most others moved to more efficient columns. The property is now a large-scale industrial ruin, having been shuttered by its last owner, Beam.

VERSAILLES & LAWRENCEBURG

CASTLE & KEY SMALL BATCH WHEATED BOURBON

A nice bourbon, but very middle-of-the-road for an ambitious project incubating for so long. Balanced whiskey, cinnamon, and a touch of tropical fruit, but still a staid, even elegant whiskey. Creating a bourbon worthy of their distillery is a challenge I'm glad I don't face.

100pf	$85	C	NT	Independent

WOODFORD RESERVE STRAIGHT BOURBON

Woodford is a fine mid-shelf bourbon from Brown-Forman, the company that knows American whiskey best. This might as well be the template for Kentucky Straight Bourbon.

90.4pf	$35	C+P	HB	Brown-Forman

WOODFORD RESERVE STRAIGHT RYE

If the bourbon was set up to be a classic in 1996, the rye, launched in 2015, wasn't quite as perfect. Unbalanced and meek sound too harsh, but ultimately this one disappointed me.

90.4pf	$35	C+P	HB	Brown-Forman

Some of the barrel warehouses are still used by Beam, but Glenns Creek is an upstart project run by David Meier, a devotee of alt-malts and pot stills. The OCD and Café Olé bourbon are unlike anything you've ever had, terrific examples of the buttery richness that pot stills provide and a counterpoint to the commercial projects surrounding it.

Continue on and the road becomes McCracken Pike, and you'll pass the old E. H. Taylor Distillery, now operating as Castle & Key (the contemporary Taylor brand is owned by Sazerac, hence the new name). Once a ruin nearly as dilapidated as Old Crow, the distillery has been undergoing a decade-long refurbishment, one that is gentle enough to

WOODFORD RESERVE STRAIGHT MALT

Woodford used to get attention for its experimental series made on their pot stills. One of the best of these was a duo of classic malt and straight malt in used and new cooperage, respectively. This is a fun, affordable, big-brand twist on the American Malt category at 51% malt.

90.4pf	$35	C+P	HB	Brown-Forman

FOUR ROSES BOURBON

Once called "Yellow Label," this bottle shows up in a lot of cool spots as the entry-level bourbon. With more body than comparably priced peers, it's a decent low-shelf bottle and a good mixer in volume cocktails.

80pf	$20	C	HB	Kirin

FOUR ROSES SMALL BATCH

Four Roses has a logical and well-priced portfolio. The Small Batch is a mid-level bourbon that bests peer whiskeys in blind tests and doesn't have a lot of baggage.

90pf	$35	C	HB	Kirin

preserve the patina of time, as well as the original details that made this the first truly visitor-oriented distillery in the country. The new owners hired Marianne Eaves, then the master blender at Brown-Forman, to be their master distiller, a move hailed as a first for a woman in Kentucky (since Prohibition, perhaps), a position that brought a lot of visibility to the project until her abrupt departure in 2019. The breakup appears to have not been amicable, as Marianne's limited public comments have made clear, and the distillery hasn't found quite the same footing without her. A tour is still worth the money, as it is a significant site in bourbon history and although a bit long, it is a comprehensive experience not to be missed.

Pot stills are a rarer sight in bourbon, but the Woodford Reserve distillery was modeled on a single-malt distillery to give its whiskeys a more premium association in the mid-1990s, when bourbon was just beginning to recover from a drought.

Town Branch also uses pot stills situated in a dramatic open space at a convenient location near downtown Lexington, but the adjacent brewery and barrel-aged beer tasting are the highlight of a visit.

The last distillery to inhabit a historical structure on McCracken Pike is Woodford Reserve, a well-financed project of the Brown-Forman company (Old Forester, Jack Daniel's) for a new bourbon launched back in the mid-1990s. Built inside the Old Oscar Pepper distillery near Versailles, Kentucky, Woodford is essentially a 20,000-liter single-malt distillery complete with six Forsyth* pot stills meant mostly as showpieces, since very little of what is produced there could end up in a brand as large as Woodford. By my estimate, even at maximum capacity, only a quarter of the liquid in Woodford bottles is distilled at this location, though a trio of stills was recently added to address this discrepancy—not necessarily enough to make a meaningful difference.

A visitor should look for the Master's Collection, which often includes creative whiskeys that are distilled exclusively on the pot-still setup and are often more interesting and well-made than the main brand. As airport whiskey goes, Woodford is a more satisfying option than similarly situated

* If Vendome is the premier American still manufacturer, Forsyths is the Scottish alternative, specializing in pot stills (though like Vendome, they build all varieties). The factory is located in Rothes, near many well-known single-malt distillers on the River Spey.

peers, and Brown-Forman is a brand that invests in history and tells its story well on this tour, one of my favorites in Kentucky.

This bluegrass around Versailles is a very magical little stretch of turf, with meandering roads, the board fences of horse farms, and the old stone fences of estates from long ago. If one were looking for a joyride in America, you'd be hard-pressed to beat a drive around Versailles. If you're going that way, stop for lunch at Wallace Station and thank me later.

From here, you could make an easy trip into Lexington, Kentucky's second-largest city and home to the University of Kentucky and its famed basketball program. Lexington's historic downtown has been gutted by years of poor planning and nearsighted projects with generic architecture, though it has recently started to come alive. A downtown visitor with a penchant for bourbon will definitely enjoy Justin's House of Bourbon, a store with a terrific collection of American whiskey and Kentucky bourbon, including dusty bottles for sale under Kentucky's Vintage Spirits Law.* There are distilleries here—Bluegrass Distillers is a true craft startup and James E. Pepper is the product of an abandoned trademark investor—but if I had time for only one in Lexington, I'd suggest Lexington Brewing and Distilling Co., which is both a brewery and distillery in one location. Town Branch is the whiskey brand here, but the beer is favored by the local audience. Kentucky Bourbon Barrel Ale is a potent product that set my standard for cask-aged beers when I first tried it more than twenty years ago.

XXX

The Wild Turkey Distillery, near Lawrenceburg, sits on a bluff overlooking a steep ravine through which flows the Kentucky River. The road crosses the river here on a thin, two-lane truss bridge that gives the only hint of human intervention in a gorge of wilderness flanked by farmland on the adjacent plateaus.

---

* Kentucky is one of the few states with a provision that allows licensees (bars, restaurants, and retailers) to buy unopened bottles of spirits from consumers, so long as those bottles are not available from licensed wholesalers or a distiller. Passed in 2018, the law allows for collectors to lawfully monetize their rare bottles; such transactions in other states are considered illegal.

Wild Turkey sits on a bluff overlooking the Kentucky River.

Wild Turkey was started by a grocer in Brooklyn, New York. The Austin Nichols Company existed in various forms as a grocery supply company beginning in 1855, but after the repeal of Prohibition, they focused exclusively on alcohol. Wild Turkey, as a brand, was born in the 1940s as a sourced whiskey that eventually pulled much of its inventory from a distillery in Tyrone, Kentucky, a town named after the Ripy family's ancestral home in Ireland.

Ripy was the first distiller on the site, but by the 1950s it was known as the J. T. S. Brown distillery. Jimmy Russell got started there in 1954 and never left, rising to the ranks of master distiller. His son Eddie now shares the role and has pushed the brand to more varied offerings. Hiring Matthew McConaughey for a stint as a spokesman and "creative director" seems to have benefited McConaughey more than Wild Turkey, and perhaps is the reason the relationship ended in 2022. The brand has been owned by Campari for about a decade, which completely rebuilt the distillery in 2012.

FOUR WILD TURKEYS

WILD TURKEY 101

Wild Turkey 101 is the flagship, entry-level Wild Turkey label. It's pretty hot and not quite what the brand used to be, but still a nice bottle for the price.

101pf	$25	C	HB	Campari

WILD TURKEY KENTUCKY SPIRIT

Kentucky Spirit has a creamy, vanilla profile without a lot of the heat or spicy notes I associate with other Wild Turkey products. A really nice, underrated bourbon that may be less fashionable but still reflects what a great bourbon can be.

101pf	$60	C	HB	Campari

RUSSELL'S RESERVE 10-YEAR

If you are looking for a well-aged, well-priced bourbon that delivers on the promise of its age, you'll be hard-pressed to find a better bottle than this. Rich, bold, and spicy with a dry finish, this is really a classic.

90pf	$40	C 10 yr	HB	Campari

LONGBRANCH

I don't know if anyone asked for this whiskey, and while it's better than the brief would suggest, I wonder if Wild Turkey is the right company to pull this off. There are pleasing notes of simple syrup and a wisp of barbecue. But with so many great whiskeys actually from Texas, this one is a pass for me.

86pf	$40	C	HB	Campari

Wild Turkey in principle has a couple of key differentiating features: a low-distillation proof and low barrel-entry proof, resulting in very little water added. While Wild Turkey eight-year from the 1980s is some of the best bourbon ever made in the history of the spirit, the recent iterations aren't as special, though there's a lot to admire about some of the specialty offerings, particularly the barrel-proof editions.

The distillery itself feels corporate and new—it's clear there was a mandate to update the facility for international fire codes, OSHA standards, and a high degree of automation, with tours routed through a windowed corridor away from most of the works. Something may have been lost in the transition—there's not a lot of soul in this factory. The visitor center is also new, but architecturally elegant and inviting; it is situated so as to finish tours with a tasting looking over the river, and the view ties in the history and the spirit's connection to the land in a way that's evocative.

If you can get your hands on an older bottle of Wild Turkey, it will be something special, but dusty bottles are increasingly hard to find. You could easily settle for the 10-year Russell's Reserve, a winning bourbon up against other comparably aged whiskeys from the big brands like Bulleit or Knob Creek. Kentucky Spirit has a little bit of a lighter profile and is a lesser-known choice that showcases the vanilla-caramel cream characteristics of low-distillation proof. For an inexpensive bourbon, you can do worse than the 101-proof flagship (conceived as one better than the 100-proof Bottled-in-Bond* whiskeys that were common when the brand was launched).

On the other side of town, Four Roses is located in a Mission-style distillery building, originally called the Old Prentice Distillery, which might be a little out of place in rural Kentucky, but as a purpose-built distillery from pre-Prohibition, it's an unusual piece of the past that was

---

* Bottled-in-Bond is an 1897 law that was an early consumer protection designed to verify a spirit's provenance. It must be from one distillery, one distiller, and one season, and must be at least four years old and exactly 100 proof. Single-malt Scotch, by contrast, need only be from one distillery and at least three years old. Bonded whiskeys, as they are sometimes called, are the most constrained form of American whiskey and were once considered the gold standard, though over time their reputation diminished. A new generation of distillers, both large and small, have found the bonded designation to be a mark of transparency and distinction.

A rickhouse at Wild Turkey.

saved from near extinction. Four Roses, once part of the Seagram empire, nearly collapsed when that company was dismantled due to risky bets in entertainment in the 1990s. The Four Roses brand, which by that point was a blended whiskey for Japanese export, was shunted to Pernod Ricard and then Kirin, who has been a good steward of the name and the facility. Credit also goes to head distiller Jim Rutledge, who believed in the product and lobbied hard for its successful renaissance as a straight bourbon.

Four Roses yellow label is one of the best value bourbons on the market, and the small batch and single barrel are both classic whiskeys that improve any liquor shelf at a decent price. With two mash bills and five yeast strains, Four Roses has preserved a lot of the Seagram-era production, designed really as blending agents, but in the current era the label gives contemporary drinkers a lot of variety, all at great quality.

XXX

The self-proclaimed bourbon capital of Kentucky is Bardstown, a sleepy little town in Nelson County. Bardstown is one of the oldest cities west of the Appalachian Mountains, and there are many examples of early architecture, including the Old Talbott Tavern, a bar that would make anyone feel at home in the eighteenth century.

When I first got into bourbon, Bardstown's claim was a bit specious, as there was only one operational distillery there: Sazerac's Barton distillery. Heaven Hill's distillery burned in the 1990s, and Willett, an important bottler, didn't actually produce any of its own whiskey. Still, Jim Beam's main Clermont distillery is not far away, as is its Booker Noe plant. Its sister brand Maker's Mark is in the opposite direction, about a half hour's drive south of town.

Yet the last decade has been transformative to Bardstown and the region around it. Willett rebuilt its distillery and began distilling in 2012. Heaven Hill built a new visitor center, and then rebuilt it even bigger and laid plans to distill again on its campus. Four Roses opened a visitor center near its Cox's Creek aging facility. Bardstown Bourbon Company, a ground-up distillery with two 36-inch steel columns, is about to add a third, just in its seventh year of existence, putting it in the top twelve American distillers by capacity. Lux Row opened a show distillery to highlight its brands, notably Yellowstone. Craft distiller Steve Beam opened Limestone Branch with a little Hoga pot still—and offers one of the best distillery tours in the region. And Independent Stave, a major cooper of bourbon barrels, has a factory in Lebanon. There is now so much within

The Old Talbott Tavern in Bardstown is a piece of history, as old as America itself and a fine lunch spot with a bourbon collection to be perused and enjoyed slowly. Time tends to stand still here.

BARDSTOWN BOURBON

MAKER'S MARK STRAIGHT BOURBON

Maker's is a classic, but a flavor profile that is a bit out of fashion. Notes of sweet caramel and toffee dominate the palate, but there's a hot finish in recent bottles that's hard to overlook. I love the brand, but bourbon has become quite competitive and Maker's has a hard time keeping up. Find a bottle from ten years ago and you'll understand why this is a beloved bourbon, lately run into the ground.

90pf	$25	C	HB	Beam Suntory

MAKER'S MARK 46

With a pretty thin differentiator (aged a little longer with added French oak staves), Maker's 46 is uninspiring as a story, but in blind tasting holds up nicely. For a woodier wheated bourbon it's a nice choice, and often overlooked in plain sight, though widely available.

90pf	$35	C	HB	Beam Suntory

BARDSTOWN BOURBON CO. ORIGINS SERIES

Bardstown began its brand with well-blended whiskey sourced from elsewhere. I was curious how this six-year release of house distillate from the fall of 2016 would fare. With notes of vanilla, sweet pepper, and black tea, and at a nice price, I liked this more than several entries from recently built, large-scale Kentucky distillers.

96pf	$50	C 6 yr	NT	Semi-independent

WILLETT FAMILY ESTATE RYE

The Willett Family Estate label used to be a good way to find great single barrels. Lately the reputation and price have gotten ahead of the bourbon. The rye, on the other hand, has been available in abundance since their own distillate came of age around 2016. Not so rye-forward, but grainy and rich and drinks smoother than its proof. Still, for its price and pedigree, is a fine proofy, mainstream rye, but so much else has come up around it.

variable	$75	C	NT	Independent

WILLETT POT STILL

An apparently polarizing whiskey online. Don't be fooled by the pot still bottle, this goes through a column first, but is young Willett House distillate, which offers better value and more interesting whiskey than its Family Estate series, which has gotten perilously overvalued. This is a fairly middle-of-the-road bourbon, heavy on caramel and not much else. But hardly a divisive profile in today's bottle.

| 104pf | $50 | C | NT | Independent |

JOHNNY DRUM

If drinking Jack Daniel's was once a sign of rebelliousness, there was a moment in the early 2010s when Johnny Drum was the hard-living, late-night cheap bourbon du jour of young adulthood in New York City. Having inched up in price, it's still a nice value relative to peers, and gets a sentimental bump here.

| 100pf | $45 | C | NT | Independent |

VERY OLD BARTON

A very simple bourbon, with cinnamon and clove on the palate and a short finish. For a few more bucks, 1792 is also made at Barton. It's a more serious pour, but for bargain bourbon, Very Old Barton is actually the steal at $15.

| 100pf | $15 | C | HB | Sazerac |

a short drive of the town's picturesque courthouse that a little guidance may come in handy.

If you were to stop at one distillery in Bardstown, my recommendation would be Willett. Situated on a flat hilltop south of town, Willett was a small distillery that opened just after Prohibition. During the energy crisis of the 1970s, the family hoped to repurpose their distillery to make fuel alcohol but continued to bottle bourbon. It was the latter business that survived, and the younger generation of Willetts (now named Kulsveens) rebuilt the distillery and began producing their own whiskeys in 2012. The youthful energy and independent spirit help distinguish Willett among corporate neighbors, and an inventory of older stock kept its Family Estate label a rotating selection of very fine old American whiskey—a little hit and miss at times, but always something to bring home as a conversation piece. And Willett's house brands like Johnny Drum, Rowan's Creek, and Noah's Mill have been reliably good pours—I speculate because they were sourced from another beloved distillery not especially known as a contract supplier.

I happen to like the distillery's younger whiskeys, especially its rye, which show the strength of its own distillate. The house-made bourbon has met with some uneven reviews, typically from sources that

The wax dripping at Maker's Mark is a photogenic stop on the distillery tour.

Barton 1792 is no longer open for tours, which is a shame, as its tours offered an intimate, behind-the-working-scenes visit to an important historical distiller.

lack much experience beyond commodity whiskey. Willett continues to source most of the whiskeys for its various brands, so make sure to read the bottle for a 100-percent house-made product. And its pot-still whiskey is only finished on a pot still (as all their house spirits are, and most Kentucky bourbons that employ a doubler), so as a pot-still advocate, I would add a marketing asterisk here. Willett has gotten hard to find, so a visit to the tasting room is high yield for things not sold everywhere.

HEAVEN HILL THRILLS

EVAN WILLIAMS BLACK LABEL

Toffee and oak compensate for some rough edges, but a good entry-level whiskey for the oak lover. I miss the vanilla and caramel of some of its peers, but that's a subjective preference. A good buy for a remarkably low price. And trading up the line for more premium versions can be fruitful with this brand.

86pf	$15	C	HB	Heaven Hill

MELLOW CORN

Mellow Corn is cheap and hot, but is really the only mainstream example of aged corn whiskey on the market at any volume. It has a special place for me, with notes of buttered popcorn, corn husk, nail polish remover, and vanilla extract.

100pf	$20	C	HB	Heaven Hill

ELIJAH CRAIG 18

Time and again, this comes up as an absolute benchmark for me, as the best a bourbon can hope to be. Compared to comparably aged bourbon, often much more expensive, Elijah Craig is distinctive and often better. For age-stated Kentucky bourbon, the richness, depth, and balance are right on target. This is the high bar.

90pf	$150 ($225)	C 18 yr	HB	Heaven Hill

RITTENHOUSE RYE

The best cocktail rye in blind tasting. Designed as an entry-level rye mostly for mixing, it serves that purpose very nicely. Craft rye is often superior on flavor, but rarely on price, which is where this bottle wins.

100pf	$85 ($250)	C	HB	Heaven Hill

For a more commercial visit, Maker's Mark is a historical distillery and an interesting story within Kentucky bourbon, the unusual outlier of a bourbon brand founded in the 1950s. There's a lot of storytelling in the founding narrative, but generally I appreciate that only Maker's Mark is made at the Maker's Mark Distillery, and it is the only source for the product—for me a good signal that the distillery is a part of the brand and vice versa. Maker's is a wheat-recipe bourbon, a style that is very popular, though Maker's is lighter on the flavor spectrum, which tends to exclude it from a lot of the obsessive whiskey conversations even as it ends up on a lot of home bars. The distillery tour is a pleasant visit but highly orchestrated—don't expect to see much behind-the-scenes or hear unscripted tidbits from guides.

Maker's has been giving every bourbon lover what they really want: customized programs to create their own barrel and a series of consumer-oriented special-release whiskeys that explore the effects of different wood on aging. Although bourboneers are clamoring for more customization and process participation, this program still seems a little underappreciated. Perhaps because Maker's doesn't carry an age statement, most whiskey fans seem to overlook it, though there are plenty of lesser whiskeys that end up mistakenly coveted by ageist connoisseurs, leaving these gems in plain sight.

For something more behind-the-scenes than Maker's Mark, I often used to recommend Barton, Sazerac's distillery in Bardstown built and improved by Oscar Getz but somewhat untouched since the 1950s. Tours were not very populated and went deep into the old brick factory for a much more revealing experience than is typical of Kentucky tours. Perhaps for this reason, Barton stopped giving tours in April 2022, which is a shame. Maybe dipping fingers in the mash, sampling new make from the still, and climbing around on catwalks inside an aging factory aren't best practices anymore, but they made a visit feel special.

The two newer distilleries in town, Bardstown Bourbon Company and Lux Row, are hard to recommend, if only because they are testaments to the capital and ambition that went into recently building them and not much else (both were acquired within five years of their construction).

Bardstown is mostly a contract producer, but I have been surprised and impressed by its Fusion series, a concept that was not particularly original but lives up to its high price and out-tastes a lot of competitors. And one small note: This part of Kentucky is light on fine dining, but the bar and restaurant at Bardstown Bourbon Company are refreshingly elevated.

I spent time in Bardstown wandering around the cemeteries looking to pay respects to famous and forgotten distillers and grew to appreciate the quietude and the occasional waft of cooked corn coming from one of the local distilleries. The songwriter Stephen Foster is said to have written the Kentucky state song in a Federal-style mansion just east of town, which can be visited today. Some will recognize the house from the Kentucky state quarter. Foster was a prolific figure, a songwriter whose music lasts to this day, despite an early death at thirty-seven, drunk and penniless on the Bowery in New York City. His legacy is complicated by the fact that his music proliferated through minstrel shows, a form of entertainment that exploited racial stereotypes and exacerbated racial animosity. Nevertheless, Foster is still celebrated here, despite his very thin connection to the town. An outdoor musical tells his story in the summertime, when Kentucky's climate perhaps seems most Southern.

When the British colonized the American continent, they established triangular trade. West Africans were enslaved and shipped to the Caribbean to grow sugarcane and refine it into molasses, which was shipped up to the distilleries of the early American cities to get distilled into rum. Many nineteenth-century Americans believed that the United States was founded on twin evils, and that abolition and temperance were the absolution to the original sin of the American project. The Civil War and Emancipation, and then later Prohibition and repeal, were landmark moments in nineteenth- and twentieth-century history meant to address that sin, and yet we as a nation are still grappling with it, all these years later, continuing to reckon with vice and virtue in ways that remain unresolved.

XXX

For something a little unusual, head out of town toward Lebanon, where there are two places of note to the whiskey fan. Independent Stave operates

The air reeks of fermentation and history in Bardstown. Here is the Samuels family plot (T.W. Samuels and Maker's Mark) in the Bardstown Cemetery.

JIM BEAM'S EMPIRE

JIM BEAM WHITE LABEL BOURBON

Jim Beam is pretty gnarly, with notes of nail polish remover, corn oil, and lumber. To its credit, the flaws are mitigated by a proper four-year minimum maturation, something craft distillers took a while to appreciate.

80pf	$15	C	HB	Beam Suntory

BOOKER'S SMALL BATCH BOURBON

Booker's was the original barrel-strength bourbon from Beam— and to some extent this whiskey built an audience for barrel-proof whiskeys. Booker's is hot and solventy, though it delivers many of the pleasures of a middle-aged, barrel-proof Kentucky bourbon. Prices have gone up in recent years, but the product remains mostly the same.

	Variable	$80 ($200)	C	HB	Beam Suntory

KNOB CREEK

For the price, Knob Creek is a stellar Kentucky bourbon that has constantly won in blinds for me, with dry baking spice and rich oak depth. You won't find a better combination of excellence and price in straight Kentucky bourbon. A classic and a value, a good combo.

100pf	$45 ($250)	C 9 yr	HB	Beam Suntory

a cooperage here and gives tours, so for those who have visited many distilleries and want a change of pace, there is a lot to learn at the cooperage. Did you know that a mature tree usually yields only two barrels' worth of wood, as the lowest limb (first knot) determines the length of the usable stave? I didn't!

Two Jim Beam plants are a short drive from Bardstown, and the Clermont location is open to the public. An overcooked visitor center

KNOB CREEK 12

A classic dram, one I often use to benchmark bourbon in the 10–15 year range, and not impossible to find. Beam's whiskeys show better with age, and this one proves that most succinctly. The 18-year version is nice too, but the 12 is a sweeter spot for value.

125–140pf	$55 (18-year goes for $199)	C	HB	Beam Suntory

OLD OVERHOLT RYE WHISKEY

A storied rye brand, long made in Pennsylvania and once owned by former treasury secretary Andrew Mellon. That lineage is in name only, and Overholt is a passable cocktail rye, but with so many more authentic options for just a few more dollars, it's hard to recommend.

80pf	$20	C	HB	Beam Suntory

OLD GRAND-DAD BOTTLED-IN-BOND

A high-rye entry-level bourbon, Bonded Old Grand-Dad is fine cheap whiskey that is hot and viscous with a cloying sweetness. A lot of bartenders like this as a base spirit for proofy drinks.

100pf	$25	C	HB	Beam Suntory

has been redone and upscaled, a metaphor for a lot of the brands under the Beam Suntory umbrella, which includes Booker's, Baker's, and Knob Creek (and Maker's Mark distilled in Loretto). Beam has an idiosyncratic two-column distillation in stainless steel, which is a neat contrast to its competitor Jack Daniel's heavy use of copper in the vapor path. The tour features a miniature distillery, but with so much to see on the bourbon trail, this is a recommend only if it's on your way and time allows.

Also nearby is Limestone Branch, a little distillery founded by Paul and Steve Beam, whose connection to the great Beam family is legitimate but distant enough that it doesn't have much of a connection to the distillery north of Bardstown that bears the Beam name. There are Beams all through Kentucky bourbon history, and Steve has made a project of collecting and cataloging that history. Steve is also a Dant, another big whiskey name, through his mother, but despite being descended from bourbon eminence, Steve had to build his distillery barrel by barrel. I once popped in early one morning to find him tending the still himself, watching a steel bucket slowly fill with heart-run distillate. A partnership with Lux Row, which owned the family's Yellowstone label and helped initiate a new label to honor Minor Case Beam, has helped the brothers grow their reach in the bourbon world. But Limestone Branch itself remains very much a craft operation—and a unique visit among mostly large column-oriented factories that are making bourbon on an industrial scale.

XXX

On a recent visit to Kentucky, I participated in a tasting event called Bourbon on the Banks, a fundraiser for Kentucky State University, in Frankfort, Kentucky's historically Black college. The city feels ancient, much like other Kentucky cities, but a little aristocratic and refined, sunken into an S-shaped bend in the Kentucky River, which gives the feeling of an old city surrounded by high walls.

On this trip, I got to know the city as an adult, visiting its watering holes and enjoying the street life on a vibrant summer weekend. Bourbon on Main is an old tavern that has an unfussy feel. Goodwood Brewery is a nice, if corporate, brewpub chain, and Buddy's Pizza is a classic college-town joint that feels homey. Sig Luscher Brewery specializes in barrel-aged beers (among others), and I spent the latter part of one evening with owner Timothy Luscher drinking brews right from the bourbon barrel and drifting further from lucidity with each glass.

A little side business on this trip would bring me to visit two newer distilleries that are slightly off the common map. First, I drove south from Frankfort to Danville, the first post office west of the Alleghenies. Centre

College, a small liberal arts college, is here, but not much else. Danville is more on the periphery of bourbon country—or it was until Wilderness Trail opened in 2013.

The business was founded by Shane Baker and Dr. Pat Heist, bandmates in high school. Heist has a PhD in microbiology and consulted to the professional spirits industry with their Ferm-Solutions company. They eventually got out of the lab and built a small distillery to make the most of their knowledge, and within five years had built the fourteenth-largest whiskey distillery in the United States, running a 32-inch column and an 18-inch column to make roughly 240 barrels each week, about the size of Maker's Mark back in 2010.

I arrived for what I thought was the noon tour, but in fact discovered I was half an hour late for the eleven a.m. tour. A man with an ambitious and singularly conspicuous goatee offered to walk me over to join the tour group, and soon I realized it was Dr. Heist himself, and we immediately got to talking as distillers. Dr. Heist likes to play two sides of his professional personality against each other—his mountain roots in eastern Kentucky and his PhD in microbiology—and the result is compelling and often unexpectedly funny, a celebrity's charisma.

He showed me his lab and production logs, the nerve center for the distillery unlike any other facility I'd seen. Yeast strains are kept frozen here, allowing for thousands of permutations, but meticulous records are kept so that any positive deviation can be traced and exploited.

Wilderness Trail distillery surrounds an old farmhouse on a sprawling property.

Pappy Van Winkle was a salesman first and always. His slogans were posted around the property at Stitzel-Weller. His "No chemists allowed!" sign appeared at a time when the bourbon business was consolidating and industrializing quickly.

The distillery itself isn't so remarkable—they run a typical Vendome column still—but get under the hood and there are little tweaks here and there that speak to the distiller's specificity of process. I was particularly impressed with a spent-grain dewatering system that used pressure instead of centrifugal force to create less environmental impact from operations.

Wilderness Trail has great ryes that are estery with a sort of pickle brine tang that suits the style. They make a wheated mash bill Bottled-in-Bond, and the bourbon is clean and nice. Most of their whiskeys as of this writing are in the five-to-six-year range, and I get the sense that what people are tasting now is not so much the tip of an iceberg but the tip of a glacier, a slow-moving monolith that is grinding year over year toward perfection.

Pappy Van Winkle was well known for his sign, "At a profit if we can, at a loss if we must, but always fine bourbon." He is somewhat lesser known for a sign elsewhere at Stitzel-Weller that read, "No Chemists Allowed! Nature and the old-time 'know how' of a Master Distiller get the job done here." But distilling is science, whether you describe it that way or not. It's fashionable in certain circles to "believe in science" but whether it's global warming or genetically modified foods, many people have a bias against science somewhere in their consciousness. It takes a very particular modern-day distiller to stake their competitive advantage on microbiology. In the case of Wilderness Trail, it works.

From Danville, I drove back through Frankfort to Sparta, a town mostly known for the NASCAR track that opened in 2000. Nearly in the shadow of the grandstands sits a small distillery in an unassuming log building, the Neeley Family Distillery. When I arrived on a Saturday afternoon, distiller Royce Neeley was busy in the still room and puttering with equipment. His mother was out working the tasting room. Neeley family indeed.

Though the distillery is in the northern reaches of bourbon country, the Neeley family has rich history in whiskey-making in southeastern Kentucky, and the distillery's tasting room features newspaper articles and artifacts from their moonshining days in Owsley County. One artifact is a pistol Royce's great-grandfather used to shoot a rival. Royce will freely say that

The stillhouse at Neeley Family Distillery is a compact operation full of steel, copper, and oak.

the lore of moonshining might have an allure to the modern sensibility, but he would be quick to point out that moonshine feuds were street wars with killer factions, and a survival mechanism in a depressed economy. The romance gives way to a bitter reality, which is that moonshining has often stoked gang warfare and bloodshed.

Family history notwithstanding, Royce has built an open-fermentation, pot-still setup that can make rich, buttery white whiskey unlike any I've had. He runs a thumper keg with spent mash for extra flavor. While I visited, he showed me the fishpond he uses as a heat exchanger to keep his still condensers cool. Everything here is done by gut and by sense. Royce is a tinkerer, trying different configurations, testing flavors, and relying on the elder members of the family for technique and suggestions.

Despite the family's deep history in moonshine, it would be a mistake to call Neeley a moonshine distillery gone legitimate. Royce has built something entirely new that takes inspiration, process, and technique from the past but adapts it for a modern craft distiller. Nothing here fell off the truck pre-engineered from the big manufacturers, but everything has been tested, tinkered with, reverse engineered, and retested again. Royce

Neeley Family Distillery has a DIY atmosphere, but this distinguishes it as one of the few distiller-led, truly small-scale producers in the state doing great whiskeys.

has full command of his operation, sized at just the scale that allows full autonomy over every aspect.

For spirits, his moonshine is authentic, but I would favor the bourbon white dog, true white whiskey that is among the best you will ever drink. Neeley makes a young bourbon that is impressive, but the distillery has only been around since 2015 and I would expect great things to come very soon as more aged whiskey becomes available.

In a way, Neeley Family Distillery and Wilderness Trail represent two poles of the future of Kentucky whiskey. One is technocratic, science driven, well financed, and aims at the industry at large (peers like Bardstown Bourbon Company and New Riff belong in this group). The other is personal, sensory driven, small scale, and authentic to a history of whiskey-making that disappeared long ago and aims to offer something commercial whiskey cannot. Both are led by charismatic, uncompromising visionaries who are working on a Saturday in both the distillery floor and the tasting room because they are in a cage fight with the status quo, the establishment, and their own legacy as distillers. They see a staid mainstream bourbon industry with a lot of inertia that might be ripe for some

new voices and some new whiskeys. They have financial independence, drive, and a credible program to bring back to bourbon something that's been missing.

Bourbon missing something? Did I say that? No, no, bourbon is immaculate and perfectly rendered already, you say, any claim to the contrary is heresy. Thad Vogler, owner of Bar Agricole in San Francisco, says it better than I could in his book *By the Smoke and the Smell*:

> *To take a tour of an American whiskey distillery in Kentucky is almost inevitably to be immersed in apocryphal horseshit, which is only appropriate, as bourbon is our nation's, "native spirit," as decreed by Congress in 1964. We are the nation of apocryphal horseshit, and at no point is this more apparent than the day I most recently arrive in Kentucky. . . .*
>
> *Bourbon is a paradox. At once the most obsessed-over spirit, with bottles like Pappy Van Winkle's twenty-year selling for thousands of dollars, it is also a pretty industrial, unremarkable spirit compared to a number that we have already tasted on our journey together. For the three thousand dollars a twenty-year-old bottle of bourbon fetches, I could fill your shelves with thirty grower-producers, wild-fermented, cask-strength, unfiltered bottles of spirit that will blow your mind.*

I have a more generous view of bourbon than Mr. Vogler, but for someone who knows distilling intimately and loves the spirit, the criticism lands heavy. This is what makes the newer distillers in Kentucky so appealing: their independence, their personality, and their determination to achieve excellence—all traits that have been quietly set aside by the commercial producers, who all make fine bourbon, yes, but it is quite possible that none of us have tasted fine bourbon like what is to come. I'll wager the bourbon of the 2010s will not stand in history's reckoning as the best the industry could make.

But to the skeptic of my analysis, I will simply say: Wait. Be patient. It's coming.

KENTUCKY'S NEW GUARD

WILDERNESS TRAIL BIB WHEATED BOURBON

Wilderness Trail is a great distillery making great whiskeys. Their basic bourbon single-barrel BiB is pretty middle of the road. Classic profile of vanilla, maple syrup, and caramel, this is a mid age-range bourbon that is well distilled and approachable, smoothly outdrinks peer bourbons, but won't necessarily stand out in a crowd. This is the gold standard bourbon that Maker's Mark used to be in the 1990s, and that's some of the highest praise in bourbon.

100pf	$55	C	NT	Campari

WILDERNESS TRAIL SETTLERS SELECT BARREL PROOF RYE

With a low barrel entry proof and a sweet mash, this is actually an odd entry from a fairly mainstream new producer. The result is a clean distillate that isn't too rye forward and has caramel and a wisp of spice. With so much rye offering so much more flavor elsewhere, I'll take this over Kentucky peers, but stop short there.

103.09 pf (variable)	$60	C	NT	Campari

NEELEY FAMILY STRAIGHT BOURBON WHISKEY

A beautiful, remarkable bourbon whiskey. Warm bread, cinnamon, not too sour, not too sweet. A very nearly perfect Kentucky straight bourbon whiskey in a style that is no longer made regularly and only at a small scale now, this bottle is a four grain (with oats, rye, and malt), is pot-stilled and thumped, and aged in a twenty-five-gallon barrel to perfection in forty-one months. At 111 proof, it's not for the weak-kneed, but it drinks easy and smooth, as its perfectionist distiller intended.

111pf	$40	P	TC	Independent

NEELEY SWEET THUMPED RYE WHISKEY

A richly made whiskey, but with a less rye-forward profile than more northerly peers, this still has some Kentucky DNA and the balance and restraint of that tradition. It's still a lovely, proofy rye that bests most of the others in this book.

109.5pf	$40	P	TC	Independent

MOONSHINE HOLLOWS

Moonshine, sometimes called white whiskey or white dog, is an underappreciated subcategory of American whiskey, but it is strong in the mountain parts of Kentucky and Tennessee, as well as in parts of Georgia and the Carolinas. Moonshine can mean any illegal spirit, but as a commercial term, it can refer to nearly anything, as the government considers it merely a fanciful term with no specific meaning.

While some may scoff, the Ole Smoky brand of moonshine was at one point selling more cases than Woodford Reserve, and its visitor center has boasted of having more visitors (4.1 million) to its various locations in the Smoky Mountains than the Kentucky Bourbon Trail and all the distilleries in Scotland combined. Take a minute with that, and you begin to understand the market for moonshine. There is a lot about Appalachia that baffles those on the coasts or even in cities, but looking at moonshine in depth can perhaps help us understand some of the virtues that the rest of the country may be missing.

First off, moonshine is a product made in a folk tradition. Folk traditions stand in opposition to academic disciplines in that they are socially generated by a particular community and adapt as they are handed down among generations. Much of what we love about American culture comes from folk traditions from the various cultures that came together in the United States. Appalachia has been an incubator for folk traditions as it remains isolated by topographical particularities. This has been greatly diminished by radio, television, and the internet, but there is much about Appalachia that remains obstinately unlike other parts of the US.

Moonshine is the embodiment of that tradition, in part because it is illegal, and the word-of-mouth nature of its practice is perfectly suited to folk tradition. It's also agriculturally derived, creating a connection to the land. Put a different way, moonshine is the ultimate farm-to-table product. It benefits from the land, the culture, and the social history from which it springs. It's also incredible when made right.

As a distiller, I am often focused on the white (or unaged) spirit being produced by another distiller as the best measure of their talent and ambition. Any spirit can be improved through aging, but white spirit, if designed for drinking, must be recalibrated or scrapped altogether if it isn't excellent. That might be a change in ingredients, recipe, or process, but only a competent distiller will have the intuition to do this work. A commercial distiller, on the other hand, may know that barrel aging will eliminate rough edges and pass along a compromised product, knowing that time and wood will solve it.

White whiskey is frowned on by a certain type of whiskey drinker, generally the kind that puts a lot of faith in age statements and doesn't do a whole lot of blind tasting. In fact, tasting white spirits is a better way to understand whiskey distillation, I would argue, than any amount of aged-whiskey tasting. For all the bourbon drinkers scoffing at moonshine, I'll wager many—even most—could not identify corn distillate from rye distillate in a blind test. White dog is a very basic building block of any whiskey, and I would argue its sensory command is the secret sauce to perfect whiskey.

People intrinsically understand that age improves whiskey. But remove that variable. Who makes the best zero-year-old whiskey? Start asking this question, and you'll begin to understand who will have the best whiskey at two years and four years and twenty years.

Still, not every moonshine aims to be fine whiskey someday or even today. Most that appears on shelves may even be corn vodka, not even classified as whiskey, or adulterated with sugar or flavorings. Many of the newly successful commercial moonshines tried to enter the national market and failed miserably, assuming what worked in Tennessee might work in Connecticut. It didn't, and a lot of retailers will get visibly agitated when the notion of white whiskey or moonshine comes up. It's not for everyone.

But just like silver tequila, white rum, grappa, and eaux-de-vie (unaged fruit brandies), white whiskey deserves a place at the tasting table. These are all distiller-focused, pot- or low-proof spirits that show how rarefied and particular distilling can be. In fact, many consider silver tequila to be a more refined and perfect version of the spirit than reposado or añejo. White whiskey's potential has been hobbled by laws that require whiskey to be aged or favor aged whiskey, but these laws are cultural and tradition-based or designed to protect commercial interests—and a little arbitrary in the scheme of history. Why can sugar, fruit, and agave yield fine white spirit, but grain cannot? It's a ridiculous notion that is based on centuries of marketing, law, commerce, and, yes, tradition. But that's not to say it can't change.

Ole Smoky and Midnight Moon are mainstream brands aiming at the widest audience, but there are some interesting high-end moonshines. Short Mountain Distillery and Troy & Sons have aimed at upscaling corn whiskey, like silver tequila. Neeley Family Distillery may be the best I've tasted in a while, but moonshine is like its makers—growing, evolving, and adapting like the folk culture it came from. And other craft distillers like Distillery 291 (and Kings County) are proud of their distillate and want to show it off as unaged whiskey to anyone who appreciates its complexity and significance.

MODERN MOONSHINES

GEORGE DICKEL WHITE CORN WHISKEY

Sour mash corn whiskey isn't common, but this bottle, which retails at the distillery and around moonshine country, is a great example of bourbon white dog. Tangy, bright, and oily, with a hint of circus peanut candy, this is the bedrock of flavor in American whiskey, a note so familiar it belongs in every whiskey collection.

91pf	$25	C	HB	Diageo

TROY & SONS PLATINUM MOONSHINE

Clean but flavorful, this is a near-perfect white whiskey. With notes of chocolate and caramel in the distillate, it's an unusually polished flavor, but nothing you'd confuse with vodka. Marketed in a way to evoke silver tequila, the association is too broad to accurately describe the sophistication of this excellent white whiskey.

80pf	$45	H	TC	Independent

DISTILLERY 291 COLORADO RYE WHISKEY WHITE DOG

A punchy white whiskey from malted rye, at 101.7 proof, it's a great proofy spirit with a pungent, malty tang that's hard to find in aged whiskey and suggests the places this whiskey will go over time.

101.7pf	$50	P	TC	Independent

CORSAIR WRY MOON

Corsair, like many of the serious early craft distillers, has moved away from white whiskeys, but I couldn't help but include this near-perfect whiskey distilled from rye malt. Grainy and dry, with notes of red pepper and sage, it shows how rye presents so much variety in American whiskey with a beautiful flavor that shows the diversity and richness of what rye can be.

92pf	$30	P	TC	Independent

Cascade Hollow Distillery sits in a quiet corner of Tennessee near Tuallhoma. Built by Schenley in 1958, it has long been home to the George Dickel brand, which has undergone a renaissance in the past few years.

5

ALT WHISKEY

While you weren't paying any attention, Tennessee whiskey came to be dominated by women. Leave out Jack Daniel's, which accounts for nearly all of Tennessee whiskey produced (indeed almost half of American whiskey produced) and a very good bit of the remaining whiskey comes from either a female distiller or a female founder of American whiskey. This is no small development in the second-most widely consumed category of whiskey and a business that has long appealed to prevailing notions of masculinity in marketing, branding, and storytelling.

Four prominent Tennessee distillers are Fawn Weaver, founder of Uncle Nearest; Nicole Austin, distiller at Cascade Hollow Distilling Co. (George Dickel); Allisa Henley, formerly of Dickel and now running the production facility for Sazerac's new Tennessee Whiskey; and Alex Castle of Old Dominick, Memphis's largest craft distiller. Luckily, three of these distilleries are a short drive from Nashville, which is a fine place to begin any tour of Tennessee whiskey. Nashville has at least two great craft distillers, but more on them after we drive south.

Tennessee whiskey is bourbon by another name, usually differentiated by maple charcoal filtration, known as the Lincoln County process. It has long stood as the alternative to bourbon, and Jack Daniel's in particular has positioned itself as something different, though with bourbon surging in popularity (and Jack's sales stalled), they have been doing a lot of messaging to remind everyone that Jack is bourbon just as much as it is whiskey. They just don't call it that. But the contrarian streak remains, visible in many of the distillers operating in Tennessee today, stoking a rivalry going back decades or more. These whiskeys generally make the most of the idea that they are an alternative to bourbon, whether that means a staid, heritage rebel like Jack Daniel's or the wild creativity of Corsair's Triple Smoke.

I visited Tennessee in the fall of 2019 for the Nashville Whiskey Festival and made some time to go see distillers before the event. First on my list was my former colleague Nicole Austin at George Dickel. The smallest of the heritage distillers, the brand has always played spoiler to the much, much larger Jack Daniel's in the category of Tennessee whiskey. Mismanaged and maligned for years, George Dickel makes a bright and buttery distillate, one of the best in the business, and their Number 12 has long been a favorite spirit of mine, in spite of a clunky brand name. For decades, the distillery has been owned by spirits giant Diageo, whose main interest in Tennessee whiskey is as a foil to Jack Daniel's, which vies with Diageo's Johnnie Walker for global whiskey hegemony.

All of that feels far away when you arrive at the distillery, which sits in a little hollow outside the town of Tullahoma. The distillery dates to 1959 and was built by defunct spirits giant Schenley after Jack Daniel's owners at Brown-Forman refused to sell the brand to Schenley's belligerent owner, Lewis "Lew" Rosenstiel. In this way, the distillery has always played a little bit of a funny role in American whiskey as an alternative to the most mainstream American whiskey for more than a half-century.

Now legally defined by state law, Tennessee whiskey is simply bourbon that is maple charcoal filtered before barreling, a process that isn't closely regulated. While Jack Daniel's aggressively filters their whiskeys with maple charcoal, the vats at Dickel aren't changed out nearly as often, diminishing its effect. The distillery is a compact enterprise but has a lot of character, as very little has changed over the years with ambivalent corporate owners.

At our visit, we tasted through some of the expressions, including Nicole's first project for Dickel, a Bottled-in-Bond that would go on to win *Whisky Advocate*'s Whiskey of the Year that December.

I first met Nicole in August 2010, the day Kings County first launched at retail at a wine shop in Brooklyn. She loved whiskey, wanted to work in this industry, and offered to work for free until we could pay her. She quickly carved a place for herself as our head blender, something not all American distillers would have prioritized, though smaller production and smaller

Fermentation vats at Cascade Hollow. The Lincoln County process is followed here, but vats are changed infrequently for less impact.

barrels especially demand it. While many distillers will bottle purely by age, we bottled by flavor profile, establishing a range of products from four different whiskey recipes that differed in proof, age, and fullness of flavor. That requires a fair amount of sensory training and sensory specificity when assembling a whiskey blend, and I attribute Kings County's early success in part to Nicole's diligence (and stubbornness) around flavor profile. She trained Ryan Ciuchta, our current head blender, in the same mold, and I can say the diligence, stubbornness, and excellence all continue.

Nicole's ambitions extended beyond our own distillery, and she worked also for Dave Pickerell, a former distiller at Maker's Mark who remade his career in connecting brands to sourced whiskeys, including WhistlePig, Widow Jane, Hillrock, and others. He also helped on the technical and engineering side for startups like Woodinville, which has been the best steward of his legacy. Nicole then went on to serve as commissioning engineer at Tullamore D.E.W. in Ireland for their new column still. But it is her latest job at Dickel, where she holds a fair amount of autonomy, that suits her talents best.

FOUR FROM CASCADE HOLLOW

GEORGE DICKEL NO. 12

One of my favorite all-time drams, this is a really evocative pour for the price—with a sour honey, roasted peanut, and rich oak character that is hard to find at this price. Dickel's whiskeys are polarizing, perhaps, but to me this one is a classic. Out-drinks whiskeys with a lot more hype and twice the price.

90pf	$25	C	HB	Diageo

GEORGE DICKEL BOTTLED-IN-BOND

This whiskey was Nicole Austin's first project for Dickel, a 13-year BiB for $35. Rich depth of character but a sour peanut brittle note may not be universally loved. A great BiB and inarguably excellent value.

100pf	$35	C	HB	Diageo

GEORGE DICKEL SINGLE BARREL SELECT

The squat bottle ("barrel select") has sometimes been a sleeper gem for the Dickel brand. This single-barrel version is a 15-year bottled at 40% 80 proof. The most age for the price you can get in today's market, if you don't mind the barely legal proof. A different approach and a bit of a flex from the distillery, though not necessarily an especially memorable whiskey.

80pf (variable)	$55	C 15 yr	HB	Diageo

GEORGE DICKEL 17-YEAR

A delicious whiskey, with rich oak, barrel spice, and heft, and not a lot of the typical peanut brittle Dickel note. There are less expensive and younger whiskeys with a comparable profile, but for a fine old celebration Tennessee whiskey, you won't do better.

92pf	$200	C 17 yr	HB	Diageo

On our visit in fall 2019, Nicole hosted a small group of us, and we got to climb around inside the distillery, looking out over grain bins and mash vessels and up into the tower that houses the 48-inch column still. Dickel is a polarizing whiskey for many, and some point to a vitamin-like quality in the aged spirit. I tend to like more oak-forward Dickel, though the Bottled-in-Bond is a very classic style, if actually a touch on the lighter side for its age. For the retail price, it's hard to find a

Fawn Weaver read an article about Nearest Green in the *New York Times* and built the fastest-growing whiskey brand in America around the story of the man who taught Jack Daniel how to distill.

more perfect whiskey, and nearly all of Dickel's whiskeys are underrated, including the barrel select and some older editions. If you travel through this part of Tennessee, I highly recommend the stop.

Not that far away is an old horse farm that is currently being transformed into the Nearest Green Distillery. Nathan (or Nearest) Green was relatively unknown to the official history, though anyone studying Jack Daniel (the man) closely would have found his name, often misspelled as "Nearis." Jack Daniel was an enigmatic figure, from what I can gather, even in his own time. The youngest of ten kids, orphaned at a young age, and small of stature, he went to live with a local minister where he learned the distilling business from an enslaved man, Green. After the Civil War, Daniel set out to build a distillery and a brand and worked closely with Green and his descendants in the role we might today call a master or head distiller. Daniel was a dandy and a salesman, and certainly had unusual interactions with women, which seem bizarre and performative, even by the standards of the day. Jack Daniel found religion coinciding, maybe a little too coincidentally, with the start of Prohibition in Tennessee, and in 1909 vowed never to let his name appear on another bottle of whiskey ever again.

That, of course, didn't happen, and Green's legacy was overshadowed by others who were important to the label's later development—Daniel's nephew Lem Motlow and then Frank Sinatra, who turned an obscure brand into a global one. But for all Black Americans have contributed to whiskey, there's been an unfortunately long tradition of bourbon winking at the Old South, seen in brands like Rebel Yell, Early Times, and Southern Comfort. Brown-Forman, to its credit, began to reshape its own narrative history away from Motlow (who posed some problems to anyone bothering to dig into his story) and toward Green.

After a *New York Times* article about Green's overlooked legacy, Fawn Weaver, a Los Angeles entrepreneur, set out to learn about Green and eventually began to build a new brand of Tennessee whiskey around him. I heard her speak at a craft distillers convention and have never been in a room of 1,500 people so electrified. Whiskey is good storytelling after all, and Nearest Green's tale is a fascinating one. It didn't hurt that Weaver's previous career was as an author.

My host for the visit to the Nearest Green site was Sherrie Moore, who appeared to be single-handedly building the distillery, save for a crew of workers who were beautifying one of the buildings. Moore was asking

Jack Daniel seated with one of Nathan Green's sons at his right hand in 1904

questions and soliciting feedback on everything from display literature to whether or not she was going to splurge on agitators for her fermenters. As of my visit, there wasn't much to see (a public opening was planned for later in the month), but it was clear that big ambitions suited the site, a sprawling complex of green-roofed barns and stables.

Nearest Green has a core expression (Uncle Nearest 1856) and a lower-priced, lighter small batch (Uncle Nearest 1884). Both are more typical of a bourbon than a Tennessee whiskey and are no longer sourced from Dickel (as was once the case), but from a purpose-built contract distiller in Tennessee. A rye expression is sourced from WhistlePig's stock of Alberta Premium Rye, then finished in Tennessee.

If you are driving around this part of rural Tennessee, which is really the only way to get around here, it's worth imagining yourself in an earlier era, before railroads and paved highways, when whiskey was distilled in a copper pot or even a hollow log, sold by jug or small barrel over land by wagon.

I got to know this area very well as a little boy. My surrogate grand-parents, the Gallaghers, lived in Winchester, Tennessee. We'd travel down to visit them on long weekends and shop for toys in the local hardware store, Hammer's, which carried everything a rural county could need. Rural America has changed, Hammer's is gone, and so are the Gallaghers, but I came to love their Tennessee home with its fall colors and hilly landscape, geologically similar to Kentucky's bluegrass region. When my brother went to college, he chose nearby Sewanee in part to continue the cave exploring he enjoyed at home in Kentucky. Caves mean limestone, and this region has the same type of sandstone/limestone combination that has historically been associated with good whiskey.

Just down the road is a very famous cave in Lynchburg, and around it lies the Jack Daniel's distillery. Jack is the largest brand of American whis-key by any measure and sells more than double its closest competitor, Jim Beam, through line extensions and other expressions. It runs seven massive column stills and puts away more than 2,400 barrels a day. The modern brand is owned by Brown-Forman, the Louisville-based spirits giant.

Jack Daniel is a singular figure in whiskey history, as he had no dis-cernible philosophy other than to stubbornly make good whiskey the

NATHAN GREEN & JACK DANIEL

UNCLE NEAREST 1856

Tropical fruit, maple syrup, and honey on the palate make this a nice whiskey for sipping or for mixing. A versatile pour for any occasion—and a welcome entry to a small category of Tennessee whiskeys

93pf	$50	C	SW	Independent

UNCLE NEAREST 1884

This is a lovely whiskey. Rich toffee and butterscotch on the nose, warming spice on the palate. This is a whiskey that's well put together and one of the few sourced whiskeys with a story worth telling.

100pf	$60	C	SW	Independent

JACK DANIEL'S OLD NO. 7 TENNESSEE WHISKEY

What a strange whiskey to be America's most popular! Thin with notes of diluted campfire and creosote, the charcoal strips a lot of the corn oils that give corn-based whiskeys so much texture. But who am I to disagree with the world?

80pf	$20	C	HB	Brown-Forman

old-fashioned way. When Lem Motlow, the heir apparent, suggested they make peach brandy, Daniel would have none of it (though there is evidence enough that Jack sourced whiskey from other distillers to prop his brand when Tennessee Prohibition loomed). Today, many brands are based on figures that make this claim, but Jack lived it, and there's enough documentation of his life to support the claim. Jack represents something that is mostly lost in American whiskey: the cantankerous perfectionist who controls both product and financial decisions for his company. In many ways, most of commercial American whiskey up until the recent

GENTLEMAN JACK

The slightly more rounded version of Jack, it's still thin to my taste, but there's a little more cinnamon and marzipan on the palate. Still, for the proof and price, this is a hard whiskey for me to love.

80pf	$30	C	HB	Brown-Forman

JACK DANIEL'S SINGLE BARREL SELECT

If you want a quintessential Jack Daniel's product for sipping, this is probably the one. It has the Jack Daniel's wood-forward dry palate, but some more complexity and body at a proof that isn't timid. Other Tennessee whiskeys want to be bourbon, but this is distinctive and the best Jack gets without losing its identity.

94pf	$35	C	HB	Brown-Forman

JACK DANIEL'S BOTTLED-IN-BOND

Whisky Advocate's 2022 Whiskey of the Year, this is maybe 1 part Jack, 3 parts rich and buttery balanced bourbon. This rounds out a collection of BiBs (or Tennessee whiskeys), and it's a nice whiskey that shows that Jack can be whatever it wants to be.

100pf	$35	C	HB	Brown-Forman

craft boom was dedicated to preserving the illusion that single makers had such power (through the elevation of master distillers as traveling salesmen), when only a handful had any hand in product direction in the old sense. Which is why Jack Daniel stands out.

In many ways, the modern brand honors much of that spirit. Jack is still filtered through maple charcoal before it is aged, an expensive process, and unlike other Tennessee whiskeys, Jack commits to this filtration, changing out its vats frequently. This is a way to jump-start the aging process (after all, charcoal is what lines every charred new oak barrel) and a way to make younger whiskey taste better. Jack Daniel's has rarely been sold with an age statement, though a 10-year hit the market recently, keeping up with a modern audience obsessed with age as the measure of whiskey. An excellent Bottled-in-Bond has also now arrived, and when white whiskey had a vogue moment a decade ago, Jack had the best one on the commercial market. But recent moves toward higher-proof and age-stated expressions show that Jack is pressing for legitimacy in a crowded market obsessed with bourbon, which Jack has long marketed itself away from.

But is Jack good? It's a drier, woodier product than comparably aged bourbon. It's thin on the palate, which I take to be the result of rectification and filtration working together. Gentleman Jack is a modest improvement, but stylistically, the fashion in recent years has gone for more flavor, rounder mouthfeel, and higher proof. If I am trapped at an event with limited American whiskey options, it's always a pleasant reminder of something familiar, but not beloved.

The fact that the largest American whiskey brand and the fastest-growing American whiskey brand can be traced back to a formerly enslaved man and an orphaned boy in a forgotten corner of Tennessee, who made a run at the whiskey business together back in the 1860s and 1870s, is quite remarkable. I think both men would be baffled by the modern products, but at least a little proud of what their names have come to represent.

XXX

If you are down in this area, a side trip to Chattanooga is worth your while. Chattanooga is a city like Austin, Texas; Athens, Georgia; or even a bit like Nashville without the bachelorettes. It has Civil War and civil rights history, but a younger creative identity than other southern cities. You can enjoy hot chicken here too, and then head to Lookout Mountain for a funky hodgepodge of national historic Civil War park, Victorian fairy-tale architecture, old money, and roadside attraction.

The local distillery, Chattanooga Whiskey Company, is formidable, having upgraded from a pot-still microdistillery near the Choo Choo (there is such a place) to a 24-inch column still in a custom-built facility

The Nashville skyline has changed since the 1969 Bob Dylan album. There are more buildings, biscuits, bachelorettes, and hot chicken, but still lots of country music.

downtown not far from the aquarium. The brand was mostly built on sourced whiskey, but they've done a good job of moving out and away from it. An excellent high-malt bourbon is just one example of why it should be on the radar of anyone watching Tennessee's newer distillers.

On the other end of the state, Old Dominick is the most established whiskey maker in Memphis, and its distiller, Alex Castle, does a nice job as ambassador as much as maker, bringing a background in engineering from the University of Kentucky to her work in the factory and education events. It's early for their whiskey, but a house-made Tennessee whiskey finally landed in October 2022, and it's a bottle I'll be keen to find when supply opens up.

XXX

Music, like whiskey, is something that can become fiercely regional. As long as people have enjoyed coming together for a nice meal, good drink and live music have served to provide conviviality. In some rare moments, a city's music culture can accelerate and amplify, as happened with Motown in Detroit or grunge rock in Seattle. Nashville has done a good job of marketing itself as the home of country music, though one feels that only vestiges of the apparatus of the country industry remain—its financial infrastructure has rolled up into other entertainment capitals.

The bit that remains feels a bit ossified, and the touristy megabars of Broadway feel as though they are paying homage and fetishizing history while their real aim is pumping young tourists full of cheap beer and sugary drinks, the morning-after stench of which taints the putrid air. But the Country Music Hall of Fame is here and worth a visit, as is the new National Museum of African American Music.

Nashville has also always been a college town, which provides good incubation for young bands. It also provides Nashville's justification for its older nickname as the Athens of the South (not to be confused with the actual Athens of the South, in Georgia). A cement replica of the Parthenon in Centennial Park is certainly one of the more enduring American garden follies of another time and reinforces the city's vision of itself from more than a century ago.

Nashville in the last decade has completely transformed, as young people from around the South flock there to begin careers. Its decadent food culture and party atmosphere have secured it another title as the "Bachelorette Capital," a title I would have assumed to be exaggerated if I hadn't seen the hordes for myself when visiting distilleries. Music, intellectual curiosity, young love, and whiskey all make for a heady stew, and Nashville will nourish like few other cities.

There are two distilleries in town worth a visit, Nelson's Green Brier and Corsair, and luckily they are located in the same building complex. Nelson's Green Brier was founded by two brothers who set out to revive an old family label. They have done so mostly with whiskey sourced from elsewhere, but with some creativity and verve. Their Belle Meade was intended to be the sourced brand before their own house-distilled Green Brier label came out. Current labels of Green Brier suggest sourcing after all, and the still on-site is mostly a showpiece, so don't expect much in the way of novelty here. But barrel-finished editions and special releases have earned high praise from credible sources.

The former Marathon Motor Works in Nashville is home to two craft distillers: Nelson's Green Brier and Corsair.

TENNESSEE CRAFT WHISKEY

CORSAIR TRIPLE SMOKE

One of the original craft spirits to push the boundaries of American whiskey, this is an all-malt whiskey smoked with beechwood, cherrywood, and peat. Perfect with barbecue, this has a sweet, malty base that's lightly oaked with a heavy note of smoke in the middle that calls to mind leather and tobacco (and Islay Scotch).

80pf	$47	P	TC	Independent

CORSAIR DARK RYE

This is a dank, almost hoppy rye whiskey, a little edgy and dissonant, but full of flavor and richness in spite of a younger age statement. Cinnamon, cola, and a red-peppery finish round out this very flavor-forward entry, distilled from malted rye and chocolate-malt rye.

85pf	$47	P 2 yr	TC	Independent

BELLE MEADE BOURBON

For me, this is a nearly perfect bourbon, made in Indiana and bottled in Tennessee. Go figure. But a good example of how commodity whiskey in the right hands can be molded to nice outcomes.

90.4pf	$45	C	SW	Constellation

NELSON'S GREEN BRIER TENNESSEE WHISKEY

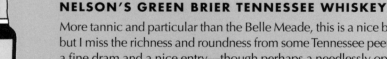

More tannic and particular than the Belle Meade, this is a nice bottle, but I miss the richness and roundness from some Tennessee peers. It's a fine dram and a nice entry—though perhaps a needlessly opaque one. Distillery exclusives and brand extensions may be the better way.

91pf	$35	C	S	Constellation

CHATTANOOGA CASK 111 HIGH MALT BOURBON

A bourbon that drinks like a Tennessee Whiskey (from Tennessee), this is a limited edition of at least 25 percent specialty malts (found via Seelbach's). It's proofy and barrel-forward for a younger whiskey, the very thing you can expect from adventurous, creative distillers.

111pf	$50	C 2 yr	TC	Constellation

Corsair was a well-deserved early darling of craft distilling, earning accolades for an expansive variety of creative spirits.

The real gem of Nashville distilling is Corsair, one of the most significant players in the craft movement and a leader in expanding the category of American whiskey. Corsair actually has two locations in Nashville; the one near Nelson's Green Brier runs a small still and taproom at the Marathon Building but does most of its production out of a facility in the Wedgewood neighborhood. Corsair has released dozens of labels over the years, all manner of gins, moonshines, liqueurs, absinthes, and whiskeys—though its whiskeys demonstrate best what the distillery can do. Focused on alt whiskeys, the brand's labeling nods to indie film, though the current bottle design has gone more mainstream.

Corsair is probably best known in the whiskey world for its triple smoke, a whiskey that marries beechwood, cherry wood, and peat-smoked malts in a recipe that makes an American malt whiskey that's brash and complex and unlike any Scotch whisky. Corsair has been leading with this whiskey, but their rye is some of the finest produced by any distiller.

Oatrage, an oat whiskey, and Buck Yeah, a buckwheat whiskey, are great finds for the whiskey hunter looking to the absolute frontier of American whiskey, where few travel and the rules of tradition are loose. Corsair does not fool much with corn, but a four-year Tennessee whiskey I once tried at an awards show proved that founder Darek Bell's team of distillers can work their magic in any genre.

I count Darek as a friend and had the good fortune to visit both of his Nashville distilleries and his malthouse, as well as the family farm where he is cultivating grains for the whiskeys and even fruit for brandies. Darek couldn't care less about Kentucky bourbon and Tennessee whiskey, believing them to have been corrupted long ago. His distillery has inspired many of his workers to begin their own projects, and Corsair has a rightful place as a founding father of craft—Darek even wrote a book called *Alt Whiskeys*, a remarkably open document that expands the horizon of American whiskey.

Still, commercial distilling, even at a small scale, has its pressures, and Corsair has streamlined and grown up in recent years. A Kentucky location closed in 2018 in favor of a new expansion in Nashville, but you

A small selection from the shelves at the Nashville Whiskey House

can be sure that whatever Corsair becomes as it matures, it will stay true to its polymorphous roots.

Perhaps the best spot in all of American whiskey is in Nashville. It's neither a distillery nor a bar, and I can't even tell you its exact location. It's just called the "Whiskey House." There are many great temples of American whiskey: Justin's House of Bourbon in Lexington, Canon in Seattle, Old Hickory in Pensacola, Jack Rose in DC, and Brandy Library in New York. But they are all bars with employees and rent and other economic pressures. The Whiskey House isn't a bar, or even a club. It's a private collection, and a whopper, with close to 5,000 bottles of whiskey, mostly focused on Kentucky and Tennessee whiskeys, with respective rooms for each. Another room is a sort of doomsday bunker with vials of the last bits of every bottle that has ever been consumed in the Whiskey House, including some whiskeys that are long gone in traditional channels.

I had the good fortune to visit two iterations of the Whiskey House, which were first installed in houses that were stuck in Department of Buildings limbo before being cleared for renovations. The new location is in a commercial building, and access to the house is governed by a loose committee of enthusiasts. But the real oligarch of the Whiskey House and its liquid fortune is John Brittle or "JB," who created the Whiskey House and had the biggest hand in building its collection. He is a curious enthusiast, a mad collector, and a hospitable force. Social media is banned here, but the multiplicity of rooms lined with bottles are a sight for any American whiskey lover to behold.

Access to the Whiskey House is through charitable donation, and if you are a person of means, or know someone who is, find out which charities the Whiskey House is supporting and make a contribution generous enough for access and a personal tasting. I won't have steered you wrong, and we'll all have done something good for the world.

WHISKEY RECKONING

"I don't know if it's PC to offer this," a friend recently said as he handed me a glass of E. H. Taylor, worried about inadvertently glorifying the Confederate South. Kentucky was never a part of the Confederacy during the war but all too frequently embraced the Lost Cause after the war, and the question says a lot about what the bourbon business has become. So many whiskey brands have depended on antebellum imagery (Early Times, Southern Comfort) or outright Confederate sympathy (Rebel Yell, a brand that only in 2020 dropped the Yell) that it's almost impossible not to look at bourbon differently in an era when monuments to Confederate figures are being torn down and narratives of the Old South are being reconsidered.

Cognac is more popular in the United States than in France, and mostly because Black Americans since the two world wars have preferred its international flavor as an alternative to bourbon's unapologetic southern affinity. It's a cultural divide that is only just now starting to soften as groups like the Black Bourbon Society consider bourbon, in spite of its past, for a new era.

Bourbon brands, more than other types of booze, tend to be named after people, and people are often judged by complicated legacies. Still, politics is relative. Is the lowly Confederate foot soldier more despicable than the robber baron industrialist who built fortunes exploiting tens of thousands of laborers? And how much can we forgive people for being a product of their own time? The slaveowner in 1790 is rightly despicable, but what contemporary failures will we come to judge harshly someday? Which figures were progressive or forward-thinking within whiskey? Which marginalized entrepreneurs succeeded despite the challenges? Who had privilege and used it to exploit venal desires, and who used spirits as a way to escape and transcend society's prejudice?

COLONEL E. H. TAYLOR

Taylor was not a Confederate leader, as his title suggests. Kentucky has a tradition of bestowing the honorary title of colonel on community leaders and businessmen (most famously on fried chicken magnate Colonel Sanders). Taylor avoided service for either side during the Civil War but instead began his career in banking before getting into distilling. Later he became a skilled Democratic politician serving as mayor of Frankfort and as state senator. One online sleuth found Taylor being thanked in a ceremony to dedicate a Jefferson Davis memorial (Davis's first wife was a Taylor relative). It's unequivocal that Taylor was a great advocate for bourbon and protecting the tradition that made it what we know today at a moment of crisis for American whiskey. He was also raised by a wealthy and connected family, litigious, and made and lost fortunes over his lifetime, causing financial harm to himself and others. For bourbon, he is an elder statesman; as a man, his legacy is mixed.

OLD FORESTER

Brown-Forman has always insisted that the Old Forester brand was named for a Louisville physician, Dr. William Forrester. At some point the brand dropped the second "r" in the name for reasons that remain murky. Still, the name bears a close resemblance to Nathan Bedford Forrest, third most famous Confederate and the first Grand Wizard of the KKK. Would it be a stretch to assume that many Southerners liked the brand because of this subliminal association? Harry Harrison Kroll sums up that very sentiment in his profoundly regressive 1967 book *Bluegrass, Belles, and Bourbon*: "I have heard tell the whiskey was named in honor of General Nathan Bedford Forrest, who tipped a ready bottle of whisky as well as trafficked in slaves, and slaughtered Yankees as a pastime. Why some character who thought he could spell correctly changed the word to one "r" is not for me to say."

Amid the reckoning with Southern history that has defined the last few years, this association is impossible to ignore. Did Brown-Forman benefit from this subconscious association? They recently liquidated iffy brands like Southern Comfort and Early Times, but doubled down on Old Forester, hoping that pushing the official history might steer the public away from a coincidence that—viewed with a modern lens—is a little too close for comfort.

FOUR ROSES

Paul Jones, the brand's founder, was a Confederate soldier, but not a very successful one. Still, if there is plenty of antebellum imagery and problematic framing in early Four Roses marketing, can the modern brand be forgiven for its past sins? Four Roses stopped being sold in the United States for a stretch in the 1980s but became revered in Japan, where it is now owned and managed, creating enough distance from its early past that one can't credit any present-day success to legacy affinity.

GEORGE T. STAGG

If you want to avoid Confederate whiskey but like a classic Kentucky bourbon, you can't go wrong with Stagg. Union Captain George Stagg devoted himself to the bourbon business and built the distillery that is today known as Buffalo Trace into a powerhouse after separating from E. H. Taylor. It's great whiskey that doesn't require an asterisk.

OLD OVERHOLT

Old Overholt became a modern behemoth through the stewardship of Henry Clay Frick, a robber baron who took rye whiskey profits and invested in coal and coke ovens to make steel. Frick was deeply reviled by his workers and survived an assassination attempt and many unionization efforts through the support of armed Pinkerton guards. If that weren't enough, a poorly maintained dam at his private hunting club collapsed, flooding a whole Pennsylvania valley and killing 2,208 residents in the deluge. He also donated his priceless art collection of Old European masterworks to the public for posterity as the Frick Collection, a remarkable museum in New York City. History is complicated.

PAPPY VAN WINKLE

Pappy probably had little to do with the Rebel Yell brand, conceived as a personal project in 1936 by his business partner Alex Farnley's brother Charles, who would be mayor of Louisville from 1948 to 1953 and later a congressman. Charles was an eccentric who conceived of the brand somewhat ironically, a nuance that appears to have gotten lost when Pappy's son rebooted the brand in 1961; the opportunism in that venture is a little more starkly rendered and unforgivable, tarnishing the Van Winkle legacy for this consumer.

UNCLE NEAREST

As a boy, Jack Daniel learned distilling after leaving home to live with Dan Call, a minister and seasonal distiller like many farmers. Call was a Lutheran minister, a Confederate, and slaveowner, and Nathan Green, himself an enslaved person until Emancipation, ran the stills for the farm. Jack was drawn to this aspect of farmwork, and with Green's expertise in distilling and Jack's salesmanship, they built a burgeoning whiskey business. By 1875, Jack went into business with Call as an independent distiller, with Green's adult children running the distillery. Nathan Green's place in the business was well documented, and unlike photographs of other distillery crews of the era, a well-known image of Jack Daniel is seen proudly seated with George Green, a Black man, at his right hand—a remarkably progressive visual for its time. Mostly forgotten, this history resurfaced in 2016 in a *New York Times* article, as Brown-Forman began to embrace Green's legacy. Entrepreneur Fawn Weaver found the article inspiring and built a whiskey brand off of Green's story. It would appear that the largest and fastest-growing brands of American whiskey converge on an unlikely friendship between a Black man and a white boy in rural 1960s Tennessee.

BERNHEIM AND I. W. HARPER

With so many "great men" of bourbon either supporting the Lost Cause narrative or enjoying profits from brands that were built on it, it is refreshing to learn about Isaac Wolfe Bernheim, a German Jewish immigrant who built up a fortune in the spirits business and used his wealth to purchase and donate 16,000 acres of forest land to the people of Kentucky as a permanent park. He stipulated that "no distinction will be shown between rich or poor, white or colored" and banned discussion of religion, politics, and business in the arboretum. He also insisted that the American flag be flown to ensure the "story of liberty" be retold for children. Philanthropy from another time can be cringey, but it's hard not to appreciate the gesture. Both Bernheim Wheat Whiskey made by Heaven Hill and the I. W. Harper brand from Diageo are derived from this important figure in bourbon's history.

GEORGE DICKEL

Dickel was a blockade runner smuggling liquor past Union-held precincts in Nashville during the Civil War. He was an opportunist who ran with an unsavory crowd, but the modern brand doesn't try to make any connection to the historical figure. As run by Diageo and distiller Nicole Austin, this is, for me, a fine business to support.

BULLEIT

It's one thing to debate a modern brand that evolved from dubious circumstances. It's quite another for a living figure to pose very contemporary problems for a brand that's less than forty years old. Hollis Worth publicly accused her father, Tom Bulleit (founder of the brand), of homophobia and ostracism from the family and business, as well as abuse over a series of social media posts in 2017. Anyone in the spirits industry around that time knew Hollis to be a fervent promoter, breaking down the image of Kentucky bourbon as straight, white, and backward. So the accusation landed especially hard for those who had appreciated her perspective. Tom Bulleit, for his part, responded with a belated and terse letter in the *Louisville Courier Journal* expressing his love and clarifying that he was not a homophobe. An inter-

view with Tom Bulleit in the *Bourbon Review* paints a complex portrait, but one that hardly insulates him from criticism (court-documented allegations of domestic violence are particularly troubling).

If that's not enough, a bourbon blender at Bulleit, Eboni Major, filed a lawsuit accusing Diageo of racial discrimination. Eager to promote a progressive image in the wake of the Tom Bulleit scandal, the company promoted Major as a public face of the brand, while the lawsuit alleges, among other slights, that Bulleit failed to provide proper compensation for both her work and the dissemination of her image as an antidote to Bulleit's former woes. Diageo disputed these claims, and the suit was eventually withdrawn and the parties settled through arbitration.

MAKER'S MARK

Founder Bill Samuels's grandfather built a distillery in Deatsville, Kentucky, in 1844, and while sheriff rounded up a posse of Confederate raiders and forced them to surrender. He confiscated arms from the men, including a pistol from a man named Frank James, who with his brother Jesse would go on to infamy as a bank and train robber. Remembered as a populist hero, Jesse (and his brother) were less well known for war crimes and torture during the Civil War. Their popular image traded on Confederate sympathy in the West, much of which has been forgotten today. Frank's arrest, just after the end of the Civil War, is of genuine significance to the Union cause, and the pistol is said to be one of the last weapons of the conflict. The pistol is on display at the Samuels House, a bed-and-breakfast run by the Maker's Mark founding family.

The Ross & Squibb Distillery in Lawrenceburg, as it is formally known, is better known as MGP, and makes about 70 percent of rye sold in the US and many other white label whiskeys sold under different brands.

6

RIGHT BANK WHISKEY

Most people have focused on the "left bank" of the Ohio River, Kentucky and Tennessee, but historically the right bank made just as much whiskey, especially in distilleries around Cincinnati. The same limestone water can be found on both sides of the river, and all the geological and climatic aspects of Kentucky's position on the map apply to its northern neighbors. Fleischmann, Gaff, Squibb, and Ross were all big names on the north side of the Ohio before and after Prohibition.

While many of these distillers built businesses that have been folded into mainstream brands over the years, only George Ross's Rossville distillery in Lawrenceburg, Indiana, continues today. Formerly a major plant for Seagram, the distillery was known for a little while as LDI and has been purchased since by the descriptively named MGP (Midwest Grain Products) Ingredients as a white-label producer of whiskeys.

In 2014, an article ran in the *Daily Beast* with the headline "Your 'Craft' Whiskey Is Probably from a Factory Distillery in Indiana." This wasn't the first publication to call out the glaring hypocrisy in the then-nascent niche of craft spirits—but in an era when headlines ripped around the internet via social media, it was the tipping point when the average curious whiskey drinker became aware that most of the whiskey appearing in seemingly independent, craft bottles came from one industrial source. So many publications ran versions of this article with slight variations on the theme that within two years a public sense of being duped took hold. Templeton was sued for deceptive marketing and eventually settled, paying customers partial refunds. Labels for other brands were quietly revised. People didn't like being misled, and in those early days, brands were far less transparent, and consumers collectively pushed back.

Forthright distillers and critics (notably Chuck Cowdery) dusted off section 5.36(d) of the federal code, a passage that requires the state of distillation to be disclosed on a spirits label if it is distilled in a different state than where it is bottled, an arcane protection against, say, a Brooklyn distiller buying barrels in Indiana to claim a Brooklyn product. Or, perhaps more as the law was intended, people in Kentucky buying Indiana bourbon and labeling it a Kentucky product (how the times change, right?). Overnight, labels began appearing with new language, "distilled in Indiana."

Several grain-to-glass distillers got in on the criticism, myself included, appearing in articles such as NBC's "Behind the Misleading Claims Fueling America's Bourbon Boom" or the *Wall Street Journal*'s "Craft Whiskey Is in the Eye of the Beholder." When Senator Chuck Schumer, of New York, made the gaffe of giving the gift of a supposedly excellent Brooklyn-born bourbon to bitter rival Mitch McConnell, of Kentucky, the whiskey media were quick to smirk, knowing the bottle as one typically sourced from Kentucky or Indiana but merely bottled in Brooklyn, causing some embarrassment to Schumer's office and undermining his joke. Duping US senators is not a great business model, and it was a stark illustration of the thorny issues around sourced whiskey and transparency.

Another view of Ross & Squibb, showing Seagram signage still visible on the rickhouses

Why did grain-to-glass distillers get so bent out of shape to begin with? As Pappy Van Winkle once quipped, "It is very important to see these four words on a bottle: 'Distilled and Bottled By.' Because any fool with a funnel can bottle whiskey!" And indeed, the amount of work that goes into distilling a whiskey from scratch versus buying a commodity whiskey barrel is very different, one that Pappy knew full well as a small independent distiller in the 1950s and '60s.

MGP makes fine whiskey, and many defenders have stood by this point, which nearly everyone concedes. But as craft grows up, how will it hold up to the small-scale producers? MGP's then master distiller, Greg Metze, didn't exactly address this question but told *Cincinnati Magazine* in 2016, "[Home whiskey makers] just don't have the equipment, the analytical capacity, the science," which illustrates the debate starkly (or suggests that Metze has just never had good moonshine). Either you accept that whiskey is the only consumer product to get better when made at an industrial scale (and there are many consumers who apparently believe this), or it is like most consumer products that lose complexity, texture, and flavor when it scales, like pretty much everything else. (Metze has since departed to work at a craft distillery in Colorado.)

RYE WHISKEY SALES

Rye whiskey sold 1.3 million 9-liter cases domestically in 2020, with sales of Bulleit Rye almost half of the total sold. Other Key brands are Templeton, High West, and Old Overholt. Bourbon, by contrast, accounted for almost 30 million 9-liter cases domestically and another 20 million exported.

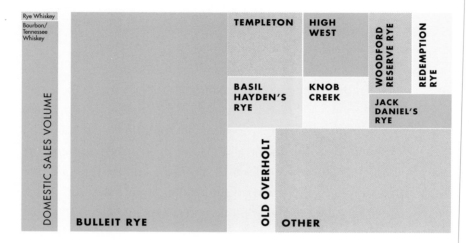

Regardless, that 95 percent rye, 5 percent barley rye recipe, engineered in the Canadian tradition of single, grain-forward flavoring agents, has, unfortunately, become what Americans think of when they think of rye whiskey. Even now, I estimate that 60 to 70 percent of the rye whiskey sold in America is distilled at this Lawrenceburg facility, with Bulleit just shy of 500,000 cases and brands like High West, Redemption, and Templeton contributing MGP-made rye to rye whiskey's overall 1.3 million case volume.

And MGP makes plenty of bourbon now too, which finds its way into a variety of bottles. Some producers have found ways around section 5.36(d) or are still outright flouting its requirement. And DISCUS* has lobbied the Alcohol and Tobacco Tax and Trade Bureau (TTB)† to weaken this statute,

---

* The Distilled Spirits Council of the United States, shortened as DISCUS, is the principal lobbying organization for the distilled spirits industry in Washington, DC. The organization also collects facts and statistics on spirits and their economic impact.

† TTB is the US government agency tasked with creating rules around the labeling, sale, and taxation of alcohol. Formerly part of the Bureau of Alcohol, Tobacco and Firearms (ATF), the taxation department was split when enforcement duties were reconfigured into the Department of Homeland Security. While many aspects of alcohol regulation are left to the states, labeling, classification, licensing, and the collection of federal excise tax remain part of TTB's purview.

CINCINNATI DISTILLERS

NEW RIFF BOURBON

A very classic bourbon with a clean palate of cinnamon and sweet vanilla. With so many established distillers in this range, New Riff proves its place with this bourbon, which hits a sweet spot but may not be a game changer . . . at least not yet.

100pf	$55	C 5 yr	NT	Independent

NEW RIFF RYE

A soft rye with a nice oak balance. This doesn't stray too far but doesn't necessarily make a strong case for itself. I've had New Riff rye that was very flavorful and full of dill and twang like a steel guitar. But this BiB from 2016 is pretty straight edge and maybe not quite as fun as I remembered.

100pf	$55	C 5 yr	NT	Independent

GEORGE REMUS

Setting aside the wisdom of naming a whiskey after an abusive murderer, this is MGP's (sorry, Ross & Squibb's) flagship. With so many whiskeys distilled from this distillery wearing various other labels throughout this book, this one doesn't quite rise to the challenge.

95pf	$55	C	HB	MGPI

a move that would make it easier for Brooklyn "distillers" to undermine Brooklyn distillers and for Indiana bourbon to undermine Kentucky bourbon, both of which are probably bad for distillers and consumers, but not bad for shareholders.

In 2021, MGP merged with Luxco, a St. Louis–based company that had a stable of successful brands—Ezra Brooks, Yellowstone, and post-yell Rebel—but only a couple of small and young Kentucky distilleries of their own. After some weak attempts to brand their own whiskey, the merger is probably good for MGP, which has struggled somewhat to make a case

OLD FIRE COPPER

Bourbon likes to claim traditional and heritage methods, but nothing from this article in 1870 sounds remotely like contemporary production processes or equipment.

This article discusses six types of bourbon whiskey production, as reprinted from the *Louisville Commercial* in the *New York Times* in 1870. They are:

- sour mash, pure copper (small mash tub, double pot distilled)
- sour mash, log and copper (stripped in a wooden chambered still, doubled in copper)
- sweet mash, pure copper (small tub mashed without backset, pot distilled)
- steam copper (direct steam injection mash, chambered still)
- bourbon steam (chambered still with wooden thumper, most common in bourbon country)
- high wines (undiluted spirit made with cheaper grains aged in uncharred barrels)

If bourbon producers want to use true heritage methods, this article is the key to articulating the old sour mash, small-tub fermentaton that is clearly a mark of quality and distilling in pure copper pots (and presumably direct-fired stills) with a wooden thumper. Very few distillers come close to this technique today, but hopefully this is a challenge that some nimble, smaller producers may take on.

Pot distillers like Spirits of French Lick, Neeley Family, Todd Leopold's Three Chamber Rye, or Coppersea (with their direct-fired pot stills) are the closest contemporary analogs to these historical styles.

SPIRITS OF THE FRENCH LICK

LEE SINCLAIR FOUR-GRAIN BOURBON

This is a really beautiful whiskey, a standout that redefines what bourbon can be. Lots of rich texture, out-drinks older and higher-proof whiskeys. There's just a broader flavor spectrum and nice balance of sweet and spice that edges a lot of whiskeys from over the river.

107pf	$57	P 5 yr	TC	Independent

MATTIE GLADDEN STRAIGHT BOURBON

Great nose of ripe fruit, but a body of all caramel and kettle corn, with a touch of black pepper on the finish. Spirits of French Lick is carving their own place and putting most of Kentucky bourbon to shame from Indiana! Apostasy, and yet—it's definitive. There is so much flavor in this whiskey, and all of it just right.

101.7pf	$57	P 5 yr	TC	Independent

OLD CLIFTY HOOSIER APPLE BRANDY

Apple brandy, or applejack, is a historical specialty of southern Indiana, and distiller Alan Bishop has set out to bring it back. You can count the bonded apple brandies that have been released in the US on one hand, but it's a pity, as the genre deserves a wider audience. This example is no apple liqueur, but a refined spirit comparable to French Calvados. I could sip this all day.

100pf	$40	P 4 yr	TC	Independent

SOLOMON SCOTT RYE WHISKEY

A more biting rye whiskey, with a backdrop of black pepper. The nose has the familiar bouquet of rye funk, but the palate is spicy and brisk.

100pf	$50	4 year P	TC	Independent

for itself as a traditional distillery, where brands and storytelling are far more important for customers than the product itself (especially when that product is in fifty different bottles already).

Lawrenceburg is really a suburb of Cincinnati, the last great Gilded Age city where an incredible amount of historic architecture, beautiful parks, and grand public institutions have survived. Cincinnati's distilling industry did not fare as well, and the last remnant, a DeKuyper schnapps bottling plant owned by Jim Beam, was set to close only about a decade ago.

Covington sits on the Kentucky side of the Ohio River across from Cincinnati, and I spent a balmy summer evening walking around its Mainstrasse Village, a time-kissed rowhouse district with pastel 1800s architecture that looks like a European hamlet. Old Kentucky Bourbon Bar, one of the original whiskey library bars, is a bourbon lover's highbrow dive. There aren't many neighborhoods like this, protected by time and years of good judgment, where you could imagine yourself in any era of American history and still enjoy a vibrant street culture today.

New Riff is a distillery in Newport, not far from Covington on the all-important Kentucky side of the river. A liquor store owner, Ken Lewis, saw the surge in bourbon coming from the retail counter and opened the business in 2014. The brand was an early example of neo-traditional Kentucky bourbon, with a 24-inch column still (that they have already outgrown). New Riff makes reliably good whiskeys, and barrel picks are often a good find. Their O.K.I. bourbon, sourced from nearby MGP, helped the distiller build distribution while waiting on the flagship product to age—though it is in different hands now.

Ohio has a couple of other distillers you should know: Middle West and Watershed, both in Columbus. Middle West is of the neo-traditional format, making its OYO Bourbon and other whiskeys, while Watershed is more of a typical craft distiller. Both are well distributed in Ohio and not very much beyond but have been pioneers in craft distilling. Cleveland Whiskey, a brand that made some noise around rapid aging a decade ago, should be considered cautiously, but more on rapid aging and synthesized whiskeys later.

Downriver, Indiana has been eyeing the action. Indiana has a number of vineyards that have transitioned to distilling. Huber's Starlight, in

Borden, is one that is becoming more well-known through an accessible barrel-pick program, and deserves a stop, but on a chilly December day in 2021 I decided to continue on to visit Alan Bishop at Spirits of French Lick.

West Baden Springs is a former resort surrounding the mineral springs in French Lick. An old hotel reminiscent of the Coronado in San Diego, the Ocean House in Watch Hill, or the Grand Hotel on Mackinac Island, the resort is a remarkable time capsule, built in 1902 with rooms arranged in a circle around a soaring atrium (the largest in the world until 1913). The hotel has been restored and is open for business. I visited the French Lick Winery just down the street, where Alan Bishop has been spearheading the spirits program for several years. Using only pot stills, Alan makes bourbon and rye, but also apple brandy, a local staple before Prohibition. The apple brandy is great, but I was most impressed with one of the few mature pure pot-still bourbons available in the United States. I had been sipping on a bottle of Lee Sinclair at home, but during my visit the Mattie Gladden impressed. Along with Royce Neeley, Alan is making American whiskey in an authentic old tradition, and the products show what good bourbon in an earlier era would have tasted like, an experience mostly lost to time but for the few new practitioners keeping it alive.

Spirits of French Lick, in Baden Springs, Indiana, won't win any beauty pageants for its distillery, but as a workhorse facility tucked behind a winery, it's emerged as one of the most idiosyncratic pot still distillers in the country.

ELSEWHERE IN THE SOUTH

With so much enthusiasm for bourbon coming from the South, admiration and respect for the traditional spirit may have kept some innovation from happening adjacent to traditional bourbon country, but I'll call out a few distillers here that are making great spirits.

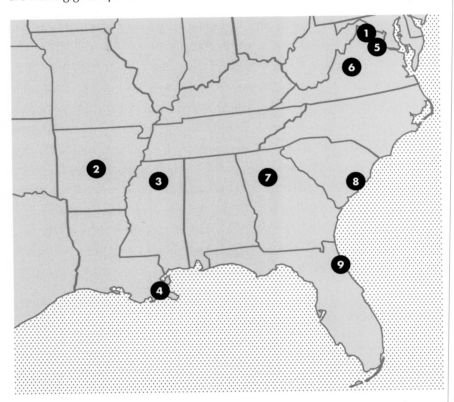

1. CATOCTIN CREEK
PURCELLVILLE, VIRGINIA

This distiller of rye and fruit brandies in the Shenandoah Valley not far from Harpers Ferry has been a crucial player in the Virginia distilling scene. Distiller Rebecca Harris has been active with national guilds and often represents small distillers' interests on national issues. The rye is accessible and authentic.

2. ROCK TOWN DISTILLERY
LITTLE ROCK, ARKANSAS

Rock Town has been under the radar for a long time, but they've been making rock-solid bourbon and rye whiskeys with unusual malts, sweet and sour mash, and peated recipes. It's a grain-to-glass bourbon that has big ambitions and a distiller's perspective. They've been winning awards and innovating for years. If only there were enough—alas, the Little Rock audience scoops this up before it has the chance to get out to the wider world.

3. WONDERBIRD SPIRITS
OXFORD, MISSISSIPPI

No whiskeys to be found here, but a surprisingly delicious gin made from rice that speaks more to the southern provenance and terroir than many whiskeys on the market.

4. ROULAISON RUM
NEW ORLEANS, LOUISIANA

No whiskeys here either, but you've never had rum before trying this pot-distilled, molasses-based rum that is flavorful and funky to an extreme degree. A former distiller for Kings County, Andrew Lohfeld has done for rum what we aspire to do for whiskey, and with definitive panache.

5. A. SMITH BOWMAN DISTILLERY
FREDERICKSBURG, VIRGINIA

An odd footnote in whiskey history, a historic distillery dating to the 1930s that has been run since 2003 by Sazerac as a contemporary craft distillery. Running low wines* trucked in from Buffalo Trace on an odd, air-cooled condenser still, this distillery has always been hard to categorize, even if its spirits fall toward mainstream on the flavor spectrum.

6. VIRGINIA DISTILLERY CO.
LOVINGSTON, VIRGINIA

Located in the highlands not far from the Blue Ridge Parkway, Virginia Distillery Co. makes malt whiskey with Forsyth pot stills. A little out of place in moonshine country, this distillery showcases one of the most ambitious East Coast single-malt brands.

7. ASW DISTILLING
ATLANTA, GEORGIA

I first heard about ASW while working the Atlanta market. The distillery had just released its first whiskey, and bartenders were talking in hushed tones, hoping to get a crack at the next release. The intervening years have gone well, and they've expanded both products and well-appointed facilities. Ultimately most interested in malt whiskeys, ASW perhaps has more in common with the Pacific Northwest than Atlanta, but that just secures its idiosyncratic place.

8. HIGH WIRE DISTILLING
CHARLESTON, SOUTH CAROLINA

High Wire is mostly a medium-sized hybrid distillery in Charleston, but they make whiskeys that are pushing boundaries. Their Jimmy Red Corn Bourbon, with its peppery notes, may be the best use of an heirloom grain in American whiskey so far. Any whiskey from High Wire is carefully crafted, and they have earned high prices in my estimation.

9. ST. AUGUSTINE DISTILLERY
ST. AUGUSTINE, FLORIDA

Set in the historic Florida village, St. Augustine is oriented to tours. Dave Pickerell had a heavy hand in setting up this distillery, which is best appreciated from the vantage point of a public tour. The spirits aren't widely distributed, but it hardly matters, as this is really the showcase of how a visitor-serving distillery with a steady audience can make good spirits and a fine business without playing the conventional distribution game.

---

* Low wines are the result of the first pass on a double-distillation system. The oily, funky liquid is still too impure to drink and must be redistilled a second time in order to make a palatable spirit. This in-between, unpotable liquid (usually at a middle range of alcoholic strength) is known as the "low wines."

A WORD ON DUSTIES

If you linger in the places where whiskey lovers like to congregate on the internet, you'll hear the word "dusty," originally referring to old bottles of vintage whiskey that sat collecting dust in a forgotten liquor store. These bottles have been scooped up by collectors, as the whiskey itself never goes bad and can be a window into the way bourbon used to be made.

We think of brands as having the same flavor profile year over year, day in and day out. But it simply isn't true, and flavors will drift over time as distilleries gradually tinker with their processes, recipes, and emphasis. Wild Turkey used to be made in a crumbling facility that was not necessarily the most sanitary factory but made fine whiskey. Its newer whiskey, from what I can tell, simply doesn't taste the same. 1980s Wild Turkey has richer notes of caramel and molasses. Even Jim Beam from the 1960s was more like Jim Beam Black today, more body and richness. Other brands have completely disappeared, but their whiskeys live on in bottles that remain. Bottles from Stitzel-Weller, the shuttered distillery in Louisville, are highly prized. I can't personally say that 1960s Old Fitzgerald lives up to the hype. But vintage whiskeys (perhaps a more accurate name) are always a fun journey into the past. Even if American whiskey wasn't aged like Scotch whisky, the rarity of dusties can provide the same sense of adventure as drinking a 25-year or older Scotch. I've even had some pre-Prohibition whiskey, which was gorgeous.

If you've read this far, we've covered all of the heritage distillers, and if your poison is fine old Kentucky bourbon, you can stop reading here. If, however, you've tried vintage bourbon or rye and found a richness, a depth, and a texture to those whiskeys, read on. We are about to venture into the frontier of American craft whiskey, and many of those notes of well-aged vintage bourbon can be found in well-aged craft whiskey—there just hasn't been that much of it until recently. Now as craft distillers reach maturity, it's easy to understand the antecedents of today's bourbon in craft producers, who may use non-GMO corn, do not have temperature-controlled fermentation, distill with seasonal variation based on cooling temperatures, or age in slightly smaller barrels—all more common practices in mainstream bourbon just a few decades ago.

I love sipping dusties, as a consumer and as a distiller, because it combines so much of the pleasures of whiskey. That pre-Prohibition whiskey, bottled by the American Medicinal Spirits Company fifteen years after it was distilled, was dank—it tasted of chocolate and lacquered wood. I imagined being in an Elks Lodge in the dead of night, or a law-school library after hours. A hallowed place, liminal, between a past impossible to recover and a very present elixir. I've never had anything like it before or since.

The remains of the Commonwealth Distillery, long defunct, were briefly owned by Julian Van Winkle, who used some of its old stock to fill his Pappy Van Winkle whiskey lines.

The Hoga pot stills at Coppersea. Of all the distillers claiming traditional techniques, Coppersea has the most credibility.

7

HIGH RYE AND BLENDED RYE

Think of the American Northeast, and whiskey is about the last consumer product that will spring to mind. As a New York City distiller, I am too often reminded of a television commercial where a group of cowboys sitting around a campfire threaten to hang the cowboy who had the nerve to bring picante sauce made in New York City (hilarious, right?). Until recently, whiskey could have been the butt of the same joke. Indeed, Van Winkle Jr. at Stitzel-Weller at one point had conceived of a whiskey called "Battle Hymn" purportedly distilled in Massachusetts and meant to appeal to northerners, a concept apparently so laughable in the 1960s that the mere idea was a joke meant to glorify bourbon—and a particularly Old South flavored version of it.

Times, fortunately, have changed, but it has been a long climb to acceptance. Perhaps when craft beer emerged, people scoffed at the idea that beer could be made outside of Milwaukee or St. Louis? Whiskey is still associated with the "heartland," a mythical American place where warm apple pies appear on tables of hewn logs while fires kindle in stone hearths. Wherever it is, it is most certainly not Boston, New York, or Philadelphia, where distillers first congregated in this country. These cities are in fact so old, they are more likely to have been distillers of rum, America's first poison, along with the slave trade that sprang up to support its commercialization by the British. But after the Revolutionary War, many distillers turned to whiskey, a commodity that could be produced domestically (even locally) in the Northeast, where the population at the time was most concentrated.

In 1840, census documents show New York made 11.9 million gallons of whiskey, while Kentucky made 1.7 and Tennessee 1.1. The New York whiskey boom was fueled by Irish immigrants landing in ports and making good work of cheap and voluminous whiskey. In 1842, 11,000 barrels arrived in New York from the Hubb Distillery in Lawrenceburg, Indiana, marking the beginning of a long transition to the Ohio River valley as the distilling heart of the United States. And it's not an ironic footnote that Lawrenceburg's remaining distillery (MGP) is often still a thorn in the side of many a legitimate urban distiller, as its proximity to grain farms offers a cheaper alternative whiskey source all these years later.

By the 1880s, corn surpassed rye as the dominant whiskey grain of choice, and distilling in the Northeast has been on a slow decline ever since. After Prohibition, it reemerged in the Allegheny Mountains and in Philadelphia, but not much beyond. Even then, the Overholt Distillery closed in the 1960s, and with it went the last significant rye production in the Northeast. Michter's hung on too but fell into bankruptcy in 1989, and its buildings remained until they were finally torn down in 2014, around the same time the plans to rescue the Old Taylor Distillery were being hatched by the founders of Castle & Key. Which is just to say that bourbon's renaissance came too late to have the same effect on rye's great historical distillers, and only by a hair.

The brands have continued. Overholt, Michter's, Fleischmann's, Pikesville, and Rittenhouse were all storied rye brands that got bought, merged, shuffled into bourbon distillers that ran rye whiskey two production days a year and bourbon every other day. To the consumer, rye has been mounting a comeback, as the craft cocktail movement exhumed old cocktail texts from the late 1800s and early 1900s, many of which called for the whiskey of the era, rye. And there were plenty of brands on the lower shelves that remained, creating an illusion of continuity to that older time.

But to the distiller, rye production got shot in the back and died in the street. And only a handful of little distillers have begun to try to piece together what rye was historically and what it should be today. Many of us feel that it should not be the high-corn, column-distilled ryes made in bourbon distilleries or MGP's 95-percent rye recipe, produced as a blending agent and never meant to be sold as purpose-made straight rye, both examples of rye in name, but hardly historical styles. In the land of the blind, the one-eyed man is king.

FIG. 4.—THREE-CHAMBER CHARGE BEER STILL.

In its heyday, before the 1840s, most New York whiskey was made on a three-chamber wooden still, and would have been rye whiskey or a rye and sugar mash.

Today, most of the whiskey made in the Northeast is produced where it thrived historically—in New York, Pennsylvania, and Maryland—and I will focus on those places for this chapter. And while the contemporary distillers of the Northeast make all kinds of whiskey, from bourbon to single malt, the rye whiskey stands out most not just because it tells a nice story, but because it really is that much better.

XXX

After heading to college in the Northeast, I felt more than a little bit of a culture shock as someone born in Appalachia and schooled in the Deep South. Yale is a grand old institution, and it was hard not to fall in love with both the college and the funny Old World charm of New England. To this day, the drive from New York to Boston on a crisp fall day, when the leaves are at their peak of red and gold, the wind is blustery, and a slight drizzle paints everything in starker contrast, remains one of America's best road trips, complete with stops for lobster rolls and coal-oven New Haven pizza.

Upon graduation, I moved to New York City to seek my fortune, living first on the Upper West Side, then Hell's Kitchen, before moving to Brooklyn. New York is not a place that shouts good whiskey, but there are two things about the city that have made it a surprise hotbed of whiskey enthusiasm.

The first is that there is a lot of wealth in New York. Conspicuous accumulation and deployment of wealth is what New York City does best. The second is a lively nightlife culture born of the density of a city where tiny apartments are ill-suited to entertaining and all the communal life takes place in eating and drinking establishments. The work of making cocktails means something different in New York, where the bar and restaurant scene is simply the richest, the most diverse, and superior to that of any other American city, full stop. It is the thing that New Yorkers miss most when they leave, and the best enticement for new blood to seek fame and fortune in the Big Apple.

So, it was inevitable those bars and restaurants would look for local spirits, and many aspiring distillers would set up shop in the city. The years 2009 to 2011 marked a period where the colluding forces of the internet, social media proliferation, and the spread of the farm-to-table ethos conspired to create an easily mocked environment of "artisanal" brands of coffee, chocolate, pickles, salsa, and yes, whiskey. It can be difficult to remember it now, but the internet made the costs of starting a business much lower, and therefore, would-be entrepreneurs were everywhere, a trend that we may take for granted today but was not as obvious at the time.

Spirits were seemingly a good fit, especially in New York State, where laws prevented chain liquor stores and grassroots salesmanship would be better received than in some other states. So it happened that the frothy, energetic youth culture of late-aughts Brooklyn gave birth to some of the more well-regarded craft distillers of the movement.

Brooklyn distillers have long concentrated along the waterfront, and modern craft distillers are no different.

It can be difficult to write about my closest competitors. Many of the distillers here are crosstown rivals, and my perception of them has evolved quite a bit over time. Business changes fast, and the whiskey business, though slower than some, changes just as fast as New York City real estate. Add in the pandemic, and a lot has been scrambled.

I'll start with the New York City distillers in rough order of formation. In this book, my own distillery would fall here, Kings County Distillery, and I certainly think we make fine whiskey. I can't objectively compare us to my peers and colleagues. I can only recommend you consider us with our peers in your own travels. In terms of distinguishing factors, as New York is a melting pot of world cultures, we borrow from various distilling traditions around the world to make creative whiskeys that still are distinctly American. While I think all our whiskeys are quite good, I'll specifically flag our moonshine, peated bourbon, and Bottled-in-Bond as personal favorites that are especially distinctive and close to my heart.

Kings County opened in April 2010, and later that month Brad Estabrooke started Breuckelen Distilling in Sunset Park. Brad started with a wheat-based white spirit for his gins but has really focused on whiskeys

The Kings County Distillery barrel room, when we were focused on smaller sizes. We now use more practical 53- and 30-gallon barrels, which aren't quite as picturesque.

New York Distilling Company in Williamsburg, Brooklyn.

in ways few craft distillers have so far, coming out with well-aged, creative, well-made whiskeys that are singular and quite often overlooked. Breuckelen had a tasting room early on, but dispensed with visitors when space constraints demanded more distillation equipment. With wheat, rye, corn, and malt whiskeys, his offerings make up a classic palate.

Moving north is the Red Hook neighborhood, an industrial lobe of Brooklyn that is hard to reach by any form of public transit. It's a quirky, vibrant neighborhood that is home to two whiskey distillers. The first is Van Brunt Stillhouse, founded by former *Daily Show* editor Daric Schlesselman, which focuses on a variety of American whiskeys often made with brewer's specialty malts: a four-grain, a rye, a bourbon, and even some smoked corn whiskeys. The tasting room is very friendly and casual, well worth a visit if you are in the neighborhood.

A few blocks north is Widow Jane, opened by Daniel Preston in 2012. In contrast to most of the New York distillers, Widow Jane sources most of its whiskeys from Kentucky and Indiana but has played up a token on-site still (that runs infrequently) and limestone water from a mine upstate. Anyone who knows mining would think this sounds disgusting, but here in the big city, a quaint selling point! Preston in one way or another annoyed most of the other New York distillers through eliding labeling rules, copying packaging,

BROOKLYN WHISKEY

BREUCKELEN 77 WHEAT

Made from 100% New York wheat, this is a whiskey I'm proud to share a borough with. I don't think there's a better wheat whiskey on the market, with a nutty, bready balance and clean wheat profile that's rich and memorable.

90pf	$45	H 2 yr	TC	Independent

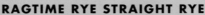

RAGTIME RYE STRAIGHT RYE

A nice rye for a nice price, and dependable. Go for the Bottled-in-Bond version for a more mature flavor profile, but this is a clean rye that has simply gotten better and more complex in recent years.

90.4pf	$40 ($55 BiB)	C 3 yr	SW	Independent

APPLEJACK FINISHED RAGTIME RYE

A cool concept for a whiskey (made in the Big Apple!) that doesn't quite land; the finish doesn't add that much besides some residual sugars.

100pf	$40	C 2 yr	SW	Independent

and illegally selling out-of-state whiskey in his farm tasting room, among other grievances. Even the historical society that owns the Widow Jane mine complained they never supplied any water and had no commercial relationship with Preston, sparking a lawsuit that is worth a read for those who want whiskey labels to accurately reflect what's in the bottle (the suit was dismissed, and later owners would abandon any dubious practices).

VAN BRUNT EMPIRE RYE

Edgy and brash, this whiskey punches heavy for a two-year 42% 84 proof. Obvious rye notes, but toffee and malt separate this from the column-stilled Kentucky rye, both old and new. Lots of richness that older whiskeys wish they had.

92pf	$69	H 2 yr	TC	Independent

KINGS COUNTY PEATED BOURBON

Maybe a little complicated to comment on my own whiskeys, but Kings County's peated bourbon is mostly a bourbon with the finish of an Islay malt, a wisp of scotchiness that transforms a young bourbon into something very different and distinctive.

90pf	$70	P 3 yr	TC	Independent

KINGS COUNTY BOTTLED-IN-BOND

Kings County BiB has notes of dark chocolate and molasses, and represents an older expression of pot-still craft whiskey that's hard to find anywhere else. One of the first bonded craft whiskeys, the 2023 batch adds a hint of cherry cordial.

100pf	$99	P 7 yr	TC	Independent

KINGS COUNTY EMPIRE RYE

The most barrel-forward (and my favorite) of the Empire Rye whiskeys, this is a hefty whiskey at 102 proof that opens with chocolate and toffee with touches of grass, crème brûlée, and a hint of mint. But consider the source—a little bias is surely at play here.

102pf	$99	P 3 yr	TC	Independent

Preston sold the business to Samson and Surrey, a sort of investment fund for craft spirits. Lisa Wicker, a relative newcomer to craft whiskey, was installed to manage the brand and the token distillery on-site, but the label has always been mostly trading on the Brooklyn provenance, an early cache of well-aged barrels, and a market hungry for high-priced bourbon. Lisa has done a good job trying to sanitize the brand and give it credibility, but it has been an uphill climb with peers who have a long memory (she departed the company in October 2022 for Town Branch, after Heaven Hill acquired Samson and Surrey). Still, the contracts for whiskey were established early and Widow Jane seems to keep landing on shelves with high age statements when few others can regularly produce them.

On the other end of Brooklyn, in Bushwick, resides New York Distilling Company, whose co-founder, Tom Potter, was once half of the duo that founded the Brooklyn Brewery, essentially craft beverage royalty. His business partner, Allen Katz, is a cocktail and spirits savant and one of the nicest people in American whiskey. Together, they opened New York Distilling Company in the Shanty, a shed of corrugated metal in Williamsburg, before moving to the current location. The Christian Carl hybrid still on-site mostly distills the gins—they have a couple of varieties. The whiskeys are produced by contract elsewhere in New York. Ragtime Rye is the flagship, and for a long time played catch-up with some of the other New York distillers as a young whiskey priced for mixing. Still, on a recent Empire Rye producer's retreat, a bottle of Ragtime Rye took the room for me, a striking entry on a table full of great producers all making rye the old way. It was a remarkably good rye whiskey and one that I won't forget for a long time.

Widow Jane and Ragtime Rye are a study in opposites. Both are primarily sourced brands, but they go about it completely differently. Widow Jane sources from MGP and large Kentucky commodity producers. Ragtime Rye is made by other craft producers upstate. Widow Jane charges double what Ragtime Rye charges. Widow Jane was founded by an industry outsider who played loose with the rules and the truth and looked for a quick exit. Ragtime Rye is a labor of love for two spirits-industry veterans who were out to revive rye whiskey in New York cocktails. It's not a mystery what I'd put in my glass.

One other New York City distiller of whiskey I'm obliged to mention is Great Jones Distillery, two years old as of this writing and really a four-story restaurant with a bourbon brand attached. Founded as a project of Proximo Spirits, the company behind Jose Cuervo, Bushmills, and Stranahan's, the company is billed as the first whiskey distillery in Manhattan (Our/

New York built a miniature still before them, not to mention two dozen distilleries in Brooklyn, Queens, and the Bronx). Proximo went on a buying spree in New York, buying Warwick Valley Winery and its Black Dirt bourbon to produce for Great Jones, and Owney's Rum for the distilling talent. Money can buy an ersatz, retro-styled building, but it can't buy authenticity. Somehow this project took a solid craft whiskey in Black Dirt and branded it beyond recognition with Great Jones—a boondoggle that may have been a little late for a craft-jaded retail scene.

There are certainly other distillers that should be named, including Port Morris Distillery in the Bronx, Barrow's Intense Ginger Liqueur, Greenhook Ginsmiths, Forthave Spirits, and others mostly outside of whiskey. And as I've said, New York's restaurant and bar culture is unparalleled, though the city has lost more whiskey bars lately than it has gained. Brandy Library in Manhattan and Travel Bar in Brooklyn are good mainstays, as is Cardiff Giant, for a program that highlights only New York brands. Down & Out, an East Village haunt founded by a former Kings County distiller, has a beautiful collection of whiskeys.

XXX

New York is a strange union of places. Its topography along the Appalachian Mountains is not very different climatically or geologically from that of Kentucky, at least not so much as our politics would suggest. Still, the map of New York looks like a bizarre gerrymander from some back-room compromise: a block of mountainous terrain covered in deciduous forests over a huge landmass that tapers to an area less than three miles wide—its most densely populated—and then stretches out on the funny little flat foot of Long Island. Could this amalgam of territories define a distinctive whiskey culture? The distillers of New York believe it will, and there is evidence to suggest we may be right.

Leaving New York City and heading upstate always gives me a feeling of relief. Most often I take the Henry Hudson Parkway, with its broad views of the Hudson River and the Palisades. It doesn't take long to reach a more agrarian landscape, though the land around here is usually too valuable for commercial farming. This is an old part of America too, and one where

The tasting room and shop at Tuthilltown Spirits, makers of Hudson Whiskeys

different eras of artists and visionaries and dilettantes found refuge from the city in exchange for a conjured—sometimes utopian—idea of country life. The farm-to-table movement found its strongest cultural advocacy here, as places like Blue Hill at Stone Barns most notably found new ways to look at produce and farming (as well as cooking and restauranting) in a contemporary landscape of long-commercialized production. Sometimes precious and overbearing, sometimes salient and disruptive, the farm and food culture of the Hudson Valley feeds the vibrant restaurant culture of the city and vice versa; the relationship is an important one, and a historic one. Three Hudson Valley distillers are worth including here, and all are an easy drive from Poughkeepsie, a convenient destination by car or train from New York City.

Tuthilltown Spirits Distillery, in Gardiner, New York, is one of the pioneers of craft distilling in America, but also a cautionary tale. Tuthilltown is better known as the maker of Hudson Whiskey, whose Baby Bourbon captivated whiskey culture when the idea of bourbon being made outside of Kentucky was apostasy. Tuthilltown scraped together a distillery with a Carl still and parts from a dairy and started producing very fine bourbon and rye whiskey after opening in 2005. Hudson worked small:

Using small-format barrels and 375ml bottles, the brand worked at half scale to make something that really hadn't been witnessed outside of a handful of other existing distilleries that were mostly focused on single malts. This was a new program for a craft style of whiskeys, made from familiar grains, but altogether different from its Kentucky peers. It cannot be overstated how significant the Hudson whiskeys were to broad acceptance of craft—as well as a rediscovery of traditional Kentucky bourbon as a sort of reaction to Hudson (and others outside of Kentucky trying to expand American whiskey).

Founders Ralph Erenzo and Brian Lee worked scrappily, and Ralph's late son Gable became a critical ambassador for the brand. Ralph has worked as godfather to New York's craft spirits industry, lobbying for legislative changes like the farm distillery license, and Gable became the young face of the brand, leading tours and tastings. By 2010, Hudson was on fire, and William Grant & Sons acquired the whiskey portfolio.

Business stories are often like relationships. At first, it appeared as though William Grant would be a good steward of the brand, but a move to larger 750ml bottles at a more affordable price alienated customers who had been paying not much less for half-sized bottles. Product reviews were all over the place, growing more inconsistent under Grant's ownership. In 2017, Grant purchased the distillery outright. A bizarre rebrand attempted

Taconic Distillery in Stanfordville runs a respectable column-still setup in a bucolic setting.

HUDSON VALLEY WHISKEY

HUDSON BRIGHT LIGHTS BIG BOURBON

I like a bourbon that presents differently from Kentucky bourbon, and by that measure this hits a sweet spot, though its butterscotch nose, buttered-corn palate, and glyceriney sweetness don't quite add up to a home run. Its 95 percent corn mash bill is an oddity, now priced well for a true-craft product. The reformulation drinks better than its reputation, but an unusual bourbon that even I, lover of strange whiskeys, have a hard time fully embracing.

92pf	$40	H 3 yr	TC	William Grant

HUDSON DO THE RYE THING

With apparently no apology (and no royalties) to Spike Lee, this is Hudson's contribution to the rye tradition in New York. Dill forward and a little tannic, this whiskey has a big molasses flavor, but it fades quickly. A worthy bearer of the Empire Rye seal, good value, and probably the most disseminated example of northeastern rye out there, but for a few more dollars in this category there are others I'd ask for first.

90pf	$40	H 3 yr	TC	William Grant

TACONIC BOURBON

Taconic started as a sourced whiskey, but switched over to making all their own spirits (a feat that many promise and few deliver). This is a very clean distillate with gentle spice, a nice bourbon from New York that's easy to appreciate.

95pf	$45	C	TC	Independent

TACONIC RYE

A very light rye whiskey from a state earning a reputation for big, brawny rye whiskeys. Next to these, this whiskey tastes pretty pale, but has a soft approachability.

95pf	$45	C	TC	Independent

to recast Hudson as a New York City product—a move that may have been aimed at Grant's European audience more than locals. Baby Bourbon and the brand's iconic packaging are gone, leaving behind a sort of marketing project that delivers some middle-of-the-road whiskeys. Of these, the rye is best, but if you are looking for New York rye, there are others I would recommend first. Still, Hudson is readily found all over the country and can be had at a good price.

Another small distiller, Taconic, has taken a different approach. Running an eighteen-inch column from Vendome, Taconic makes bourbon and rye a little more in the Kentucky style than is typical for a Yankee distiller. Indeed, distiller Brandon Collins came to New York from Kentucky, where he worked at Buffalo Trace in production. Until recently, he managed all aspects of distillation, maturation, and blending for Taconic. Some intriguing barrel finishes keep the program varied, but the standard bourbon and rye are quite good. Taconic began the brand with sourced whiskey, which is not usually a way to win my interest, but the distillery is an impressive operation that's well run and producing a nice product, much of which I credited to Brandon. When he left Taconic, I offered him the job as distillery manager at Kings County, where you'll find him today.

The state motto of New York is simply "Excelsior," meaning "always upward," and that motto is a mantra at Coppersea.

Christopher Williams inside the historic barn that acts as the tasting room at Coppersea, just a few miles north of New Paltz, New York

Still, my favorite distiller in the Hudson Valley, and probably my favorite distiller overall, is Coppersea, which is everything that you would want from American whiskey. Coppersea grows (sometimes) and malts its own grain. Coppersea open ferments in beautiful wooden vats and uses pot stills, but not just any pot stills: direct-fired pot stills, causing pyrolysis in the wash (or, put a different way, caramelizing the sugars in the still). Essentially, Coppersea is making whiskey in an eighteenth-century way in the twenty-first century, and there are very few (if any) other examples of this type of whiskey being made today. For people who like the idea of whiskey heritage, Coppersea is the distillery they don't even know they need.

But to understand why Coppersea is so special, one must look at the long decline (or business evolution) of American whiskey. I'm reminded of the article from the *Louisville Commercial* (see p. 132) describing the six types of Kentucky bourbon, essentially charting the evolution of distilled-spirits technology from direct-fired copper pots to wooden three-chambered stills, all the way to column stills run on steam fitted with doublers, the type typical of nearly every Kentucky bourbon made today. Very few distillers are using pot stills, and very few of those are using

THREE FROM COPPERSEA

COPPERSEA BONTICOU CRAIG STRAIGHT RYE MALT

Incredibly fragrant, this is a rich, round rye that is quite singular in the rye world, or even the whiskey world as a whole. The rye malt is very grain forward, but balanced with a dark piney woodiness with black tea, for a luscious, viscous rye whiskey, that compares to nothing else in American whiskey.

96pf	$65	P	TC	Independent

EXCELSIOR BOTTLED-IN-BOND BOURBON

If you like bourbon, this bottle is the closest anyone will ever get to tasting pre-Prohibition, direct-fire, copper pot bourbon. While most bourbon leads with corn and toasted oak, this is an earthy whiskey that leads with coffee, chocolate, brown sugar, and sourdough bread.

100pf	$99	P	TC	Independent

PX FINISHED RYE

This may well be the country's most flavorful rye whiskey. Malted rye mash, direct fire, pot distilled, small barrel aged, then finished with a Pedro Ximénez cask. It's a beast of a whiskey that you give yourself over to, like a symphonic orchestration of grunge metal.

107pf	$70	P	TC	Independent

direct-fired. And no one is doing floor malting, direct-fire, and estate-grown grain. So, if you are looking for a whiskey that makes no compromises, Coppersea is about as good as it can get.

Do all these things make for better whiskey? To my palate, yes. The old-fashioned way is not only romantic or nostalgic, but also usually less efficient and more flavor-centric. In distilling, character is often sacrificed for yield. Craft beer was a flavor improvement over the commercial watery beers that existed in the 1980s. Third-wave coffee focused on ingredients

OTHER YANKEE WHISKEYS

HILLROCK SINGLE MALT

Hillrock's solera aging system is a pretext to sell whiskey made elsewhere, but the house-distilled single malt is actually the gem from this distillery, a whiskey that makes the best of a category dominated by West Coast players.

98.6pf	$120	H	TC	Independent

MCKENZIE RYE

A slightly more refined rye from New York, this doesn't have as much of the rye funk that can define the Empire State, but has a gentle graininess and balanced oak profile that's the mark of a considered spirit.

91pf	$40	C	TC	Independent

MCKENZIE SINGLE BARREL EMPIRE RYE WHISKEY

A more barrel forward, cinnamon rye. All the beauty of McKenzie's entry-level rye, but a little less grain character and a more singular profile. Hard to pick a favorite with McKenzie, one of the best American craft distillers that isn't widely known.

101pf (variable)	$55	C	TC	Independent

and sourcing as well as specifics of production. You might find the notion of "craft" to be quaint, but craft beer and third-wave coffee are different from their commercial predecessors.

If you want to know what rye whiskey from the 1800s tasted like, Coppersea is as close as you are going to get in America today, and you won't regret a drop of it. Coppersea does a lot with malted rye, which adds even more particularity to their flavor profile, though it may not be for every palate. The bourbon also is a stunning window into what bourbon used to be—I can't recommend it enough.

MACKENZIE BOTTLED-IN-BOND BOURBON

With a nose that reminds you of a beautiful old barn full of corn and hay, this is another sleeper bourbon giving Kentucky a good run. This BiB is quite impressive and proves the case for Yankee bourbon as much as rye.

	100pf	$55	C	TC	Independent

BLACK BUTTON EMPIRE RYE

A sweet-spot rye that's full of flavor and gets the nutty, funky rye character. A touch of dill and mint gives some complexity for a rye whiskey that bests nearly any commercial offering. Lots of flavor despite a lower proof too, one mark of a skilled distiller.

84pf	$70	H	TC	Independent

WHISTLEPIG 10 YEAR

It's hard to get past the gimmickry of this brand, but the sourced Canadian rye in the bottles that built its reputation is no joke. Resin, cedar, fig, oak, sour rye grain combine with a touch of savory heft in the body. As a whiskey, it's interesting if you can bypass the fact that this brand is trying to insult the goodwill of its customers with sleight of hand. I cannot, but maybe you can.

	100pf	$80	C 10 yr	SW	Semi-independent

Christopher Williams, the lead distiller at Coppersea, is a distiller in the best mold: an intellectual, a bon vivant, a storyteller, and a stubborn mule. I recall a conversation with a group of New York distillers on the topic of exogenous enzymes that lasted way longer than it should have but began with Williams's provocation that such enzymes were a form of a cheat, an esoteric position for an American distiller but no less fervently defended. I am rarely jealous of other distilleries, but Coppersea has credibility I can't achieve in Brooklyn and have conceded as we've scaled.

Woodville is a historic museum outside of Pittsburgh and was once the home of John Neville after a raiding party burned his first home, just up the street, at the Battle of Bower Hill, the most significant skirmish of the Whiskey Rebellion.

The last New York distiller I'll mention is one I haven't visited in person yet, but I know Brian McKenzie, its founder, well enough. Finger Lakes Distilling is one of the old guards in the state and has been operating at a significant scale for a while, giving them good stocks of well-aged whiskey. A 10-year bourbon I sampled in 2021 rivaled anything I've ever had from Kentucky, including 15-year Van Winkle, a strong statement for a relatively young New York bourbon. But their whiskeys have always been strong and lead with age, making them a little bit of a sleeper distillery.

There are other distillers of note, including Black Button in Rochester, that have been a part of the Empire Rye project from the outset. And Hillrock is a distiller of note, even if I feel their signature story of solera aging is a pretext to sell sourced whiskey as their own; to me, their single malts are more compelling. Long Island Spirits has done some interesting whiskeys in the past as well; the Pine Barrens malt whiskey is a dark horse in the world of New York spirits.

Looking beyond New York State I don't include a lot of distillers in New England here, not because there aren't good options, but they are small and idiosyncratic. I'm thinking of the Notch Nantucket single malt, a limited-edition malt that's been made on Nantucket for a quarter-century as a side project of Cisco Brewery and Nantucket Vineyard. Or even Privateer rum, which is not whiskey, but certainly a craft distiller of note in Ipswich, Massachusetts.

You might have noticed I left out WhistlePig, which is probably the most successful rye whiskey brand in the Northeast by case volume and dollars. While the whiskey is fine, I have always found its marketing to be misleading, once trying to bury the fact that its whiskey was sourced. Mercurial and bombastic founder Raj Bhatka, a former *Apprentice* contestant, was ousted from the company in 2016 by investors in an ugly divorce. Marketing antics always seem to be a little shrill; for example, a Tales of the Cocktail party in a house filled with sex toys, or trotting a live pig through a sales meeting. Dave Pickerell was a genuinely positive founding force, but with his passing and its original leadership gone, the brand is trying to remake itself as a farm product, promoting its distillery-made line of spirits. However, the still on-site is too small for a brand their size, and inevitably only a token amount of their own distillate is going into these releases.

In my view, even their recent whiskey releases are bungled. A pig-shaped decanter put the focus anywhere but the whiskey inside. A "barrel aged" canned cocktail hoped you wouldn't notice it's a *fermented* beverage, not a *distilled* one. And a product called Beyond Bonded, bottled at 100.1 proof, manages to elide the rules of Bottled-in-Bond while benefiting from its good name, somehow whiffing on the bedrock of consumer trust in American whiskey. If the idea was to be a hashmark better than 100-proof bonded whiskey, Wild Turkey 101 has been playing that hand quite well for eighty years, and manages it with aplomb and credibility, a playbook WhistlePig could read quietly in the corner and learn something from.

XXX

The Oxford Companion to Spirits and Cocktails argues that American rye whiskey's heritage probably came via German immigrants, not necessarily the Scots or Irish (or the Scots-Irish), who often get too much credit for whiskey history in the popular imagination and even in considered historical narratives. Many of the Pennsylvania Dutch, as German-speaking immigrants came to be known, would have been familiar with this style of whiskey and would have promulgated it in the New World where they settled, in the Pennsylvania colony.

Mennonite Henry Overholt (born Henrich Oberholtzer) and his son Abraham were founders of the Old Overholt brand in West Overton, Pennsylvania. Abraham's grandson, Henry Clay Frick, learned the whiskey business early and parlayed his business acumen into a grand fortune built of steelmaking and various industrial concerns. The brand is still a leading rye label, second only to Bulleit. The endurance of rye whiskey and its ability to build fortunes is a great credit to the spirit itself. Grassy and funky rye, when full-bodied, can add heft to a cocktail and is even better on its own as a complex spirit. Often maligned and neglected by corporate owners, American rye fell to 150,000 case production in 2006, but with the enthusiasm of craft cocktail makers and small distillers, it ramped up to an estimated 1.13 million cases in 2022.

I first visited Pennsylvania as a distiller to explore the sites of the Whiskey Rebellion, an important moment in the American story that lays that stage for a birth and death of rye whiskey. Like a lot of early whiskey history, geography plays an important role here. Seeking inexpensive, arable land, settlers pressed past the Allegheny Mountains and built subsistence farms with a little extra to make into whiskey to barter for necessities.

Meanwhile, Alexander Hamilton, industrialist and first secretary of the treasury, proposed a tax on distilled spirits that favored large distilleries. For a country that had fought a war in protest of British taxation on various goods (tea, most notably), the idea of taxing anything was not palatable, but whiskey was perceived as perhaps the most achievable—and urgently necessary to pay down Revolutionary war debts. Hamilton orchestrated the tax to favor industrial distillers, hoping to engineer a stable industry and stream of revenue for the government.

On the frontier, in western Pennsylvania, where federal benefits were few and whiskey was a practical means of agricultural production as a commodity, the tax did not sit well (perhaps predictably), and a small band of farmer distillers started organizing against collection officers. The rebellion concentrated in and south of Pittsburgh, and consisted mostly of political activity, though a tax collector was tarred and feathered in Westmoreland County, and later, an armed confrontation at tax collector John Neville's house resulted in the death of the rebel's leader, James McFarlane, who appeared to have been the victim of a cheap shot during a cease-fire. Enraged, the rebels treated McFarlane as a martyr and organized 7,000 citizens strong at Braddock's field with speeches and threats to secede.

President Washington sent a military force of 13,000 at a time when New York City had only 33,000 residents, a dramatic show of force for a domestic disturbance. But upon its arrival in Pittsburgh, many of the rebels had fled. Only a handful were arrested, and only two men were convicted of treason, and even those men, Philip Wigle and John Mitchell, were pardoned by Washington in an effort to move on from the crisis.

Eventually, the whiskey tax was scuttled until the Civil War, when it came back as an emergency wartime measure. By then, distilling in Pennsylvania

PENNSYLVANIA WHISKEY & RYE

DAD'S HAT RYE

A nice spicy rye, proofy and rich with a tangy, almost savory dill note like a whiskey you found in the back of your grandparents' liquor cabinet. Flavorful and evocative, definitely an outlier in rye whiskeys. An odd note that I can't place; certainly an acquired taste, but a beguiling one.

90pf	$50	H	TC	Independent

WIGLE PENNSYLVANIA RYE

A nice, bright rye whiskey with a balanced profile. Not too funky, not too spicy, but approachable and flavorful to rival a lot of column-distilled peers that get more visibility.

84pf	$47	H 2 yr	TC	Semi-independent

WIGLE DEEP CUT RYE WHISKEY

A rich, round rye hitting all the right notes, and a very classic rye from the cradle of the style. There's a beautiful funk on the nose, but a clean and spicy palate that solidifies a treasure in any collection. Wigle often plays with how they run the still, and this shows the apotheosis of that art.

118.6pf	$85	H 5 yr	TC	Semi-independent

had become big business, with rye distillers making Monongahela rye, a high-rye-styled whiskey, the dominant form. As in Kentucky, distilleries grew and consolidated, and brands were traded over the years, but Pennsylvania rye remained a strong consumer concept, much like Tennessee whiskey today. Distillers like Overholt in Broad Ford, and Finch in Schenley, were large, but small distillers remained. When whiskey dried up in the 1970s and '80s, rye production completely sputtered in Pennsylvania, and ended completely when Bomberger's (Michter's) closed in 1989.

LIBERTY POLE MONONGAHELA RYE

A very flavorful rye with notes of caramel, honey, toasted almonds, and toasted wheat bread, this is a beautiful whiskey laying full claim to Monongahela heritage—and doing so with aplomb.

92pf	$47	**P 2 yr**	**TC**	Independent

LIBERTY POLE PEATED RYE

Whoa! Peated rye is a remarkable fusion of Monongahela and Islay flavor notes. Heavy barbecue-forward peat character laid over an amazing rye whiskey base (see above). Rich, smoky, and still a little sweet, this is a bucket-list whiskey for the adventurous drinker.

110.6pf	$47	**P 2 yr**	**TC**	Independent

STOLL & WOLFE

Compared to some of the other Pennsylvania ryes, Stoll & Wolfe may be playing it cool for now, with a middle-of-the-road, clean rye. With the only claim to any trade knowledge of rye whiskey through Michter's distiller Dick Stoll, this brand is built on a treasured expertise that is rare from new distillers.

90pf	$48	**H**	**TC**	Independent

It would be twenty-five years until rye production began again. Dad's Hat was most likely the first distiller to bring rye back after the drought, opening in 2010 and releasing early barrels not long after, a debut not marked with as much fanfare as the moment deserved. Founder Herman Mihalich grew up on the banks of the Monongahela in prime Whiskey Rebel territory, but would later launch Dad's Hat in Bristol, north of Philadelphia. The whiskeys have always been well-made, solid examples of what a detail-oriented craft distiller can do, and the focus on rye stood apart from other early craft

Wigle is one of the most relentlessly creative and curious distilleries in the United States, with a staggering portfolio of genuinely differentiated spirits, including some classic rye whiskeys.

distillers that focused on bourbon or single malts. The whiskeys should be on anyone's list of best rye and best small distillers in the country.

Philip Wigle was one of the men charged with treason during the Whiskey Rebellion and he serves as the namesake for Wigle Whiskey, a fascinating distillery in downtown Pittsburgh known almost excessive for variety and creativity. When I visited, in 2017, I must have tried twenty-five different spirits, most of them whiskey. Wigle began as a multigenerational family business, and I met Mary Meyer, the matriarch, on my visit, though a recent acquisition in 2022 by Pittsburgh Pirates owner Bob Nutting may change the dynamic.

Wigle has a creative energy that spills into their products; the owners have even written a book on the Whiskey Rebellion. Wigle is also a quintessential urban distillery, a compact operation that nonetheless has a recently expanded tasting room. A visit leaves you with the impression that Wigle isn't so much building a brand as a community—using whiskey and other spirits to bring people together and connect with history, making it all look fun and limitless.

Wigle's whiskeys are polarizing, perhaps, for the traditionalist, and I've even tried some whiskeys I outright loathed. But I would argue that if you can't find a whiskey you like here, you must not be trying very hard, since variety is part of the point.

Another Pittsburgh area distiller is Liberty Pole, based in Washington, south and west of the city. Liberty Pole makes a peated rye and peated bourbon, which are products close to our hearts at Kings County. Still, Liberty Pole takes a very different direction with a more heavily peated offering—demonstrating that there's still a lot of variety left in emerging styles of American whiskey. Their whiskeys are well-made and worthy of the region's historic prominence—a true Monongahela rye that earns its designation.

While Pennsylvania distillers were using the state's rye history as a starting point, Stoll & Wolfe began with the person best positioned to provide a living bridge between the rye of the past and the present: Dick Stoll, former distiller at the Michter's distillery and an apprentice to Charles Everett Beam, who ran the plant until 1972. Stoll became head distiller and oversaw some improvements to the visitor experience, including the installation of a pot-still system, but was forced into retirement when the distillery closed in 1990. Erik Wolfe, then living in New York, planned a return to the Lancaster area to open a distillery and sought Stoll's expertise, and eventually partnered with him to open a craft distillery. Stoll died in 2020, but not before laying the groundwork for the Pennsylvania rye with the best case for bridging the gap between past and present.

Nearby Lancaster is a lovely town to visit, a sort of farm-to-table fantasia where Amish bakers and hipster locavores blend into a small-town charm that feels neither contrived nor preserved in amber. The central market in downtown Lancaster is a remarkable forum that puts more famous and beloved markets to shame. I visited Lancaster twice trying to peddle whiskey (mostly unsuccessfully, owing in part to Pennsylvania's tough liquor laws), and stumbled into Thistle Finch, a distillery making rye and a few other spirits. Their white spirit floored me, and I vowed to follow up when the aged whiskey is ready.

Rye has grown tenfold over the past decade. Bulleit Rye, distilled at MGP, is almost half of the cases sold in the US. It sells seven times the second-place contender, Old Overholt. Brands distilled at MGP mostly populate the list, and it's easy to estimate that 70 percent of rye is made at that one distillery, often from a 95-percent-rye mash bill, long a canard for a rye lover, who longs for a more historical recipe meant to be consumed as straight whiskey rather than blended away. The Pennsylvania brands all together might add up to 25,000 cases sold, but all this is to say there's still a lot of opportunity in American rye when the average consumer wants to get past the mainstream homogeneity that currently dominates the market.

XXX

Rye is also often associated with Maryland, but what constitutes the difference between Maryland rye and Pennsylvania rye is a debated topic. While many sources suggest that Maryland rye had a higher corn content than Monongahela and other Pennsylvania rye, making for a softer, more accessible whiskey, *New York Times* journalist and author Clay Risen argues that Maryland may not have defined a style so much as a provenance, a contention that holds water when looking at something like Tennessee whiskey (if you accept it as bourbon by another name).

Historic whiskey advertising suggests that Maryland seems to have promoted more blended whiskeys than straight whiskeys, and this may be Maryland's heritage, more than any recipe or process tied to a straight whiskey. Maryland Club, Lord Calvert, and Baltimore Pure Rye were all labels that traded on geographic association, which was also a subtle way of appealing to a demographic—niche marketing for its day. Colonial Maryland started as a haven for Catholics fleeing religious persecution in England, and Catholicism has always had a cozier relationship to alcohol than Protestantism, dominant in many of the other early American colonies. Maryland Catholics might have been easier to target in marketing, and whether the regional audience built a particular style of whiskey or vice versa may never be known.

As with Pennsylvania, Prohibition killed off most distillers in Maryland, but some stubbornly remained. Baltimore Pure Rye, a Seagram plant in Dundalk, closed only in 1985, a relic from the "big four" era when four companies controlled most spirits production in the US. From what I can gather, the Baltimore facility produced neutral spirits for blended whiskeys, including Seagram's Four Roses when it was a blend.

Today, only a handful of craft distillers are at work in Maryland, hoping to rejuvenate the heritage of rye, but like Pennsylvania rye, there are no

Near Mount Vernon, George Washington's restored distillery is the only re-creation of a historical distillery that actively produces. It's a fascinating window into the whiskey of the very late 1700s, when the distillery was active.

historic Maryland brands that continue to be produced in Maryland (and I can only find Lord Calvert as a Canadian import now). Pikesville is an old Maryland brand now made by Heaven Hill, but there is nothing in marketing materials to connect the contemporary product to any historical one. A new company is trying to bring Maryland Club back, but the product is sourced elsewhere.

The distiller best positioned to reclaim Maryland whiskey is Sagamore Spirits, in a purpose-built facility in Locust Point, not far from Fort

The recreation of George Washington's distillery near Mount Vernon is a window into distilling before electricity, plumbing, and other modern methods.

McHenry National Monument and Baltimore's inner harbor. Baltimore has the makings of a great whiskey city, with highbrow and lowbrow culture in equal measure, white- and blue-collar jobs side by side. Locust Point and neighboring Federal Hill are fascinating neighborhoods where divey watering-hole bars cater to a diverse spectrum of residents and exist in good harmony with upscale farm-to-table and craft-cocktail fine dining.

Sagamore is a well-financed project, founded by entrepreneur Kevin Plank, whose Under Armour sportswear business is a point of local pride, having grown to be the number-two sportswear brand in the US after Nike. Under Armour has faltered somewhat in recent years, and Plank has stepped down as chief executive, but his Baltimore loyalty is unquestionable.

Sagamore's ambitions are a good fit for Baltimore, but most of the whiskey sold was sourced from elsewhere. This was nothing to be ashamed of on its own, but the grain-to-glass marketing and spring-water storytelling fall a little flatter than they need to. The brand's namesake Sagamore farm, once a breeder of racehorses, exited the thoroughbred business in 2020, according to a press release, so its acreage could be devoted to growing grain for the distillery—suggesting that maybe the whiskey business has done better than sportswear or horse breeding and a true grain-to-glass whiskey may be coming soon.

Even if Sagamore is a slightly imperfect vehicle to steward the Maryland rye renaissance, there aren't a lot of smaller contenders waiting in the wings. My favorite Maryland distiller has stopped making whiskey to focus on a Chesapeake Bay rum. Founder Jamie Windon began the St. Michaels–based grain-to-glass Windon Distilling, making rum and rye from scratch, but has lately focused exclusively on rum and barrel-aged rum (often in Kings County ex-bourbon barrels). Rich and complicated, the rum is so good we can only hope Jamie may get the whiskey bug again, but we are perfectly happy to enjoy a Chesapeake dark and stormy in the meantime.

Jack Rose Dining Saloon in Washington, DC, is a temple bar for the whiskey lover.

MARYLAND RYE

SAGAMORE SPIRIT RYE

This bottle still lists Indiana provenance, so even seven years on, this is MGP spirit with a lot of Maryland dressing. Still, I'll say it has a very mellow presentation with a little bit of sour melon, nutmeg, and simple syrup. The label says hand-bottled, so there's that. Maryland should reclaim its rye heritage (and that may mean sourced and blended rye), but it's still a hard bottle to get too excited about.

83pf	$35	H	NT	Illva Saronno

BALTIMORE SPIRITS CO. EPOCH RYE

A beautiful, flavorful rye that argues better for Maryland Rye than any historical yarns or marketing bluster. Rich with notes of toffee, buttered brown sugar, and nutty rye grain, this is a rye lover's luxuriation in the richness and texture that mark the best of the genre.

100pf	$65	P	4 years TC	Independent

In Washington, DC, Republic Restoratives is a crowdfunded women-led distiller making edgy (mostly sourced) products that has a nice tasting room, if not much distribution outside the District.

The real star of DC's distilling scene is George Washington's Distillery at Mount Vernon, rebuilt recently with money from the spirits industry lobbying group DISCUS. With re-created custom stills by Vendome and hand mashing in barrels, there's a lot more to learn and appreciate here than on your standard distillery tour. Many distilling luminaries have passed through and tried their hand at mashing, fermenting, distilling, and aging all without electricity, boilers, pumps, and the kinds of heat exchangers that populate even very old-fashioned pot-still distilleries.

Perhaps one of the few distillery tours where you can bring the kids along, it's a welcome stop for those who appreciate a healthier dose of history with their whiskey-making. And Mount Vernon itself is an interesting stop that has done a better job with Washington's complicated legacy in recent years.

If you don't have time to make it out to Mount Vernon, Jack Rose is one of the premier whiskey bars in America, with lots of easter eggs for those who know what to look for. I remember trying a bourbon from the Hoffman Distillery in Lawrenceburg, Kentucky, long defunct. Readers will know it as the distillery once owned by Julian Van Winkle III, who set up a bottling line and aging warehouse for the family whiskeys, which included some of the Hoffman stock. I was prepared for excellence and came up with surprisingly middling whiskey, but such is the fun of hunting. Jack Rose has thousands of bottles on offer, a little something for every palate and proclivity.

Since most American whiskey draws from three somewhat standardized bourbon recipes (rye, high-rye, and wheat), many consumers have drilled down on the barrel as the key differentiator in whiskey. And this is a legitimate way of looking at whiskeys—much of what distinguishes one bourbon from another is merely time in the barrel and dilution proof—though this ignores the work of the blender in placing barrels into assemblages to create differentiated spirits.

And indeed, it appears that barrel-forward whiskey is in vogue, and no amount of barrel can ever be enough. If there is a horizon to barrel aging in the popular consciousness, we haven't discovered it yet as distillers. I like to think of the work of the barrel as a little bit like salt as it relates to cooking. It enhances flavor, and more is often better. In cooking, the moment when there is too much is easily identified, but in whiskey it is less obvious. Some of the whiskeys in this book are over-salted to my palate, but they remain very sought-after whiskeys.

Another function of contemporary whiskey culture is barrel-proof bourbon. While barrel-proof whiskeys have been around—and may have originated when Booker's hit the market in 1989, they have certainly gained traction in recent years, especially popular in the swath of bourbon country that stretches from

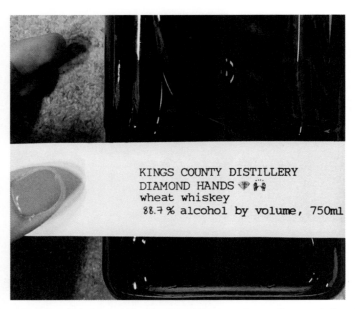

We made a private barrel of wheat whiskey for Alexis Ohanian, who was then merely founder of Reddit and not yet the husband of Serena Williams. It took seven years before we agreed to have it bottled. The angels had drunk all but three 750ml bottles of the whiskey, leaving behind a viscous spirit that floated the hydrometer at 88.7% alcohol, or 177.4 proof. I don't know if there have been higher-proof whiskeys before, but definitely nothing like it in the world of whiskeys. Was it a great whiskey? It was superlative, and maybe that's all that need be said.

Kentucky to Texas. The advantage of barrel-strength whiskey is that it gives the drinker the opportunity to dilute the whiskey at their pace and preference, but I have no doubt that plenty of consumers are drinking these neat and undiluted just as often. There is some intrigue in those concentrated flavors that only time and seasons coming and going confer, refining the whiskey and concentrating it, most often, into a potent tincture that can be as much as three-quarters alcohol.

The TSA prohibits flying with anything over 70 percent alcohol, and so 140 proof has become a small obsession among barrel-strength believers. These so-called hazmat barrels have become a sought-after curiosity within barrel-strength whiskey, adding a quantifiable desirability in an era when few aged-stated whiskeys are findable and affordable.

Of course, a hazmat is a good whiskey only if it's a good whiskey, just as age alone is no indicator of quality. I have no doubt that some tenacious distiller will recognize this trend and aim their whiskeys toward the hazmat designation, with dubious results. Bourbon barrels are limited to 125 as an entry proof; to climb to 140, there must be an unlikely series of circumstances that may affect only a small number of barrels, even if everything else about them is the same. Gaming a spirit for high proof sounds like letting a very niche internet cart drive a very real horse.

But the hazmat trend only serves to illuminate a larger condition in the bourbon market: the disappearance of well-aged whiskeys at reasonable prices. I don't think anyone would be talking about extreme proof if well-aged (10-year or older) bourbon was readily available at an affordable price. As bourbon has boomed, prices for older whiskeys tripled or quadrupled. Can these higher prices be justified?

Barrels work in both subtractive and additive ways. First the barrel subtracts the most volatile compounds (most solventy flavors) by letting it evaporate as angel's share. Then the barrel removes the least volatile fusel oils* that get absorbed into the porous charcoal. Those subtractive processes happen almost entirely in the first years of age. Then a barrel becomes additive, adding oak character defined by the increasingly older sap and caramelized sap that continue to add color and flavor summer after summer as the barrel ages. One thing our friends in Scotland have long understood is that old wood makes better whiskey than young wood does. That can be a tricky truth to square with bourbon's requirement for a new barrel, but with the right patience, old wood makes great whiskey (and a great secondary finish if done correctly). American single malt is a proving ground for old cooperage, as it makes no requirement for new oak, opening up fertile territory for experimentation that will likely have an impact on the broader taste and culture of American whiskey.

But to answer the question: Is the depth and complexity of well-aged bourbon worth the price? That's more of a matter for your budget, since the broad dynamics in the bourbon industry aren't going away soon, and a ten-year-old bourbon is worth much more than it used to be. Whether your wallet and palate agree is a secondary, very personal question.

---

* An imprecise and archaic term for the oily, estery chemicals that characterize the late part of a distilling run. These compounds have a high boiling point and give the tails part of a distilling run a skunky, soapy, or floral character.

The Carousel Bar at Hotel Monteleone is a classic that has patrons at all hours of the day.

7½

VIEUX CARRÉ

It might seem like whiplash to travel from the Northeast to New Orleans, but for whiskey history, these were early capitals of the spirits trade (and spirits consumption). New Orleans has old history like Boston, New York, and Philadelphia, and its distinctive culture has been both preserved and iterated for almost three centuries.

New Orleans is not known for its whiskey distillers, but the traveled bourbon drinker may find it is the most hospitable drinking city in the Union, and bourbon holds a special place in the culture. Its most famous street, after all, shares a name with the beverage.

Here, one comes not for the distillers, but for the cocktails. And any book on American whiskey should acknowledge the role New Orleans has played as a hub of commerce for American whiskey in the first half of the country's history and as an incubator of cocktail culture for much of the second half. So, we will pause here on our journey where east meets west and old traditions will yield mostly to new ones, while we savor a whiskey cocktail in the city of its invention.

All river traffic west of the Alleghenies and east of the Rockies dumps out in New Orleans. The eastern continental divide was a significant boundary before railroads, and while whiskey could travel over the mountains by wagon at places like the Cumberland Gap, it was easier to sell whiskey downriver. Pittsburgh, Maysville, Cincinnati, and Louisville all became important hubs where whiskey brokers bought and sold whiskey before sending it on flatboats to New Orleans, where it would reach a broader world. It takes about twelve bushels of grain to make a barrel of whiskey, and a 400-pound barrel of bourbon was a lot easier to trade than a ton of grain. As a result, New Orleans has been awash in liquor since before the steamboat era. Of course, many businesses that depended on

New Orleans has a lot to offer the whiskey fan, as a city that has been hosting drinkers since long before the United States was a country.

liquor, like restaurants, saloons, and brothels, created a culture of hospitality that took on a life of its own.

For the whiskey drinker, the new but terrific New Orleans Bourbon Festival is as good as any in the business, run with an eye toward inclusion from distillers of all sizes. There is also Tales of the Cocktail, the annual bar tradeshow in the syrupy hot days of July, when a handful of bartenders and thousands of alcohol-industry executives, ambassadors, and salesmen congregate in New Orleans to enlighten and intoxicate each other.

To its credit, though, "Tales," as it is foreshortened, honors the lowly spirits writer with a platform to sell and sign books at a healthy remove from the blowout parties sponsored by the big brands. The whole thing feels quite sordid after day three and it lasts much longer, so I try to get beyond the hosting hotel as much as possible. New Orleans has a great place to drink on every corner, so it would be impossible to list them all, and whole books have been written about the culinary and nightlife culture of New Orleans. It is far beyond the scope of this book.

New Orleans is a small city that is always swollen with tourists, and it is a fine thing to give in to here, wandering around the French Quarter. There is no place in America that feels quite so old, even in old cities like New

York, Boston, Philadelphia, Charleston, or Savannah. The French Quarter feels both well-preserved and timelessly present. A stop at the quintessential dive Old Absinthe House, the ancient watering hole Napoleon House, or the timelessly kitsch Carousel Bar at Hotel Monteleone, all offer rewards that I struggle to find in New York, where novelty is favored over the staid. Muffulettas and beignets are simply an added bonus.

I spent a week in New Orleans one August with my son, then only about a year old, and saw the city from a completely different perspective, joyriding on the trolleys and going to the zoo and the children's museum. Any local will tell you the real New Orleans exists exclusively beyond the French Quarter, and I have vivid memories of so many epic meals it would be impossible to relate them, though shrimp stuffed inside ground beef stuffed inside a pork chop at Jacques-Imo's, quotidian low-key sandwiches at Cochon Butcher, or brunch at Café Degas stand out.

Still, as much as there is to enjoy with children, the perfection and exuberance (and abundance) of cocktails in the city are worth the effort of finding a sitter. Even for the straight-whiskey drinker, the cocktails of New Orleans are an excuse to set aside habits of neat pours and embrace the cocktail.

MINT JULEP

Like bourbon itself, the julep is more a drink of process than ingredients. Its only parts are bourbon, sugar, mint, and ice, though the particularity of the ice and frosted silver cup is crucial to a successful julep. General Simon Bolivar Buckner compared the making of a julep to "simply carving an elephant from a block of wood by whittling away the parts that don't look like an elephant," which is to say there is some artistry and practice required. Many would say the mint syrup is crucial to a julep, but the right consistency of dry, crushed ice is actually most important.

> 2 oz bourbon
> 1 oz mint simple syrup
> Mint sprig

To make the mint simple syrup, boil 2 parts sugar with 1 part water with mint leaves. Strain and set aside to cool. In a julep cup, add mint simple syrup, crushed ice, and bourbon. Top with crushed ice in a mound using an ice cream scoop to shape the top. Garnish with a generous mint sprig. If done correctly, the cup should frost over on a warm day, indicating the drink is ready for consumption.

OLD FASHIONED

Ask for an Old Fashioned at the famed Brown Hotel in Louisville, and they will ask you if you want the official version, akin to a fruit salad, or a more contemporary version. This is one of the oldest cocktails in any book, so its iterations have been numerous. If you come by Kings County's tasting room, this is how we'll serve it:

> 3 dashes Angostura Bitters
> ¼ oz simple syrup
> 2 oz peated bourbon

Build in a rocks glass. Add a brandied cherry and an orange peel to garnish.

PENICILLIN

Typically, the penicillin calls for Scotch whisky, but this is a book on American whiskey, and many American single malts bridge an interesting gap between traditions.

> ¾ oz lemon juice
> 1 oz Ginger Honey Syrup
> 2 oz American single malt

To make the ginger honey syrup, boil 7 ounces fresh ginger, cut into coins, in 1 pint water, then combine with equal parts honey. For the cocktail, add ingredients to a shaking tin. Add ice and shake vigorously. Double strain over fresh ice and garnish with a lemon peel.

MOONSHINE MARTINI

This is definitely a drink that bends tradition, but the moonshine martini (or white Manhattan, if you prefer) is a drink that answers the question posed by moonshine or unaged whiskeys—spirits full of flavor, but novel and not yet standardized into canonical cocktails. Yet this one has been around for almost two decades in some form, first made by the bar at Marlow & Sons in Brooklyn.

> 2 oz white whiskey
> 1 oz Dolin's Blanc vermouth
> or similar

Build in a mixing glass. Add ice and stir. Strain into a chilled glass. Garnish: Long, neat lemon twist. The twist should coil around the inside of the glass.

MANHATTAN

The Manhattan is the best of the whiskey drinks—the one I'm most likely to make at home. It's essentially a bourbon martini, a potent libation to be consumed judiciously. With any two-ingredient cocktail, so much depends on the bourbon and the vermouth. Like whiskey, vermouth is having an American renaissance, and there are great options local to much of the country (we've used Uncouth Vermouth, Little City, and Atsby). Or you can make it the Van Winkle way with Carpano Anitca (before that gets allocated too!).

> 2 oz bourbon
> 1 oz sweet vermouth
> 2–3 dashes aromatic bitters

Build in a shaker tin, shake for 1 full minute, and strain into coupe glass. Garnish with a brandied cherry, traditionally, or a lemon twist.

BOULEVARDIER

I tend to roll my eyes at versions of the negroni, the Campari-funded favorite drink™ of every bartender in the last decade plus. It's an easy one: 1 part bitter aperitif, 1 part sweet vermouth, and 1 part American whiskey, preferably bourbon, which is one of the reasons it is so popular. One nice thing about the craft spirits revolution is that many distillers have opted to make alternatives to the global hegemony of Campari. St. George, Leopold, and Forthave spirits in New York all make better substitutes to the candy red liqueur, each colored with real cochineal as Campari used to be.

> 2 dashes Peychaud's Bitters
> 1 oz Atsby Sweet Vermouth
> 1 oz Forthave Spirits RED Aperitivo
> 1 oz bourbon or rye
> Grapefruit peel

Build in a mixing glass. Add ice and stir. Strain over fresh ice. Garnish with grapefruit peel.

IRISH COFFEE

Like the Irish Goodbye, Irish coffee could be construed as a slur on the fine culture of Ireland, where at least they know how to spell whiskey properly. For the everyday drinker of black coffee, the union of coffee and bourbon may sound unappealing: two intense flavors competing with one another. The secret is sugar and hand-whipped cream, which is easier than it sounds if you have the bar tools nearby. This recipe was inspired by a trip to the Dead Rabbit, where the drink is a specialty.

COFFEE
¾ mug hot black coffee
2 oz bourbon
Simple syrup (optional)

WHIPPED CREAM
½ oz simple syrup
3 oz sugar
¼ cup heavy cream
Vanilla bean
Cinnamon

In a mug of hot black coffee, add the bourbon and simple syrup, if desired. For the whipped cream, scrape a vanilla bean into the simple syrup. Strain. Add sugar and shake with heavy cream. Top the coffee with the cream and sprinkle with shaved vanilla bean or cinnamon.

HOT TODDY

The hot toddy is a classic vehicle for whiskey, a winter warmer without parallel.

2 oz any whiskey
1 oz lemon juice
Honey
Hot water
Cinnamon stick

Add the whiskey, lemon juice, and honey to a large mug and add boiling water. Garnish with a cinnamon stick and let stand until drinkable.

It takes grain to make whiskey. A 55-pound bushel of corn will make approximately 5 gallons of whiskey at 100 proof. Kings County sources corn, wheat, and oats from Lakeview Organic Grain (above). But more than any other region, the distillers of the Midwest have used proximity to farmers as a differentiating advantage.

8

FARMER DISTILLERS

One of the enduring myths of whiskey history is that Kentucky has always been the center of whiskey production in America. We've already dismantled that myth by looking at the Northeast, but an important, forgotten era in whiskey history is the first great industrial age of bourbon, when whiskey production expanded in the 1880s, culminating in the rise and fall of the Whiskey Trust, headquartered in Peoria, Illinois.

There are many cities that can claim to be hubs of whiskey production in the United States. St. Louis, Pittsburgh, Louisville, and Cincinnati all have good and credible claims. Still, the city with the most production capacity of all time may have been Peoria, where the Great Western Distillery Company turned grain into whiskey by the tanker rail car starting in 1866.

Great Western's president, Joseph Greenhut, saw an opportunity after whiskey prices crashed in the mid-1870s, when European winemaking recovered from a blight that had improved the fortunes of American distillers in the export market. A glut of whiskey distressed many distillery owners, and Greenhut moved to organize the distillers into a trust that would control the supply, the price of whiskey, and the profit participation of its principals. The trust was able to control whiskey production such that 90 percent or more was under the auspices of the trust, but not without stories of violent retaliation against distillers that refused to join. George Gibson, the trust's secretary, was arrested in a sting operation, offering to pay an undercover agent to bomb an uncooperative distillery. Facing anti-trust legislation and economic crisis, the trust relinquished much of its power in the 1890s. The constituent distillers of the Whiskey Trust stayed around in modified form as National Distillers and eventually its assets were absorbed into today's Beam Suntory.

The whiskey being produced in the distilleries around Chicago was not whiskey in the contemporary sense. Most produced something more like grain alcohol or *cologne spirits* as it was called—an industrial product with many uses, not always beverage alcohol. Some of these plants did make something like grain whiskey, which middlemen known as rectifiers would use to cut straight whiskeys or stretch other types of spirits. Rectifiers were not unlike the sourced whiskey brands of their day, though their spirits were sometimes cut with more than grain alcohol, including adulterants like caramel coloring, glycerin, wood shavings, formaldehyde, and other chemicals. Before the Bottled-in-Bond Act of 1897 and the Pure Food and Drug Act of 1906, spirits were largely unregulated by the federal government, and consumers had a very hard time trusting the whiskeys.

After Prohibition, some of these plants reopened, with Hiram Walker in Peoria the largest, with at least some whiskey production continuing until the 1990s, and still operating today to make fuel ethanol. One of my favorite whiskeys in my collection is a Hirsch-branded 20-year Illinois corn whiskey—something that probably we won't see much of for a while to come.

If this is the cultural history of whiskey in the Midwest, its contemporary distillers have leaned on their proximity to grain farms as the distinguishing feature. Like other areas where distillers once thrived, no historical beverage-alcohol distillers continue here, so it has been left to craft producers, all of which have opened in the last fifteen years, to define what Midwest whiskey should be.

Abundant rail and water transport, proximity to farms and grain, and location central to much of the country's population helped propel the areas around Chicago into whiskey history. The modern inheritors of this storytelling use the same advantages, but rather than a neutral industrial product, they have made niche spirits that challenge the hegemony of Kentucky bourbon.

The most obvious of these inheritors is Koval, a distillery started by husband and wife Robert Birnecker and Sonat Birnecker Hart. Robert's family history led to his interest in distillation, and he not only founded a distillery but also worked as an operational consultant to startup distillers using Kothe stills. Sonat left academia to manage the business as its CEO.

Sonat and Robert Birnecker run Koval, in Chicago, a boutique maker of elegant, grain-forward whiskeys.

The distillery is like peers Clear Creek and Leopold Brothers in relying on European traditions of distilling fruit and grains in pursuit of their purest expression. The portfolio is wide and varied, but the whiskeys are what may be most interesting. Bourbon and rye are available, as well as a four-grain whiskey, but also whiskeys made from millet and oat. All of Koval's products are certified organic, not an easy feat for spirits, and they truly reflect the considered approach of its founders.

This leads to a different place than most whiskey distillers, and the oat is a fun whiskey to try, if maybe not one that will end up on a list of all-time favorite whiskeys. Koval has a lot that makes it the quintessential distiller of American craft spirits: beautiful, art-world packaging that continually evolves; charismatic and intellectual founders; a portfolio of spirits that challenge expectations; an urban site and community; and, as a consultant to a still manufacturer, a behind-the-scenes role in setting up other craft distillers.

The other Chicagoland whiskey distiller of note is FEW Spirits. Tucked into an Evanston alley, the speakeasy nature of their small urban industrial space fits with a brand named after Frances E. Willard, second leader of the

CHICAGOLAND WHISKEY

KOVAL BOURBON

Koval is a little before its time, coming out with creative whiskeys before the market was ready. They have recalibrated with more mainstream offerings, but this single-barrel bourbon, distilled from barely legal corn and 49 percent millet, is hardly ordinary. That mash bill suggests something strange, but with butterscotch, caramel, and toffee—this is what a bourbon wants to be and my favorite from the region.

94pf	$52	H	TC	Independent

KOVAL OAT WHISKEY

Not many distillers have experimented with oats, but you can make whiskey from any breakfast mush (grits and cream of wheat being more common in whiskey) while oatmeal gets the silent treatment. This is an argument for it: nutty and earthy but not so unfamiliar you'd even guess this was a whiskey from a very avant-garde grain. A refined, almost-floral whiskey from a funky source, it's a pity this has been downgraded to a seasonal release. This is an adventurous drinker's must-have bottle.

80pf	$49	H	NT	Independent

Women's Christian Temperance Union, and a major figure in the history of Evanston, notably a dry city from its founding by Methodist ministers until 1972 (and perhaps better known as the home of Northwestern University).

FEW draws on iconography from the World's Columbian Exposition in 1893, a world's fair that proved influential in architecture, industry, and American identity, so to borrow from this local story is a canny move to connect to history without being particularly explicit. FEW uses a column and hybrid pot still, as well as a variety of barrel formats to make the classic styles of American whiskey, bourbon, rye, and single malt, as well as gins.

KOVAL BOTTLED-IN-BOND RYE

One of the great pleasures of writing this book was rediscovering Koval. After a lot of very similar Kentucky whiskeys, these are a breath of novelty and excellence. A lot of intense flavors here: caramel, toffee, and butterscotch. Like a kitchen after a great meal with bread in the oven, there is a lot that appeals to the senses. This has the rye tang on the nose, but the body is rich and viscous with chocolate and cream. An all-star rye.

100pf	$65	H	NT	Independent

FEW BOURBON

A musty bourbon that is both woodsy and a little floral, FEW Bourbon is a craft staple in a lot of bars, a beneficiary of good distribution, if not always with the most grassroots support—which is a pity since FEW has an interesting complexity and deserves true partisans.

93pf	$45	H	TC	Heaven Hill

FEW RYE

A very soft, caramel-forward rye whiskey with a touch of spearmint on the finish. A fine whiskey, not straying too far from its lane, but also carving out flavors that distinguish a solid craft rye.

93pf	$50	H	TC	Heaven Hill

FEW's success is attributable in many ways to its founder, Paul Hletko, a lawyer by trade but a brewer by blood. His folksy, down-to-earth manner has carried the brand since its founding in 2011, and he's been an important figure in the industry with the American Craft Spirits Association.

FEW was an early acquisition of Samson and Surrey, the accelerator for craft brands, and as such it got wide placement around the US. It used to break my heart that the only grain-to-glass craft whiskey in most Brooklyn bars was often FEW, which speaks to the power of distribution. It takes only a handful of people to make whiskey, but it takes an army to sell it, and

FEW ended up with opportunities many brands dream of. In late 2021, it was announced that Heaven Hill would buy Sampson and Surrey, giving Paul new bosses. How much opportunity Heaven Hill sees in protecting FEW remains to be seen, but as I look to the future and regionalization of whiskey, they would be foolish not to protect the brand and its distillery.

XXX

Though I grew up in Appalachia, my parents were raised in western Michigan, in territory settled by my Dutch ancestors who liked flat, soggy land and going to church as often as possible. It turns out Holland, Michigan, which I frequented as a boy visiting Windmill Island (the only historic Dutch Windmill to be rebuilt in the United States) and Dutch Village, a sort of creepy theme park with a wooden shoe factory and candle dipping, has a fine craft distiller in New Holland Spirits.

Holland itself is a charming, small lakeside and college town—even a Christian college town has a little bit of edge, or what passes for it in these parts. New Holland started out as a brewery but branched into spirits with a variety of interesting whiskeys, perhaps most notably bourbon finished in beer barrels.

New Holland Brewery and Distillery celebrated its twenty-fifth anniversary in 2022.

It's not uncommon for beer to be aged in whiskey barrels—the residual high-proof whiskey helps prevent the kinds of contamination that can ruin a beer as it rests. Aged beer is never stored very long compared to whiskey, and a steady supply of used barrels has made bourbon-barrel ales a common product from brewers big and small.

It's still relatively rare for the reverse to happen, though that is a big part of the product line at New Holland, where various whiskeys are aged in the Dragon's Milk stout barrels and vice versa. Zeppelin Bend single malt is perhaps my favorite of the lineup, a proper American single malt if there ever was one.

Head south of Holland along the Lake Michigan shoreline and near the Indiana state line, where Journeyman Distillery in Three Oaks has built a great portfolio of whiskeys and a destination distillery in the highest class. Journeyman's whiskeys are always well made, and more than any single standout, they make a variety of classic whiskeys to a high standard.

Michiganders describe their state as a mitten, and near the tip of the ring finger is Traverse City, a resort town known mostly for cherries, which grow here in abundance. It's also Michigan's wine region and home to a pair of distilleries. Traverse City Whiskey Company is widely distributed and mostly or entirely sourced from the usual suspects. Grand Traverse Distillery, on the other hand, is the real deal—a family-run grain-to-glass distillery making everything from peated rye to, yes, cherry bourbon.

Michigan is a miserable place to sell whiskey, at least from a distiller's point of view. A control state (with a heavy government presence in the middle), liquor stores sell all the sins—beer, wine, liquor, tobacco, and lottery tickets—creating a sordid vibe around the whole enterprise. And there are too many of them, so they are all fiercely competitive—but with mandatory state minimum pricing, so the competition is to either the top in terms of the shopping experience, or the bottom, and mostly in my experience the latter. I'm impressed with anyone who has taken on the challenge and won, especially those from Michigan. And there is no more cutthroat sales environment than in Detroit.

Detroit is a city with a manufacturing heritage that has been adopted by a few brands, though its craft distillers occupy slightly less cultural share

MITTEN WHISKEY

JOURNEYMAN FEATHERBONE

Light and sweet, this is a clean distillate with simple syrup and a buttery finish. A light-bodied wheated craft bourbon that's a step up from entry-level wheaters from Kentucky that get a lot more fuss.

100pf	$40	H	TC	Independent

JOURNEYMAN CORSETS, WHIPS & WHISKEY

A deeply flavored, rich and viscous wheat (!) whiskey. Certainly nothing close to this from commercial distillers. It's a detail-oriented distiller's fantasia of flavors, all I'd not usually associate with timid old wheat whiskey. This is chocolate, molasses, honey, and a little pot-still funk.

123.4 (variable)	$65	H	TC	Independent

NEW HOLLAND BREWERS' WHISKEY

Distilled beer as a style of whiskey is a tough game to pull off, and while I liked a lot of whiskeys from New Holland, especially the Zeppelin Bend, this bottle is an especially zany twist on malt whiskey that at first is a little shocking, but it grows on you just the same like a good acquired taste. Chocolate and malty tang dominate the finish with a funky backbone and lots of oak.

90pf	$40	P 6 mo	TC	Independent

than some of their more rural Michigan peers. Two James Spirits has done a nice job of building artfully sourced whiskeys and some house-distilled spirits from their facility, and people line up for the annual release of Pączki Day Vodka from Detroit City Distillery.

But the real story in Detroit whiskey is just over the river, the behemoth Hiram Walker in Windsor, a Detroit suburb in Ontario, Canada. The largest distiller in North America, maker of Canadian whiskeys like Lot 40 and J.P.

The Hiram Walker distillery faces Detroit from Windsor, Canada, and is the largest distillery in North America, making a variety of Canadian whiskeys.

Wiser's, Hiram Walker also makes more unlikely spirits, like Malibu Rum (if you don't think of the Detroit River when drinking Malibu, now you can).

Hiram Walker's master blender, Dr. Don Livermore, is a science nerd who is quick to argue for the Canadian model of whiskey-making, which may not be fully appreciated, even among sophisticated American drinkers. Canadians distill their grains separately and then blend the whiskeys later, versus the American model, where the grains are mixed into a recipe, or mash bill, at the beginning. If you've wondered how 95 percent rye became the standard recipe for American rye after its collapse, you have Seagram's legacy production as it was being carried out by the Lawrenceburg, Indiana, distillery to thank—a Canadian whiskey process becoming hallowed by American whiskey purists who appreciated the high rye content.

Hiram Walker has pot as well as column stills, and true to Canadian tradition, they begin with the blender as the author of the whiskey, who selects from pot stills and columns stills, as well as various grain distillates to make their products. Canadian whiskey may have up to 9.09 percent other spirits or blending adjuncts added into whiskey without losing its whiskey status (or 10ml of additives in a 100ml graduated cylinder).

This may seem like heresy, but few Americans realize that single-malt Scotch may have coloring added, or that US vodka can have citric acid or sweeteners added to a certain threshold without disclosing it on the label. I've even seen a popular tequila's lab analysis revealing a secret ingredient: salt. Canadian whiskey is hardly alone in allowing additives. And if that addition was fortified wine or brandy (as was traditional), is it destroying the integrity of the whiskey? Is that any different from the American trend of "finishing" a whiskey in a brandy or wine barrel, allowing some of the former contents to mingle with the aging spirit? Some American finished whiskeys have flavorings added too, because they are classed as "Distilled Spirits Specialty" by the government and no longer are bound by the rules of straight whiskeys. Some mass-market finished whiskeys include flavorings because they can.

XXX

Many in the whiskey industry have their eye on Minnesota-based O'Shaughnessy Distilling, who recently hired Brian Nation as their distiller. When I met Brian, he was leading the Midleton Distillery in Ireland, makers of most Irish whiskey, including Jameson, Powers, Paddy, Green Spot, Redbreast, and most of Tullamore D.E.W. for now, as well as many other labels as a contract provider. No individual distiller at the time had as much authority over so much of a country's output. Midleton is owned by Pernod Ricard, and a corporate grind (I assume), and Nation, for his part, has said he was excited for a change and to start something new. It probably helps that Americans revere the distiller as the author of whiskeys (in Ireland or Scotland, it would be the blender), and that Americans have made Irish whiskey one of the fastest growing genres of spirits.

At O'Shaughnessy, Nation is working with three large pot stills (there are column stills for other spirits). Nation built a "microdistillery" inside Midleton for training purposes that's larger than all but a handful of American craft distillers, so he's comfortable with scale. O'Shaughnessy is large by American craft distiller standards, but perhaps just the right size for an ambitious Irish distiller striking out on its own in American craft.

Its first whiskey, Keeper's Heart, is a blend of American and Irish whiskeys (all sourced) and joins a handful of distillers experimenting with

Irish distilling traditions on American soil. I trust Nation as someone who will do it credibly, though I will wait until the distillery-made whiskey is out to render a judgment.

When the protests around George Floyd's murder broke out in 2020, a small footnote of that narrative was that looters had set fire to a craft distillery. That distillery, Du Nord Craft Spirits, then well established and busy making hand sanitizer in the early days of the pandemic, was the first Black-owned distillery in the country. Founder Chris Montana had grown up in the same neighborhood but set his sights beyond, as a restless polymath. After running a campaign for Congress and living for a time in DC working as an aide, Montana went back to law school in Minneapolis and, as an avid home brewer, investigated alcohol laws, including how to start a distillery. Du Nord opened in 2013.

The business ran as a more or less by-the-book craft distillery until 2020, when the pandemic, the protests, and the interest in Black-owned businesses put a bright spotlight on Du Nord. Du Nord started a food bank and then a foundation to support social justice initiatives. The business name changed, and so did its packaging with a bold, colorful

Cedar Ridge began as a winery in corn country but quickly pivoted to whiskeys.

Cedar Ridge's bourbon outsells Kentucky brands in its home state of Iowa.

presentation. Delta Airlines now serves its vodka. And their Mixed Blood Blended Whiskey takes house-distilled high-rye bourbon and blends it with other sourced whiskeys. They've been expanding, so this may only be the beginning for Du Nord.

Still, how could the first Black-owned distillery have started only in 2013? Jackie Summers started Sorel in New York earlier with a distiller's license but wasn't distilling. And having attended craft-distiller trade shows, I can verify that it has been overwhelmingly white and homogeneous in the early days of the movement. This is not to say that Black Americans haven't been making spirits—there is a long and important moonshine tradition in Black culture, and many distillers in commercial whiskey who were doing the work of running the factories were Black.

I put the question to Chris, and he simply said it took consumers demanding change for a staid industry to evolve. He was reluctant, even as protests raged outside his business, to put up a sign that said "Black-owned." But an employee did put up a sign, and that marked an inflection point for Chris's business and the spirits industry as a whole.

Given that making spirits outside of a licensed distillery is still a federal crime, there is a chilling effect on entrepreneurship and innovation that particularly impacts aspiring Black spirits makers. Consider that the American whiskey industry has never acknowledged Black drinkers while bending over backward to highlight its continuous line of Southern heritage production, and you begin to understand the picture a little better. Fortunately, this year's craft-spirits association tradeshow was more diverse than ever, and it points to a more heterogeneous spiritous future—which in this book is a very good thing.

xxx

Driving through Iowa, you might be forgiven for thinking the state is a cornfield interrupted by small towns. It was perhaps inevitable that someone would make the connection to bourbon whiskey, and Cedar Ridge did it first and has done it most credibly.

Cedar Ridge whiskeys have been around since 2010 in fine form, and you may not find a better bourbon for its age. A winery that has been

'Templeton Rye,' Once a Flood Of Iowa Whiskey Thruout U. S., Has Dwindled to Mere Trickle

Templeton, Ia., Dec. 19.—(AP)— "Templeton Rye," once a flood of red whisky thruout the country, is dwindling to a mere trickle.

In fact, it's just a memory among prohibition drinkers for the most part, a memory of a wry face, a "whos-s-s-h, that's good!"—a hangover which was distilled i̶ country around Templeton, a of 518 residents in Southern Ca county.

Once Templeton rye was sold Des Moines, Sioux City, Oma Kansas City, St. Louis, Chica Even Iowans returning from t̶ prohibition day speakeasies in Ne York City reported that Templeto rye had its place on the liquor card

the early years of prohibition, Templeton consumed its whisky for the most part.

Traveling men, people be̶ lieve, probably s̶n̶ about " ̶ d away to another town. ̶itory moved **Simple Recipe.**

His recipe, as recalled now, was simple:
"Put rye, sugar and water in a barrel. Give them 10 days to get acquainted. Then cook the mess."

The whisky comes off in steam. The steam, after condensation. was placed in charred oak barrels and allowed to age to the proper shade of redness. Residents ex- ̶ ̶ ̶ ̶ 1,000 gallons

A 1938 article gives some color on what Templeton Rye might have been historically.

dabbling in spirits since 2005, Cedar Ridge is a well-run business that has seen the opportunity in bourbon for a long time. With a thirty-dollar price in Iowa, and maybe a few dollars more elsewhere, this may be the best option for those looking for authenticity, excellence, and value. It's hard to find a true craft whiskey under fifty dollars, but Cedar Ridge is a great option. It's the number-one-selling bourbon in Iowa, besting all Kentucky comers—and that is no small feat. Bottled-in-Bond bourbon, rye from malted rye, and an American single malt round out the portfolio.

Cedar Ridge came first, but you might be forgiven for thinking of Templeton as Iowa's distillery. Of all the Midwest distillers mentioned in this book, Templeton might be the most well-known and distributed, though its fame (or infamy) is an interesting tale with business and cultural lessons still not fully settled.

Templeton is a small town in western Iowa. A recipe published after repeal in the *Sioux City Journal* in 1936 describes a barrel-aged moonshine made with rye and sugar that yielded a reddish liquor popular in

Kansas City, Chicago, and even New York City. If corn and sugar was the dominant recipe in the South, rye and sugar makes sense for northern climates, though barrel-aging gave it refinement. After more than a decade of Prohibition, many had developed a taste for the local hooch and, in the years that followed, would seek to reclaim the taste of their illicit tipple.

Scott Bush, an MIT business school grad, reimagined Templeton Rye as a small-batch rye whiskey in 2006 and set out to replicate the "Prohibition-era recipe," with Keith Kerkhoff, who had a family connection to the so-called good stuff. The brand saw a lot of initial success. Rye was just being rediscovered by mixologists who were looking into cocktail manuals from the pre-Prohibition past, and those drinks often called for rye whiskey. Templeton was a crafty* product when bartenders wanted something new (or old, as it were).

Rye whiskey sales had fallen to less than 100,000 nine-liter cases per year in 2009, almost a rounding error in American whiskey. Still, there was interest, and Kerkhoff and Bush were there for it. They had built a small distillery, but it was an open secret that all of what went into bottles came from the distillery then called LDI, now MGPI, that was sitting on

---

* A term borrowed from the craft beer world, a "crafty" product is usually a large, corporate-owned brand in craft, indie-looking packaging.

Templeton built its own sizable distillery in 2018.

PRAIRIE WHISKEY

CEDAR RIDGE BOURBON

Grassy and grainy, this is a very cool bourbon. Light for sure, but ready to give comparably priced Kentucky bourbon a run for its money. There's a reason this is the number one bourbon in Iowa, besting traditional peers.

86pf	$30	H	TC	Independent

CEDAR RIDGE BOTTLED-IN-BOND

A more classic profile, with brawny caramel and spice, the Cedar Ridge BiB still has a Cedar Ridge signature, which is lemongrass but with the heft of toasted oak. A balanced bourbon, one that shows off the purpose of the BiB designation.

	100pf	$45	H	NT	Independent

CEDAR RIDGE THE QUINTESSENTIAL AMERICAN SINGLE MALT

A very intriguing single malt, totally different from its peers from the Pacific Northwest. Grassy and grain forward, yet buttery and soft with a nice caramel and nougat, this is a well-made, very singular malt whiskey that embodies the spirit of the prairie.

92pf	$60	H	NT	Independent

piles of rye whiskey that were made to become to Seagram's whiskeys. Templeton added a story of small-batch production, found local support, and launched nationwide.

While never quite a secret (any article on Templeton in the early years disclosed the true origin), Templeton didn't say much on its bottles about sourcing, and in fact said a lot about Al Capone and a secret recipe. A group of online commentators were quick to call foul, a charge most prominently alleged by Chuck Cowdery, who pointed to their evasion of a little-known clause in alcohol labeling law, which requires out-of-state bottles to disclose

DU NORD MIXED BLOOD WHISKEY

Notes of honey, cereal, and caramel with a nice oak balance and maybe a hint of peanut. A sipping whiskey that might be mixed, but ends up well balanced—and a whiskey with a story that's much better than most from a craft distiller with something to say.

80pf	$40	C	SW	Independent

KEEPER'S HEART WHISKEY

Light and gentle, with notes of honey and cut grass. It sure tastes more like an Irish whiskey than an American one, but there's a very grain- forward characteristic that's pleasing, like sticking your nose in a silo on a hot day, in a good way. I'll watch this label (and distiller Brian Nation) for more to come.

86pf	$40	P+C 4 yr	SW	Independent

TEMPLETON RYE

A little hard to approach this one since we've been told this is whiskey- flavored whiskey. I get warm bread, brown sugar, and a little marshmallow on the finish, but not necessarily a lot of rye.

95pf	$35	C	SW	Semi-independent

the state of distillation (27 CFR § 5.36(d) if you want to look it up). Clearly a law meant to protect the provenance of Kentucky bourbon, its application now suddenly had new meaning for distillers hoping to bottle Templeton Rye, or Brooklyn Bourbon, or any other product distilled in a conventional Ohio River valley factory that wanted a halo of local production.

The kerfuffle broke into a full scandal after a class-action lawsuit alleged that Templeton was misleading customers into purchasing a craft Iowa whiskey when in fact they were getting a commodity whiskey. However, the most damaging information (for purists) came with the revelation that Templeton differentiated its whiskey with what Kerkhoff described as an "alcohol flavoring formulation," which most consumers thought was disallowed in American rye whiskey in the first place. It is in fact disallowed in bourbon and in *straight* rye whiskey (new laws in 2022 are more vague for straight rye), but Templeton was merely making rye whiskey, which to much consternation and surprise from drinkers apparently allows flavoring agents up to 2.5 percent by volume, so long as the whiskey maintains the character generally associated with rye whiskey.

Eventually, Templeton settled their lawsuit and changed their labels. And sales continued to grow seemingly unabated by controversy, making Templeton the fourth-largest rye brand in the US today. To Templeton's credit, they opened a $35 million facility in 2018 that runs a fascinating Forsyth column still, a beautiful Scotch-flavored interpretation of an American whiskey setup, finally building the distillery it had always wanted to be.

Interestingly, TTB (the government's bureau for overseeing the labeling and taxation of alcohol) as recently as 2020 asked distillers whether listing the state of distillation might be a rule that should be dropped for the modern era. Big distillers (who are most likely to profit from the contracts with small bottlers) are leading the charge to have it eliminated.

The state of distillation, if different from the bottler, is mandatory information at the least. American whiskey could learn from tequila, which must list the NOM* (or as we would say, the DSP†) number on its tax stamp, verifying the registration number of the plant where it was manufactured. Anyone with a bottle of Casamigos and an open browser can find out quite a bit of often-disappointing information. And if that bottle is Clase Azul or Casa Dragones, that disappointment can be a two-hundred-dollar pang of regret. Most consumers don't care, but the information is there for those who do.

---

* NOM in tequila production refers to *Norma Oficial Mexicana, or the standards and regulations, in this case, for tequila production. The NOM number is a certification of the distiller that produced the tequila, and all bottles of authentic tequila must list the factory that distilled it.*

† DSP refers to a Distilled Spirits Plant licensed by the federal government to distill spirits. DSP numbers are required on bonded products but are not required on most whiskeys.

YOU TOO CAN BE AN
EXPERT WHISKEY REVIEWER

This book does not rate whiskeys. Among other reasons, ratings have become so predictable, you can practically codify them. In fact, I've tried to do just that, below. Take any issue of *Whiskey Advocate* or any other source using a 100-point scale and see if this doesn't add up for you:

START AT 90 . . .

ADD 2 POINTS for a bottle over $50

SUBTRACT 2 POINTS for a bottle less than $30

ADD 2 POINTS for a Buffalo Trace product

ADD 3 POINTS for a Willett product

SUBTRACT 2 POINTS for Beam Suntory (sorry guys!)

ADD 2 POINTS for a barrel finish

ADD 2 POINTS for barrel strength

ADD 1 POINT for single barrel

ADD 1 POINT for wheated recipe

ADD 3 POINTS for age statement over 8 years old

ADD 5 POINTS for age statement over 14 years old

SUBTRACT 4 POINTS for actual craft-distilled whiskey

SUBTRACT 2 MORE POINTS for bourbon outside of Kentucky

ADD 2 POINTS for malt whiskey

ADD 2 POINTS for Texas

ADD 2 POINTS for the word "smoke" in the name

SUBTRACT 4 POINTS for New York State

ADD 2 POINTS for a picture of a dog or a horse
on the label. If you go over 100, drop to 96.

FLIGHTS

Putting together flights is a good way to narrow down the broad world of whiskey to a few smaller players. This book already excludes many whiskeys by focusing mainly on distillers. Still, in organizing the world of whiskeys, there are ways to break down the diversity of offerings into similarly situated whiskeys. Geography, price, distillation scale, recipe, and age are all good starting places. Here are some flights put together for this book that helped determine best in a range of categories.

TOP TEN BOURBONS

A common situation: You're at an airport bar, a wedding, or a hotel restaurant in a sleepy place and they have all the usual suspects—a handful of the most common American whiskeys on the market. What should you choose? In order of decreasing popularity: Jack Daniel's, Jim Beam, Evan Williams, Maker's Mark, Bulleit, Wild Turkey, Woodford Reserve, Buffalo Trace, Knob Creek, Four Roses.

BEST ALL AROUND: Knob Creek. **BEST VALUE:** Buffalo Trace.

CRAFT RYE ASCENDANT

A look at mostly small, pot-still rye producers shows there is a lot of diversity in rye relative to bourbon. Hudson Rye, Coppersea Empire Rye, Kings County Empire Rye, McKenzie Empire, Balcones Rye, Corsair Dark Rye, Dad's Hat Rye.

BEST ALL AROUND: McKenzie. **BEST VALUE:** Corsair.

MASHBILL COLUMN WHISKEYS

New distillers in Kentucky and Tennessee are attempting to best the heritage distillers at their own game with thoughtful column-distilled releases. New Riff, Wilderness Trail, Bardstown Origin Series, Castle & Key Straight Bourbon, Uncle Nearest.

BEST ALL AROUND: Castle & Key is refined while Wilderness Trail is variable, and Bardstown had an edge in my tasting. Too early to call? **BEST VALUE:** Bardstown

HALF-CRAFT BOURBON

Midsize producers making affordable <$50 bottles outside of Kentucky with panache. Frey Ranch Bourbon, Woodinville Bourbon, Cedar Ridge, Taconic, A.D. Laws Four Grain Bourbon, Balcones Bourbon.

BEST ALL AROUND: Woodinville/Frey Ranch in a tie. **BEST VALUE:** Balcones.

BOTTLED-IN-BOND

Bonded whiskey is a great way to compare apples to apples, and craft to commercial whiskey on the same terms. Dickel Bonded, Jack Daniel's Bonded, A.D. Laws Four-Grain Bonded, New Riff Bonded, Wilderness Trail Bonded, McKenzie Bonded, Kings County Bonded.

BEST ALL AROUND: I recuse myself, but hard to go wrong here.
BEST VALUE: Jack Daniel's Bonded.

WELCOME TO THE MALTIVERSE

Stranahan's, Westward, Westland, St. George, McCarthy's, Wayward, Balcones. Pioneers and practitioners of American Single Malt, the Wild West of American Whiskey.

BEST ALL AROUND: Balcones/Westland in a tie. **BEST VALUE:** Stranahan's.

EVERYDAY OLDS

Age-stated whiskeys are hard to find these days, but these are more readily available at somewhat reasonable prices. Knob Creek 12, Elijah Craig 18, Dickel 17, Knob Creek 18, Weller 12, Dickel 15.

BEST ALL AROUND: Elijah Craig 18. **BEST VALUE:** Knob Creek 12.

The Forsyth pot stills at Balcones, in Waco, Texas.

9

DESERT WHISKEY

My wife directs movies and television. Her name is Ry, pronounced like the whiskey, so sometimes we will meet people in a whiskey context, and it is one of those funny coincidences that sounds made up. Sometimes we forget and it throws us all for a loop. We both like whiskey but came to it later in life. We meet in the middle the most on our love of movies.

In fall 2019, Ry was offered a job to direct a pilot for an Amazon series that would film in Austin, Texas. This was a big one she couldn't pass up. Before we had a son, most likely I would have stayed at the distillery in New York, and we would have lived apart for a few months and Skyped in the downtime. But our son was about to turn three and Ry was pregnant with our second child. Living apart, particularly during a pregnancy, seemed like a bad idea.

I will also say that as much as I love whiskey, and being a distiller is an easy job to love, I also run a small business, which can be a grind. New York, too, can be a grind. So, we were both kind of giddy at the chance to go live in another city for three months. Kings County does decent business in Texas, a state that is always hard to tackle as a visitor because of its sheer size. I settled into doing some market work, visiting some distilleries, and eating hill country barbecue.

Austin is an easy town to like. A million people live there, but it still manages to feel like a small college town. Growth in Austin has surged in the last decade due to a burgeoning tech sector, and the current culture feels a little bit like an unholy overlay of California hippie on old Texas stature. But calling it Silicon Ranch would be too deferential to tech: Although there is plenty of avocado toast along with the breakfast tacos, people still mostly eat the tacos. Someone described it as a casual city, and that description fits. Public pools are clean and free or inexpensive;

restaurants have giant shaded gardens and play areas for the kids (there are a lot of kids), and serve flavorful versions of all the best foods. With a small family, I didn't feel out of place if I stayed away from Sixth Street and the 25-cent beers and college clubs I hazily remembered from a road trip in my twenties.

We moved into our rental, the main house on a compound of three little bungalows in the Travis Heights neighborhood. It was walking distance to parks, a free public pool, and the restaurants on South Congress. For us, it was the largest house we'd ever lived in, having been constrained by tight quarters in New York (and occasionally in Los Angeles), so every aspect of living away felt luxurious.

My first stop in Austin was to visit my friend Heather Greene, who I had known from the New York whiskey scene. She lived in Scotland and worked in Scotch whisky for a time before becoming the whiskey sommelier at the Flatiron Room whiskey bar in New York City, when the idea of such a position was a novelty (someone please invent a better name

Heather Greene, whiskey maker; Marsha Milam, founder; and Marlene Holmes, distiller.

for this job). Heather wrote a book on whiskey, but of all her accolades, the most important is that she has one of the best palates in all of whiskey.

She had recently accepted a job as a co-creator of a new whiskey brand out of Austin, to be called Milam & Greene, and Heather invited me to their launch, which I understood to be a reinvention of Ben Milam whiskey, a sourced product but with a startup distillery in Blanco, run by an ex–Jim Beam distiller, Marlene Holmes. With Marsha Milam as the founder and story originator, this is a whiskey brand that would be distilled by a woman, blended and authored by a woman, and owned by a woman, which is noteworthy in a business that is still heavily male-dominated.

The launch was hosted at the castle-like structure that remains from the former Texas Military Institute, a beautiful old sandstone building on a dramatic hill overlooking the Texas State Capitol. Heather and her partners were debuting two whiskeys: a bourbon blended with Milam's house-distilled bourbon and a Tennessee bourbon, usually a good indicator for George Dickel distillate; and a rye whiskey finished in port barrels. I am a fan of Dickel, and I appreciated the bourbon well enough, but the rye, sourced from Indiana and finished in port barrels in Texas, was the more standout whiskey of the pair. Still, I wonder if Heather might have more up her sleeve, as these whiskeys, fine though they were, seemed like an indicator of things to come (a hunch that has since been proven right).

The next week, I ran around town with Jen Blair, a New York Drammers Club regular and, at the time, a recent hire as a Kings County New York City sales rep. She was in Austin for a film festival and had lived there for ten years, so it made sense to hit the town together. Our first stop was to visit Tom Koerner at Seven Grand. Seven Grand is one of the pioneers of the "whiskey library" style of whiskey bars. First in Los Angeles and then in Austin and San Diego, the bars feature dark wood décor, pool tables, and taxidermy. They would almost feel dated were it not for the main feature of the bar, which is a wall of whiskey that offers a cornucopia for the contemporary whiskey lover, whether your taste is Scotch, bourbon, Irish whiskey, or American craft.

I had met Tom doing the Whiskey Society for Seven Grand, a series of master classes they host. Tom was on the mezcal side of the business, Las

MILAM & GREENE

MILAM & GREENE PORT FINISHED RYE

A whiskey that makes the best use of Texas aging to complicate a port-finish sourced rye. While port-finished rye doesn't necessarily sound all that interesting, this is a cool, complex whiskey with a lot of notes from all over the flavor wheel.

94pf	$65	C	SW	Independent

MILAM & GREENE UNABRIDGED BLENDED BOURBON

With so much flavor packed in their rye, this has a more subtle appeal but is hardly a disappointment. Great credentials from a prominent and erudite blending team and a nice idea in doing a blend of straights, but this may be more of a recommendation for the barrel-proof enthusiast than the generalist.

59.15pf (variable)	$40	C	SW	Independent

Perlas (the same concept, but for mezcal), and pointed me to Erin, who hosted Jen and me through some of her favorite Texas whiskeys. We tried a Balcones single-malt single barrel, which was intense; Ironroot Republic, a local distiller that is gaining some notoriety in Texas; and some of the High Wire Jimmy Red Corn, which is among the most unusual bourbons on the market and a favorite of mine that we couldn't get in New York. The Ironroot had a sweet, almost Dr Pepper taste to it, which might just be the power of suggestion—the non-alcoholic concoction got its start in the late 1800s in Austin. Maybe it's the terroir?

We also stopped in Nickel City, a dive bar with a great menu of mixed drinks, including an unlikely tiki section, and a nicely curated range of barrel picks from Kentucky and craft distillers. We tried a few barrels there, and the Kentucky Spirit from Wild Turkey was the best pour; it reminded me of older Wild Turkey when its flavor profile had more caramel and molasses. We also visited some great retailers, including Austin Wine

Merchants, Austin Shaker, and Travis Heights Beverage World. These shops all have excellent selections and are spirit-focused, which is to say they play the long game of stocking quality spirits rather than the high-priced, highly allocated middling bottles that cater to the taters.*

XXX

But the best part of whiskey Texas is its distilleries, and my first trip was north to Fort Worth. I stopped for kolaches just north of Waco at a place called Czech Stop, a bakery off the interstate with rows and rows of baked and stuffed breakfast rolls that are a regional delicacy in this part of Texas. If you like eating, Texas delivers.

I was headed to Firestone & Robertson in Fort Worth, makers of TX blended whiskey and TX bourbon. The label was rightly criticized in the early days for splashing the TX branding all over bottles that contained liquid sourced from out of state. Still, setting aside that (legally permissible) original sin, TX makes a bourbon entirely distilled on-site. The distillery is around a golf course, and the main stillhouse is a custom-built factory with a 36-inch column (compare this scale to legacy distiller George Dickel's 48-inch column). The distillery can make up to forty barrels a day and has a substantive bottling line, as well as a traditional rickhouse.

I visited with Ale Ochoa, staff whiskey scientist, who I'd met just earlier at the Nashville Whiskey Festival. She studied the effect of different corn varietals on whiskey-making as a grad student at Texas A&M. She explained that TX bourbon uses yeast that was isolated from a pecan nut off the Texas state tree. This might sound like marketing, but I did get a nutty sensibility from the bourbon and a very pleasant raisin note that can be found from other Texas distillers. Still, it's a bold, noisy bourbon. If fine old Kentucky bourbon is a finger-picked banjo, TX bourbon is an electric guitar power chord with lots of distortion.

I also tried some single malts aged in sherry and port, as well as a rye that was terrific, and a sotol, a type of spirit similar to tequila but made from the desert spoon, a plant of the same family as agave that is native to

---

* Whiskey newbies.

Texas hill country. Challenging if not prohibitive to commercialize because of the inefficiency of its production and reliance on wild plants, sotol remains a rarity in the United States, but a fascinating category of spirit. The sotol at Firestone & Robertson was much lighter than their whiskeys, almost delicate, but compared favorably to clean, narrowly distilled tequila.

Head distiller at the time Rob Arnold joined us for the tasting. Rob is from Kentucky and studied microbiology and biochemistry and published his own book about terroir in whiskey, particularly the influence of grain. We'd had some back-and-forth over the years, but this was our first chance to meet in person. Rob's calm affect belies a tenacious approach

The 36-inch column still by Vendome at Firestone & Robertson.

MAP OF TEXAS WHISKEY COUNTRY

Texas is a slow transition from the hot, humid bayous of the gulf coast to the scrubby greenery of the hill country to the dry prairie beyond. Distillers have found the state's singularity and individuality suit the whiskey-drinker's mindset, and were some of the first to find broad success in craft bourbon, rye, and single malts. A climate with wide swings in temperature helps whiskey gain barrel flavor quickly, for some brash, bold spirits.

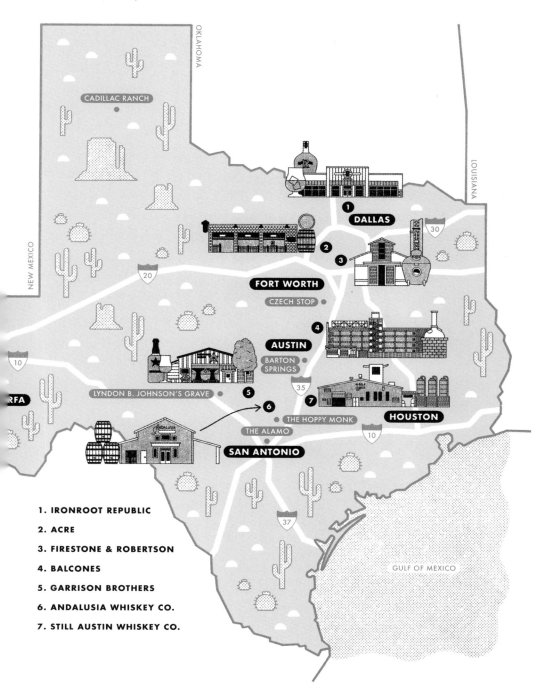

OKLAHOMA

LOUISIANA

NEW MEXICO

CADILLAC RANCH

DALLAS

30

FORT WORTH

CZECH STOP

AUSTIN

BARTON SPRINGS

20

LYNDON B. JOHNSON'S GRAVE

RFA

10

35

HOUSTON

THE HOPPY MONK

THE ALAMO

10

SAN ANTONIO

37

GULF OF MEXICO

1. IRONROOT REPUBLIC

2. ACRE

3. FIRESTONE & ROBERTSON

4. BALCONES

5. GARRISON BROTHERS

6. ANDALUSIA WHISKEY CO.

7. STILL AUSTIN WHISKEY CO.

to distilling and a perfectionist streak that left me with the impression that the best of TX whiskey came directly from Rob's attention to detail.

Another Fort Worth distillery to visit is Acre Distilling, which I visited back in 2015. Acre is operating at a more traditional craft scale and has a great tasting room as part of the distillery, which had no whiskey of their own at the time, but bottled a sourced bourbon, Longhair Jim. They have since come out with a Texas single malt and have a wide variety of spirits at their downtown distillery, in a district known as Hell's Half Acre from the saloon days of Texas's frontier history.

XXX

Head west out of Austin and the green live oaks give way to gray scrub brush hugging tightly to the ground. The yellow clay cut through with Austin's natural springs transitions to drier, whiter ground, bleached in the sun. This is the Hill Country, an area west of Austin and north of San Antonio that mediates between the rich humidity of the American coastal South and the desert Southwest. It's also Texas wine country, and while it appears unforgiving and forlorn, I was told the wine is quite good. Never mind the wine, I was on my way to taste Texas whiskey, though it's no coincidence that a distillery might thrive where wineries were already well established. Alcohol tourism works best in clusters.

Johnson City lies about an hour west of Austin and is named for the family of President Lyndon Johnson. This is where the thirty-sixth president was born and is buried. There is a national park and several historical spots around town. Just outside of this small town is Hye, a geographical designation more than any kind of recognized town, population 109, according to a sign as you pull off the main road.

Garrison Brothers distillery sits on a seventy-acre ranch just a couple of miles south of the Hye Post Office and General Store. The distillery is comprised of a handful of tin-shed and wood-cabin buildings and has the feel of a boy scout camp.

Garrison Brothers bourbon ranges from very spicy, woody, with a dry earthy quality that is quite pleasant, to oakmageddon in its Cowboy Bourbon, as far as I can tell the oakiest whiskey of any variety on the

The fermentation room at Garrison Brothers is blissfully air-conditioned.

market. Most distillers would say it's overaged, but Garrison Brothers does not apparently accept the concept. In fairness, neither does the consumer, who I can only guess takes a swig of 5-year-old Garrison Brothers, some of the most oaked whiskey ever commercially released, and says aloud to his peers on the tour, "I look forward to trying the 10-year."

Tour guides say the angel's share, the amount of whiskey that evaporates out of the barrel, is close to 14 percent each year. That suggests a half-life of three and a half years. Garrison uses only one mash bill (white corn, red wheat, and malted barley), but four different cooperages. They also use only fifteen- and thirty-gallon barrels, which is an unusual choice for a distiller that at this point in its development might think about trying to slow down its aging. But if oak-forward whiskey is the goal, then Garrison has perfected the process, and indeed the bourbon, regardless of expression, is singular and occasionally sublime. When I visited, the distillery had just come out of a statewide taste-off, and their Balmorhea had bested all the other Texas distillers, which was clearly a point of pride.

Garrison Brothers runs two 500-gallon pots with 8-plate rectification trays, and a 2,000-gallon still. They mash on two shifts a day and make 2,000 gallons of mash that ferments in the only air-conditioned room in

Garrison runs a Vendome pot/column hybrid distillation system.

open-top, square stainless totes. I also noted that they use a heavy grain bill in the cook, which yields as high as 14 percent alcohol by volume (ABV) in the fermentation.

The real magic here is the Texas climate. The day I visited, it was ninety-six during the day and went down to fifty-five at night, which is not unusual for the region. Alcohol expands and contracts more drastically than water with changes in temperature, and that creates pressurization and depressurization that moves the whiskey in and out of the charcoal layer and into the wood itself, picking up sap and caramelized sap, and leaving behind large molecules—the so-called fusel oils and less-volatile congeners* that make up the tails of the distilling run. The more volatile compounds—those with a low boiling point—are the more solventy,

---

* Congeners are chemical compounds, higher alcohols, aldehydes, esters, and acids, that are present in a distilled spirit in addition to ethanol and water. Methanol, acetone, acetaldehyde, propanol, butanol, and furfuryl are examples of common congeners.

nail-polish-remover sorts of chemicals (acetone is actually one of them), and these are the first to evaporate out of the barrel through the angel's share. The barrels are liquid-tight but not air-tight, so chemicals with the lowest boiling point evaporate off first, mellowing the whiskey by evacuating some of the turpentine notes, while scrubbing the whiskey of the oilier compounds by charcoal pressure filtration.

Because this is all a natural process that happens through changes in temperature, everything is sped up in a desert climate. Scotland, by contrast, with a cool, even climate, slows everything down (and employing used barrels helps stretch the aging process even more dramatically). Even in Kentucky there is a not-uncommon practice among large, commercial distillers of using steam-heated warehouses to cycle temperatures and expedite this aspect of whiskey aging.

As the Texas distillers grow their inventory over time, it will be interesting to see how this factor plays out. If anything, it's given Texas distillers a head start over other craft whiskeys, one that Garrison Brothers has taken full advantage of. By the time of my visit, I was told they had 18,000 barrels aging, all smaller than industry standard, but still an impressive collection for any decade-old distiller.

Andalusia Whiskey Company runs a small pot still to make lovely malt whiskeys.

For my palate, I liked the 2018 flagship Garrison Brothers the best, as opposed to the 2017, or the single barrels that were on offer the day I was there in 2019. I have tried the Cowboy Bourbon—indeed, I overindulged on the Cowboy Bourbon after the American Craft Spirits Association convention in Pittsburgh, and I can verify the hangover is no more tolerable for the $200 price tag. But it's a whiskey worth trying, as there's really nothing beyond it on the flavor spectrum, and sometimes the margins—in whiskey and otherwise—are where things get most interesting.

Andalusia Whiskey Company is not far from Garrison Brothers, just south of Johnson City. Ty Phelps, a former brewer, founded the business in 2013 and focuses on single-malt whiskeys. The distillery felt like a family affair, with Ty's wife doing all the bottling by herself.

When I visited, they had three flagship aged whiskeys: the eponymous Andalusia triple-distilled Irish Style whiskey; Revenant, a peated malt whiskey; and Stryker, a Texas-style malt smoked with mesquite and aged in a new barrel, a more American-style whiskey. All were interesting despite the distillery's youth. The Andalusia is one of the only Irish-style malt whiskeys I've seen in the US. It was the most approachable of the whiskeys and was probably my favorite of the core line. Revenant is peated directly on-site with Irish peat; as a result, it has a little more heft than most peated offerings I've tried, but there was a slight residual sweetness

The lineup at Andalusia includes Irish-style, peated, and heavily oaked whiskeys as well as brandies and barrel-finished whiskeys.

of the malt that kept it squarely away from a Scotch-style peated whiskey. The Revenant was full of flavor, sugar, and briny smoke, and was maybe less to my own taste, but it has a classic Texas profile and would be easy to sip with brisket or pulled pork.

Ty had me taste a few other things, a series of port-finished versions of the three flagship whiskeys, which added dimensionality to each, as well as a heavily peated offering. This was a whiskey not even out of the barrel—Ty disappeared for a few minutes, and I caught sight of him out of a back window in a shipping container with a whiskey thief. I felt it was ready by my palate (peated whiskeys peak earlier than their non-peated counterparts, even in Scotland), but it was an unsettled question the distillers were working on. Ty also let me try a brandy from orange wine that was full of sherbet and citrus—a brandy on an order of magnitude that is rare for any American distiller.

XXX

The city of Waco has a population of 125,000, which is to say it's bigger than you thought. Its downtown has a series of surprisingly slender high-rise buildings that loom over a grid of streets like pieces on a late-game chessboard. Balcones Distilling is housed in the Texas Fireproof Storage Building, a monolithic four-story brick-and-concrete structure in a surprisingly urban setting for a Texas distillery.

The story of Balcones is a colorful and cautionary tale, one that begins with founder Chip Tate in 2008. Tate is regarded as a mad genius by many—a sort of savant-like alchemist who cobbled up one of the most highly regarded distilleries of the early craft movement. Tate's blue corn whiskey, lightly aged in used barrels, and single malt, rich and flavor-forward but balanced and original, helped put the distillery on the map. A 2013 *New York Times* article pointed to the whiskey as a marker of American single malt's arrival (American single malt may have arrived in 2013, but it has taken a while for it to get a foothold in the popular consciousness of American whiskey, which is still hung up on bourbon).

Tate was on a rocket ship to international whiskey fame and brought on investors to help him expand a garage distillery into a modern factory

TEXAS WHISKEYS

TX BOURBON

Take a Kentucky bourbon and add a distortion pedal. Lots of Texas whiskeys have this characteristic, but maybe TX shows it most plainly. An otherwise straightforward bourbon, but Texas aging makes it brash and raisiny.

90pf	$50	C	NT	Pernod Ricard

GARRISON BROTHERS BOURBON

The best whiskey from Garrison Brothers is its most common, not that it's easy to find outside of Texas. The palate has an earthy, claylike base with leather, cinnamon, and prune layered on top.

94pf	$80	H	TC	Semi-independent

GARRISON BROTHERS COWBOY BOURBON

If oak is your thing, this rare release is one to seek out. Take regular Garrison Brothers, which is near the limits of oak tolerance to begin with, and turn it up to 11.

134.8 (variable)	$250	H	TC	Semi-independent

ANDALUSIA TRIPLE DISTILLED SINGLE MALT

The rare Irish-style whiskey from an American producer that is a perfect feat of balance. Flavorful but not too malty, sweet but not too young, and bright but not too hot, a Goldilocks blonde whiskey that would pair perfectly with a hot summer day.

100pf	$60	P	TC	Independent

ANDALUSIA REVENANT OAK

One of my hands-down favorite Texas whiskeys that tastes nothing like its barrel-forward peers, this single malt uses peat and barrel economically for a balanced whiskey that is the perfect companion to a night in the Hill Country. This has to be the most underrated American Single Malt, one that out-drinks better funded peers.

100pf	$60	P	TC	Independent

Though much in Texas is sprawling, Balcones is a vertically oriented urban distillery in Waco.

capable of servicing an international audience. Here is where things get tricky. Investors said that Tate became erratic and combative; Tate said that investors were adversarial and trying to wrest control of the company. The *New York Times* reported a salacious story (outside of Texas, perhaps) of a firearm at work and allegations of workplace threats eventually led to restraining orders, legal challenges, and, eventually, a non-amicable parting of ways (though Tate vehemently denied any hostile or erratic behavior).

The story is a business-school case study in the hazards of expanding too quickly, but Tate has built a respectable, if slightly less visible, second career making copper distilling equipment, even as he watches his brand grow from the sidelines. Whiskey-making is a long arc of time, and sometimes distillers don't get to be around when the products they design reach a wide audience.

Balcones, post-divorce, opened its new facility, one of the most impressive American distilleries in operation today, with many of the idiosyncrasies insisted on by Tate, but also protected by Jared Himstedt, now Balcones's head distiller. Like many in his position, Himstedt is a polymath whose intuition and leadership have kept the brand steady, even as it has evolved beyond the early products that earned Balcones such acclaim.

Distiller Jared Himstedt working the Forsyth spirit safe on one of the largest American pot-still setups

As for the whiskeys? Balcones is best known for its single-malt and corn whiskeys. During my tour, we tasted a rye, two bourbons, and two single malts. The rye is a more recent introduction, with notes of red pepper and cedar that for me hide a lot of the grain flavor that I tend to appreciate in rye. Balcones avoided making bourbon for a long time, but finally came out with two in 2018, both pot-stilled: a standard and a blue-corn bourbon. Both are fine, but my preference is for the standard release, a very good product for its price. The standout whiskey at Balcones is the single-malt, a cinnamon-spice malt whiskey thoroughly unlike many of its European peers. This is really a rich, round, perfect whiskey, and I prefer the lower-proof standard bottling to some of the single-barrel, barrel-proof versions I tried.

I also love the Baby Blue corn whiskey, a young whiskey that is quite refined and is a crème brûlée of creamy corn, vanilla, and just the right amount of sweetness. Corn whiskey has been sidelined for many years, and Balcones makes an exquisite entry into the category. There are other offerings: Rumble, a hybrid of whiskey and rum; and Brimstone, an overly smoky whiskey that is about as heavy-handed as you can get with smoke and whiskey.

Balcones and Garrison Brothers are generally regarded by peers as the grandfathers of the Texas craft movement. Garrison is focused on bourbon

FOUR BALCONES WHISKEYS

BALCONES BABY BLUE CORN WHISKEY

The best corn whiskey being made today with notes of buttered corn, vanilla, butterscotch, and honey, and a hint of spice. Corn whiskey is a lost tradition mostly, and Balcones has always argued for it better than any other.

92pf	$40	P	TC	Diageo

BALCONES BOURBON

It took Balcones almost ten years to decide to make a bourbon. With so many homogeneous bourbons at the same price, Balcones makes a truly distinctive one: rough and edgy, but very drinkable for its price. A pot-still bourbon that's funky and classy at the same time.

92pf	$30	P	TC	Diageo

BALCONES CASK STRENGTH RYE

A heavy-handed rye, cocoa and coffee forward, piney scrub oak. The bottle has a picture of a bung hammer, and it hits you that way. Not a subtle whiskey and not my favorite from Balcones, but surely a wild-ass whiskey worthy of the Balcones name.

130.6 (variable)	$55	P	TC	Diageo

BALCONES SINGLE MALT WHISKEY

Truly a whiskey that changed everything. A perfectly distilled single malt with the rich, briny tang of Texas maturation. Chocolate and molasses lay heavy on a rich base, without a sour or foul note. A whiskey like no other, and a great one.

106pf	$75	P	TC	Diageo

exclusively; Balcones prefers anything but. Garrison uses Kentucky-built column stills; Balcones uses Scottish Forsyth pot stills. Garrison whiskey is gregarious and brash; Balcones is rich and precise. Even the distilleries couldn't be more unlike each other—Garrison is spread out on a ranch covered in bleached dirt, scrub brush, and outbuildings; Balcones is an urban factory tightly integrated into four stories of monumental space.

And both are great.

XXX

Later in my visit, I held a tasting event at the Hoppy Monk, an establishment devoted to craft in all forms, mostly beer but a surprisingly long list of independent spirits too. The idea is simple: no Bulleit, no Jameson, no Johnnie Walker. The premise is that independent labels have a freer hand to choose quality over yield at every stage of the process. It's an interesting model, and a progressive one that I was surprised to see first in Texas. I hope it is a harbinger of an era to come.

The Hoppy Monk menu says it more clearly than I could articulate: "Every dollar you spend is a vote you make. We are proud to support only independently owned breweries and distilleries, and we thank you for

Tap handles at Hoppy Monk, which refuses to carry commercial beer or corporate whiskeys and focuses exclusively on independent labels

supporting our independent, family-owned pub." Spirits companies and cynical startups alike know that appearing to be small, handmade, and traditional is marketable, but truly indie products are worth seeking out, as different economics make different products. If you buy local and home-grown at the farmer's market, why not at the liquor store? I wince at the farm-to-table cocktail menu that takes pains to articulate the house-made syrups infused with kitchen scraps, only to then dump in an artificially colored Italian digestif from a global conglomerate.

It's a tricky project—being the arbiter of who is independent can be a fraught and imperfect process—but it's a worthy one. As wealth piles up in the hands of fewer and fewer players, in whiskey and in general, independent brands could use this support. Such a policy benefits the bar as well: Independence from mass frees up the bartenders in curating by authenticity rather than marketing influence, earning more of an honest connection to customers.

The last Texas distiller I visited was local to my neighborhood in Austin, a microdistillery called Still Austin that reminded me more of a brewery than a distillery (indeed, they share a patio with a local brewer). Opened in 2015, they use an unusual 12-inch stainless distilling column from Forsyth, though there wasn't much else in their facility to remark on. Their whiskey was young at the time of my visit, but they would concede as much, and it might be too early to judge them even now. They seem to be aiming at their local audience in the Hill Country, and that might be ambition enough.

There were other distillers I would like to have visited. Ranger Creek in San Antonio has always made good whiskeys to my palate, and Yellow Rose in Houston gets good reviews from people I trust. I wanted very much to visit Ironroot Republic, since their whiskeys deeply impressed me, but they were too far from Austin to visit easily and I felt our time in Texas getting shorter just as the nights were coming earlier and much colder.

I ran into the limits of working remotely, doing market work, and being a parent. By mid-November, it was time to go home. Our last meal in Austin was spent at Olamaie, an elevated restaurant focused on Southern cuisine headed by the husband of a former employee and permanent friend of the business, Anna Margaret Hollyman.

DESERT WHISKEYS

WHISKEY DEL BAC CLASSIC

A very well made desert malt whiskey, barrel forward and sweet. Del Bac is known for it's mesquite smoked malt, but I like this one better, rich and round. An appealing American single malt that has the scrubby, oaky tone that defines the region but a butterscotchy warm note that comes with an obsessive distiller, attention to detail.

92pf	$56	P	TC	Independent

WHISKEY DEL BAC DORADO

A light malt-forward whiskey with an overlay of mesquite smoke, an odd flavor that takes some getting used to but proves to be a fine complement to the whiskey and argues for pairing with barbecue. A little avant-garde for my taste, but a noteworthy whiskey nonetheless; a reward for the adventurous drinker.

92pf	$60	P	TC	Independent

FREY RANCH BOURBON

This is a well-made bourbon with a floral nose and an earthy palate with caramel, Earl Grey tea, and hint of black licorice. Nice viscosity and balanced booze for a great price, and on my list of craft bourbons that best comparably priced Kentucky bourbons easily.

90pf	$53 ($40)	H	TC	Independent

FREY RANCH RYE

Lots of caramel and spice with a piney tang on this very excellent rye whiskey that treads nicely between the refined flavors of column-distilled rye and the more traditional methods of craft producers. One of the best rye whiskeys for the money, this BiB is a stunner.

100pf	$65 ($63)	H	TC	Independent

We'd fallen a little in love with Austin. My son turned three in a playground surrounded by new friends. He went trick-or-treating as a coconut popsicle in a neighborhood of ranch houses and quiet, winding streets that felt like a postcard of Americana. We clambered around Fortlandia, a series of architectural constructions set up in Lady Bird Johnson Wildflower Center for kids to explore. We barely scratched the surface of Austin's culinary landscape, but everywhere we went was delicious and singular and made for fond memories.

We couldn't have known that a global pandemic was about to throw everything into disarray, that our second child would multiply the stresses of parenthood, or that the distillery would be pivoting to make hand sanitizer and sell entirely through e-commerce. It was the end of a job for Ry, and the end of an era for us both (and maybe everyone), and that night we were blissfully unaware of what was to come.

XXX

I titled this chapter "Desert Whiskey" and spent most of my time visiting distillers in Texas. Hamilton Distillers, makers of Whiskey Del Bac, is another whiskey from the American Southwest based in Tucson, Arizona. Founder Stephen Paul began his career making wooden furniture and imagined a whiskey made from malt smoked over mesquite instead of peat. With his daughter, he launched the business in 2011 and visited us in Brooklyn as the idea developed. In 2013, Whiskey Del Bac arrived as a Classic Single Malt and a Dorado Mesquite-Smoked Malt. Both are great whiskeys, but the Classic is maybe more to my preference—and still retains a smoky, barbecue richness that I associate with the desert. Colin Keegan's Colkegan sounds like an Irish whiskey but is in fact a single malt from Santa Fe Spirits.

There are two distillers in Nevada worth noting. Frey Ranch, east of Lake Tahoe, is taking a run at the established bourbon players with well-priced, well-made whiskeys that are excellent and distinctive and are getting justifiably good reviews. And Nevada H&C Distilling Company, based in Las Vegas, has made a cottage industry of aging sourced whiskey in high-desert conditions, adding lots of oak to younger whiskeys (sold as Smoke Wagon), to the delight of a subset of consumers that really like that sort of thing.

SOUR ON SOURCING

This book largely ignores non-distiller producers, or NDPs. These are bottling companies that don't distill. It may not entirely be a fair omission; distillers like WhistlePig and Widow Jane get undue credibility from a token still on-site when nearly all of the spirit is sourced. My general feeling is that distillers make whiskey, and this book belongs to them. But blenders also make whiskey, and within non-distillers, a few sourced brands stand out among their peers for their ability to deliver consistently differentiated products that have their own identity in a sea of minor iterations. Here are three that are worth mentioning.

PINHOOK

Pinhook is mostly known for its pretty, equestrian-themed bottles, but the juice inside is often sourced transparently. Lately much has been pulled from Castle & Key. Make no mistake, Pinhook is mostly graphic design and a fifteen-dollar upcharge, but it is good design and usually good whiskey that—in the case of Castle & Key—may be hard to come by from the distiller itself. Pinhook showcases lighter-bodied bourbon nicely, and there are a lot of lesser whiskeys at this price that don't look as nice on the bar. And its vertical series, offering bottles from a single run of MGP bourbon as they age from four to twelve years, is a project every working distiller should be doing too.

LOST LANTERN

Founded by husband-and-wife team Adam Polonski (formerly of *Whiskey Advocate*) and Nora Ganley-Roper (former buyer at Astor Wines), this brings credibility from New York City's spirits institutions to independent bottling. Lost Lantern lists the distiller, a big point of differentiation, and brings a fresh perspective on whiskeys as diverse as Balcones, Cedar Ridge, Watershed, St. George, and many of my favorite spirits from these pages. Sometimes distillers don't know their own stocks, and an outside perspective can yield something great.

BARRELL/STELLUM

Founded by Joe Beatrice, Barrell Craft Spirits has been earning fans the hard way: by making good whiskey day in and out. Often sourced from the usual suspects (MGP & Dickel), Barrell manages to make differentiated, superior whiskeys through patience (buying lots and holding) and blending (finding the best place for each barrel). Sold at cask strength, Barrell is a reliable source for a classic flavor profile. Stellum is a newer venture aiming at a broader audience but retains the credibility of its parent brand. Barrell has often been found on "best of" and "best in category" lists from the big competitions.

There are dozens and dozens of sourced brands, including Breckenridge, Jeffersons, Redemption, Blackened, Heaven's Door, Blue Run, Blue Note, Blueprint, Brush Creek, Jeffers Creek, Corner Creek, Bear Creek, Kings Creek, Cream of Kentucky, Kentucky Owl, Tennessee Waltz, Old Louisville, Nashville Barrel, Tincup, Widow Jane, Great Jones, Filibuster, Bib & Tucker, Joseph Magnus, Saint Cloud, Kings Family Distillery (no relation), Doc Swinson's, Penelope, Old Carter, Old Elk, Old Line, Red Line, Straight Edge, Savage and Cooke, Frank August, Chicken Cock, Backbone, Three Chord, Four Gate, Five Trail, and many, many more.

Many of these have virtues, but with a landscape of American whiskey so vast, one has to draw some hard lines. I chose to focus on distillers over brands, and all of the whiskey in each of these bottles comes from one of the makers in these pages.

The pot stills at Talnua, in Denver, Colorado.

10

MOUNTAIN MAVERICKS

By the time the West was being settled in earnest, distilling had already been established as an industry native to the Ohio River valley with a newer, larger crop of industrial distillers around Chicago. The first was the craft whiskey of its era, and the latter was the commercial stuff, more neutral and of a lower quality than what was being made in a more traditional way farther south.

This is the "whiskey" of the Wild West, which was often neutral spirits (or vodka), cut with sugar, glycerin, caramel coloring, tobacco juice, creosote, formaldehyde, and anything inexpensive that would make it look and taste like conventional whiskey. The West was won by commodity whiskey from back east and didn't build much in the way of its own distilleries, as the same railroads that brought settlers also brought the supplies to keep them fed and watered with aqua vitae, making local distilleries unnecessary for the decades before and after Prohibition.

While the rest of America's drinking palate gradually shifted to beer after the Civil War, the frontier towns needed less-perishable booze and whiskey, fueling a western migration. So, whiskey has always had a place in the mythology of the Old West, a place full of contradictions and problematic conflicts that are best left in the past. But the image persists, a hard one for America to shake, even as western cities have become modern boomtowns, growing rapidly in the last decades even as some older eastern cities shrink.

There is something enduring about the spirit of western optimism, an egalitarian temperament that doesn't care who your family is or where you come from, that gets more pronounced as you leave the small-town farmlands of the prairie and enter the mountains and deserts of the West. Old money and new money are indistinguishable and therefore less consequential. And western towns never suffered through the formative

Stranahan's has been a pioneer of American malt whiskeys and has influenced many distillers in the west.

American grievance that was the Civil War. Built around railroads and then cars, the West has been quicker to adopt new things, generally, which is why so much of the tech industry is situated here.

Craft whiskey may have thrived on the West Coast for this reason, long before it was taken seriously on the East Coast. While New York bartenders were turning up their noses at craft whiskey, entire cocktail menus made from local spirits appeared in Denver, Salt Lake City, Portland, and Seattle—and they were better and more innovative than anything happening in the stodgier cocktail epicenters of New York or New Orleans, which had found a renaissance in older, spirit-forward cocktails in the early 2000s but had lost a bit of direction after.

I'm treating the Mountain West as a region, but I'll be the first to admit that this territory defies easy categorization. You could also define the Mountain West less by its distillers and more by its audience, which was always been warmly receptive to craft beer first, and then spirits.

The first purpose-built craft whiskey distillery opened in Denver in 2004, possibly the first since Maker's Mark began distilling in 1954. Stranahan's began when Jess Graber, a volunteer firefighter, responded to a barn fire at George Stranahan's place. Somehow the conversation steered to moonshine, and Stranahan, a brewer, gave Graber the space and encouragement to begin distilling as a hobby and later gave his name to the business.

Graber ran the business until it sold in 2010 to Proximo, the spirits giant run by descendants of the Jose Cuervo tequila empire. Proximo and Graber launched Tincup, a sourced whiskey that bottled out of Stranahan's, and that adjacent investment left Stranahan's more or less as it was, preserving one of the best early craft distillers of the movement and protecting it despite early fears of "selling out" and the changes that often come with corporate ownership.

Stranahan's has a lot to recommend. It's an interesting distillery in that it makes one mash bill, a malt whiskey that, unlike Scotch malt whiskeys, is aged in new barrels like American bourbon or rye. It's a classic approach that hasn't drifted too far in the twenty years they have been in business.

When I visited in 2014, the place felt a little bit like a cruise ship without a captain, with a few employees drifting around a very large, active facility humming with bubbling stills and barrels being filled and rolled around. A pristine bottling line bolsters the perspective that Proximo has left

The stills at Stranahan's are squat Vendome hybrid pots.

THE ORIGINAL COLORADO WHISKEY

STRANAHAN'S COLORADO WHISKEY

Stranahan's is a great whiskey and has the best claim to define American single malt. It's a nice balance of brash Western heat, rich oak, and spice. This one is dialed in.

94pf	$65	C+P 4 yr	TC	Proximo

STRANAHAN'S DIAMOND PEAK

The Diamond Peak line is for cask-finished versions of regular Stranahan's. My 2022 bottle, finished in Bushmills barrels, isn't substantially differentiated from the flagship to my palate, hardly enough to justify the higher price at lower proof. Stranahan's resisted brand extensions for a long time, and with good reason. No reason to tinker with a classic.

90pf	$75	C+P 4 yr	TC	Proximo

Stranahan's alone because it needed the "bottled in Colorado" marketing angle for Tincup, but whether Tincup has lived up to its promise is a fair question. It came along when whiskey drinkers were applying more scrutiny to labels, and for all the marketing references to Colorado, the majority of the distillate came from Indiana, diluted to proof with Denver municipal water, which gives a thin shred of credibility to the Rocky Mountain provenance. I can't endorse Tincup, but Stranahan's is by now a classic of its type and pioneer in American malt whiskey. It's well made and an easy recommend.

More importantly, maybe, was that Stranahan's became a training ground and has seeded numerous other distilleries and trained staff that have built an industry in the Front Range that is more mature than many other places where craft whiskey producers are newer and less readily embraced.

Coors, one of the world's largest breweries, is also based in the Denver suburb of Golden, and has been cultivating barley growers and maltsters for generations. Denver, and much of Colorado's population, is poised between the prairie, where barley grows well, and the mountains, which still provide a mineral-rich water source.

How much of this translates into a terroir that belongs to Colorado or Rocky Mountain whiskey is an open question. But, setting aside the agriculture and the water, it is true that distilling at higher elevation will likely have interesting effects on whiskey, and certainly the dry air and cold winters will contribute very different aging conditions than those on the East Coast. And the culture of whiskey-making is more sincere, more open, and more creative than in the East in a way that is very encouraging and celebratory for this East Coast distiller.

XXX

During college, I lived for a summer in Denver. I spent my twenty-first birthday in Fort Collins, having margaritas at a restaurant that will only serve a maximum of three (a safety measure, if memory serves, but also a clear challenge). My college girlfriend and I drove across the country

Wooden fermentation vessels at Distillery 291

from New Haven, a route that took us from Ohio to camping on the shores of Lake Michigan in Wisconsin, then to the Badlands of South Dakota. The West is best experienced as a revelation by car, a slow fade from the deciduous forests of the East to the farmland of the Midwest and then to the prairie—open skies and wide-open land that inspire poetic thoughts even in very unromantic people. The Front Range of the Rockies arrives just when the inspiration of the prairie has given way to monotony.

I worked that summer for a volunteer organization that rehabilitated trails on public lands throughout Colorado, and because of that work I got to see much of the state, hiking and camping in its alpine meadows, aspen glades, and rushing creeks. Colorado has most of the "fourteeners" in the US, and climbing to that altitude, emerging above the tree line and seeing year-round snowpacks and glacial lakes, was my first clue that there was an entirely different relationship to the land in the West. There is no greater satisfaction than a hard climb to a mountain pass and crossing over to see the vastness of the Rockies and the horizon far below, in the seemingly infinite distance.

I always love an opportunity to return to Colorado (or southern Utah, where I also ventured that summer), to immerse in natural beauty and hike

The spirit still at Distillery 291 was hand-built from photographic plates.

One of the largest independent distillers in the country, A.D. Laws has been laying down serious inventory of bourbon, rye, wheat, and malt whiskeys.

the land, a very simple act of connection that is grounding and humbling. I returned to Colorado in the fall of 2022 to visit a few distilleries that I knew were making interesting whiskeys that I wanted to get to know better.

My first stop was in Colorado Springs, at Distillery 291, in the shadow of Pike's Peak—the only fourteener you can drive up—and just across the road from the University of Colorado at Colorado Springs. My host was Eric Jett, head distiller, who has worked with founder Michael Myers for eight years, almost since the distillery's inception. I first met Myers in New York. He has long gray hair and a commanding presence, even if his nature is generous and open. Myers began his career as a fashion photographer. This might sound very tangential to distilling, but the aesthetic demands of that world are intense, and taking that same focus on excellence to whiskey-making translates well.

Distillery 291, named for the Fifth Avenue art gallery in New York run by Alfred Stieglitz that gave birth to the avant-garde art movement in the early 1900s, is among the more experimental distillers in the country. They

ROCKY MOUNTAIN WHISKEYS

DISTILLERY 291 FRESH COLORADO WHISKEY

Majority corn distillate filtered over aspen charcoal. I get malty notes and a grassy sweetness that make for a sophisticated white whiskey that leans away from American tradition and toward Scotch, a true rarity for a drinkable white whiskey.

92pf	$49	P	TC	Independent

DISTILLERY 291 COLORADO RYE WHISKEY

This malted rye recipe is finished with aspen staves. This is a very flavor-forward rye whiskey with notes of leather and campfire oak over a bready distillate. Certainly an evocative whiskey, sure to be a little polarizing, but a strong argument for terroir in whiskey.

101.7pf	$75	P	TC	Independent

DISTILLERY 291 BARREL STRENGTH RYE

Like it's less potent brother, this is a rye malt mash finished with aspen staves, but at this proof, it's a big and spicy flavor bomb that shows the importance of excellent distillation at high proof. This bottle is 129.1 proof and tastes as concentrated as that would suggest, but smooth next to more conventionally distilled peers. A very cool, weird whiskey for the most adventurous.

129.1pf	$100	P	TC	Independent

use aspen staves and charcoal from aspens, the quaking, white-barked trees that cover the mountains at altitude in Colorado. That might seem like a gimmick, but its effects from my own tasting before and after stave addition were that the aspen contributes to the richness of the whiskey, if not always the flavor.

A.D. LAWS FOUR-GRAIN STRAIGHT BOURBON

A very balanced, excellent whiskey with a sour, piney note. As a well-made craft bourbon, this is richer than commercial peers. Not the most interesting offering from this creative distiller, though maybe the most accessible to the untraveled.

100pf	$65	H	TC	Independent

A.D. LAWS SAN LUIS VALLEY RYE

A little bit of cocoa, coffee, and dill make for a funky entry into rye whiskey. A little peppery funk on the finish with a very bold rye signature, almost like a Canadian rye.

95pf	$65	H	TC	Independent

A.D. LAWS CENTENNIAL WHEAT WHISKEY

Here's something special. A soft wheat whiskey, a great entry into a overlooked category. And at five years, this is aiming to be the definitive wheat whiskey in the US—and succeeds with a nice balance of grain and spice.

100pf	$85	H	TC	Independent

A.D. LAWS CORN WHISKEY

When I visited, this distillery exclusive stood out. A bonded corn whiskey made from roasted corn? A deeply weird and cool corn whiskey. The roasting gives it a hefty, peppery corn flavor that is tempered with a sweet creamy barrel profile. This was an all-time favorite (though it takes quite a whiskey geek to appreciate).

100pf	$50	H	TC	Independent

Jett showed me around their new facility, ever-growing and expanding. Distillery 291 is using a double-pot distillation with a thumper still, made from copper photogravure plates that still bear the images of photographs that were printed from them—a western landscape and the Chrysler Building are mentioned, though daily use has all but obliterated the images. This is a big part of the distillery's storytelling, but it's almost a distraction from the excellent pot distillation that goes on within the stills, a dependence on malted rye (rather than more commonly used unmalted rye grain) as a key ingredient in their whiskeys.

Distillery 291 bottles its white spirit, both a corn-heavy recipe and a malted rye recipe, and these are the best argument for their craft. Much of their whiskey is aged in small-format barrels for a year or more, but an excellent base spirit needs less from the barrel. For my palate, the white spirit and rye whiskeys were compelling, but their aged analogs are flavor-forward and wildly layered. This distillery may not be to everyone's taste, at least not yet, but they are unmistakably making excellent spirit and pushing the boundaries of what a whiskey can be, especially a regional one sprung from the Rocky Mountain conditions of its home.

The nice thing about distillery touring in Denver is that there is plenty to see, all within a short drive. I began my second day at Laws Whiskey House, founded by Alan Laws. Jake Norris, after leaving Stranahan's, set up shop here for a while, and it seems possible that Laws was going to inherit much of the independent spirit that Stranahan's yielded by selling. Laws began with a premise that all its whiskey would age for four years before being released, an expensive gamble that few bootstrapping distillers can afford. Laws worked as an analyst in oil and gas before getting into distilling (another minor theme of some of the distillers here), but it's hard to imagine the Canadian guy I met wearing a Dead Kennedys shirt and a tennis visor in a conference room. Laws has a twinkle in his eye and clearly is dead set on making the finest whiskey that can be made, and he's assembled a passionate team to make a run for it on a large scale.

My host was James Kunz, barrel manager, and we began in the distillery, a respectable 2,000-gallon system neatly tucked into an industrial warehouse south of downtown. Laws leads with a four-grain bourbon, a winning recipe I'm surprised is not more common. Like many distillers, Laws makes bourbon, rye, and malt whiskeys, but their competitive advantage is age. Few craft distillers have four- and six-year whiskeys as baseline products, and I would even argue that four years in Colorado is maybe eight years in Kentucky based on flavor, so there is a lower threshold for

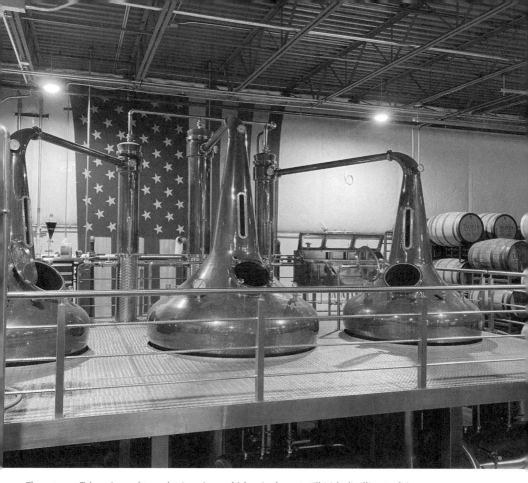

The setup at Talnua is used to make American whiskey in the pot-still Irish distilling tradition.

extraction. The distillate I tasted was earthy, and pot distillation preserves a nutty, estery spirit that has richness of texture and viscosity compared to Kentucky peers. Laws also was an early proponent of bonded whiskeys, and these will always be close to my heart.

The standouts for me on the day included a wheat whiskey better than almost any I've tried. Bourbon is a competitive category, but Laws makes a nice one. A corn whiskey made with partially roasted corn was a new product when I visited, and staff weren't quite sure what to make of it, but with few exceptional corn whiskeys in the field (usually high-corn bourbon mash aged in used barrels), I take note when one stands out.

My second visit of the day was to a newer distillery called Talnua, opened in 2019 and focused on Irish-style whiskeys. The very phrase

GEEKY STILLS: TALNUA AND LEOPOLD

TALNUA BOURBON CASK & STAVE FINISH

Essentially an Irish-style whiskey aged in used cooperage with bourbon staves added, this is the lightest offering from Talnua (and one of the best of the lighter American whiskeys). Soft and fragrant with hints of melon and nougat, but still with the backbone of the very fine, rich whiskey in the Old World tradition.

86pf	$75	P	TC	Independent

TALNUA CONTINUUM CASK

Bright and bold, continuum cask sits in a sweet spot for this triple-distilled, yet full-flavored whiskey. Buttery and grainy with a little toffee and crème brûlée, this whiskey best articulates American creativity within Irish tradition.

86pf	$50	P	TC	Independent

TALNUA VIRGIN WHITE OAK CASK

A triple-distilled barley spirit that goes into new oak, this may be the best barley whiskey for the bourbon drinker. Not overly malty, with the flavor grain dominant, this is a crazy cool whiskey that has nutty, earthy notes with the classic American profile of oak, spice, and vanilla. A hard whiskey to describe but an easy one to love.

86pf	$75	P	TC	Independent

LEOPOLD BROTHERS BONDED BOURBON

A creamy caramel corn bourbon. Leopold wants you to taste the grain here, and it comes through nicely. Not much barrel to hide flaws, but there aren't any, so what comes through is a really rich bourbon, nothing but pure gold.

100pf	$65	P	TC	Independent

LEOPOLD BROTHERS 3-CHAMBER RYE

Richly textured rye grain, well balanced with gentle oak. Butterscotch, maple, and a creamy palate of vanilla with more than a hint of dill. A lot of high-toned flavors, a very unusual whiskey, and an even more unusual rye whiskey. A cool bottle all around.

100pf	$250	Three Chamber	TC	Independent

"Irish-style whiskey" is a touchy one. Kings County has made an Irish-style whiskey for St. Patrick's Day for a few years running, but I received a nasty cease-and-desist letter from the Irish Whiskey Association, a trade group convened to protect the provenance of Irish whiskey.

What we intended and what other American distillers are doing is making whiskey that conforms to the most constrained class of Irish whiskey, once called pure pot-still but, because of labeling regulations in the US, is now just called single-pot-still whiskey. These are whiskeys that are pot distilled from a mash of malted and unmalted barley. Irish whiskeys are very often (but not always) triple distilled, resulting in a lighter-bodied spirit that is often aged in used cooperage for a shorter time than other world whiskeys. Still, the main defining feature of Irish whiskey is that it is made in Ireland, so what constitutes an Irish-style American whiskey is perhaps up to the distiller, though most of us experimenting in the space are geeky, process-oriented distillers who like the constraints of the technical file, or the legal code, to which Irish whiskeys must conform. Irish whiskey is a distiller's whiskey, and its excellence is in the production (not so much in the aging or blending), and for that reason it appeals to a lot of smaller American distillers that see it as a creative project.

Which is why, when we received the cease-and-desist, I very promptly published my response to Twitter, pushing back on the notion that a Brooklyn-made Irish-style American whiskey would ever be confused for an Irish whiskey. Indeed, our offering served to highlight the particularities of Irish whiskey, which are tricky to articulate outside the setting of a distillery. Ultimately, I argued there is Irish whiskey, which belongs to Ireland, and the tradition of Irish distilling, which belongs to the world. I promised neither to cease nor desist (though in private conversations with small Irish distillers, I have found that different but precise language might be more agreeable to all). And while we answer first to our government and not to a foreign trade association, I thought the dialogue might be useful—though I still refuse to sign their proposed treaty, as I don't wish to recognize the authority of the Irish Whiskey Association over any distillers.

The conflict exposes a dilemma that all new distillers must face, which is how to take old, sometimes faraway traditions and make them new and different, without taking away from the original tradition or seeking to profit from confusing the consumer. This is a debate going on in many parts of food culture and the culture at large, and we are hardly alone in trying to chart our respective courses.

Talnua manages to thread this needle in a way that is refreshing. With so many distillers now devoted to bourbon, rye, and American single malt, only one or two are taking their inspiration from Irish whiskey, which has a rich history that is worth repeating, as it is an important part of this story.

The Irish most likely made the first whiskey, and the island is home to the oldest operating distillery, Bushmills, in Protestant Northern Ireland. But Catholic (and arguably proper) Irish whiskey all but died out when the challenges of US Prohibition, world wars, tariffs, and changing tastes nearly killed the industry, such that the remaining brands all merged to form one company and operate one distillery to save the nation's spirit. That distillery, which made Powers, Jameson, Redbreast, and many other brands, is the Midleton Distillery, and is today owned by Pernod Ricard, which built Jameson into the workhorse brand that revived Irish whiskey, especially in the United States.

Today, other distillers have opened, and Irish whiskey is not quite so limited. But its whiskey culture is in flux just as ours is, and that makes it exciting for distillers on both sides of the Atlantic. Patrick and Meagan Miller were in Ireland on their honeymoon in 2011, watching the World Cup and sipping Irish whiskey in a pub in Galway. Romance is a strong tipple, and when the couple returned to the US, they began to think of opening a distillery that would focus less on the American single-malts that were cropping up, but on a triple-pot-distilled whiskey from malted and unmalted barley. Patrick had worked in oil and gas, but that industry is boom and bust, and when energy prices cratered in 2017, he saw a way out. He worked for Stranahan's to cut his teeth as a distiller and then opened Talnua in 2019, with a trio of beautiful copper pot stills that anchor the distillery in front of a massive American flag, lest there be any confusion as to the provenance of this whiskey.

It's early stages for Talnua, but its whiskeys are mature and well-established: A virgin oak version stood out to me, a kind of hybrid flavor

The three-chamber still at Leopold Brothers is the only one of its kind in operation, though the type was common before Prohibition.

between American and Irish whiskey. Their Cask & Stave series was one of the lightest whiskeys sampled for this book, with notes of vanilla crème and green melon that would make for a perfect summer sipper. I tried many of their whiskeys, and for a distillery that is only three years old, they are making stunning products. It was an easy favorite in Colorado.

XXX

The distiller who is likely talked about with most reverence among craft enthusiasts is Todd Leopold, who, with his brother Scott, started Leopold Brothers. The business began as a brewery in Ann Arbor, not far from the football stadium, and a fluke in a Michigan law got them into distilling as a side hustle. When the landlord refused to renew their lease, they moved back home to Colorado, where Todd, a philosophy major at Georgetown, and Scott, a process engineer who studied at Northwestern, applied their educated minds to making eaux-de-vie, amaros, and, most notably, whiskey.

Todd Leopold is an elder statesman in craft whiskey, who earned his place not by getting his start in finance before hitting up well-off friends for capital, but by going over to Germany to study beer-making traditions there. As such, the distillery does a few things that are highly unusual, including malting their own barley (so much that they now sell surplus to other distillers and brewers), open fermenting in small wooden tanks (small-tub fermentation was once a hallmark of old-time bourbon), and using a three-chambered still to make rye, built with nothing more than a diagram from an old distilling manual. Three-chambered stills were a common middle ground between the fire copper pot distillers and the more modern column distillers. First made of wood and then copper, the three-chambered still became a mainstay of rye production (and was used at Overholt until around Prohibition).

Todd approached Vendome about making one, and Vendome couldn't even verify that the still would work properly (though they believed it would). The spirit takes twelve hours to run through and produces a distillate that preserves the esters of the open fermentation but yields lower volumes than a traditional column still (or even a pot still). The distillery can produce about two barrels of rye in a run, made with 80 percent

Leopold has a collection of stills from Christian Carl and Vendome, each with a slightly different configuration.

Abruzzi rye and 20 percent floor-malted barley. It's the closest thing to history (and to the most popular spirit sold in the US in the nineteenth century) that can be found today.

Leopold also makes other fine spirits, including a very balanced high-malt, high-rye bourbon and a high-malt American whiskey from the same mash: 64 percent corn, 21 percent malted barley, and 15 percent rye. Long fermentation and low barrel-entry proof are ways beyond traditional pot distillation that Leopold is distinctive with every aspect of the process.

Additionally, they make a Campari-like aperitivo, not too sweet and gentian heavy, colored with ground red cochineal beetles as the original used to be. An orange liqueur and a cherry liqueur (essentially vodka and sweet cherry juice) rounded out the highlights of my visit. They make

TYPES OF STILLS IN AMERICAN WHISKEY

For years, bourbon and rye whiskey were made on a very similar equiptment regardless of the distillery. There are now many types of stills that make American whiskey, and knowing them is the key to understanding the spirits that come from them.

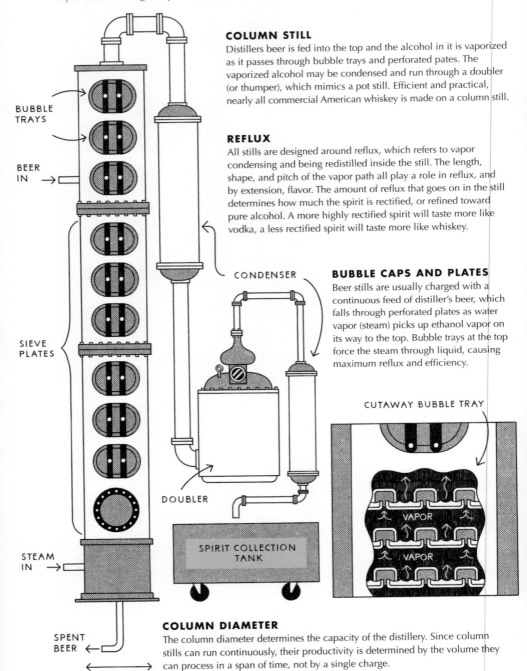

COLUMN STILL

Distillers beer is fed into the top and the alcohol in it is vaporized as it passes through bubble trays and perforated pates. The vaporized alcohol may be condensed and run through a doubler (or thumper), which mimics a pot still. Efficient and practical, nearly all commercial American whiskey is made on a column still.

REFLUX

All stills are designed around reflux, which refers to vapor condensing and being redistilled inside the still. The length, shape, and pitch of the vapor path all play a role in reflux, and by extension, flavor. The amount of reflux that goes on in the still determines how much the spirit is rectified, or refined toward pure alcohol. A more highly rectified spirit will taste more like vodka, a less rectified spirit will taste more like whiskey.

BUBBLE CAPS AND PLATES

Beer stills are usually charged with a continuous feed of distiller's beer, which falls through perforated plates as water vapor (steam) picks up ethanol vapor on its way to the top. Bubble trays at the top force the steam through liquid, causing maximum reflux and efficiency.

COLUMN DIAMETER

The column diameter determines the capacity of the distillery. Since column stills can run continuously, their productivity is determined by the volume they can process in a span of time, not by a single charge.

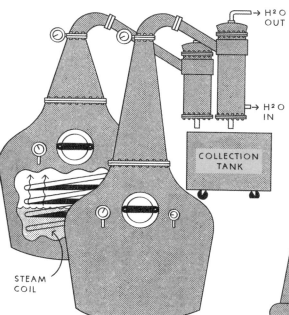

POT STILLS

Pot stills work more simply than column stills. Beer is heated in a the pot, alcohol vapor evaporates off and travels up the neck of the still, into the lyne arm, which connects the still to a condenser.

BATCH PROCESS

Pot stills are generallly a batch process. Every decision by the distiller is made each time they run the pot still, so the distiller has more control over flavor in this setup, but this is done by collecting early, middle, and late parts of distillation into separate collection vessels, a labor intensive process.

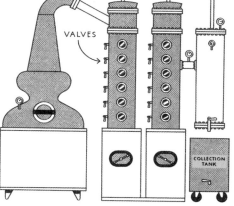

HYBRID STILLS

Hybrid stills essentially marry a pot still and a column still in a single unit. The distiller can open valves and tune the amount of rectification desired, or bypass it althogether, giving the operator maximum flexibility.

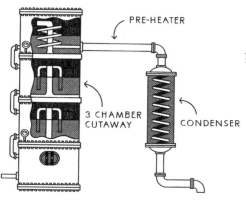

3-CHAMBER STILL

Todd Leopold has the only 3-chamber still in operation today, an 19th-century standby for high quality rye whiskey. It remains a unique throwback in distilling culture—arguably a bridge between pot and column setups.

CHARENTAIS STILL

A form of pot still peculiar to European tradition, especially in Cognac production, the charentais is easy to recognize for its steampunk look and beautiful curves. Most used for brandy, there are a handful making whiskey in the U.S.

flavored whiskeys too, so the fuss around floor malting and forgotten distillation techniques is not aimed only at the most highbrow consumers.

The distilling floor is a distiller's dream, with at least eight stills that I could count, each with a slightly different purpose or rationale. Even so, the scale is modest. Leopold is not aiming to take over the whiskey world, but to make a variety of great whiskeys well for those who can find them. A partnership with Nicole Austin of George Dickel is probably more about George Dickel, but it is also a way for Leopold to join a broader conversation than his own whiskey supply might allow. And that's not a bad thing, because Leopold is operating on a level of craft that makes most craft distillers jealous (and makes you wonder why you ever fooled with commodity whiskey in the first place).

Still, you won't find barrel-strength, oak-forward whiskeys here. And the three-chamber will set you back $250, which is a fair price for the best of craft, but it's such a different whiskey than you're used to, you might not even like it. That is what is so refreshing about the Colorado distillers.

The distillers here have all carved out clear identities relative to those in other regions, but it would be hard to categorize them as anything other than singular and determined. And superaged whiskeys don't necessarily make much sense west of the Mississippi, so there's a more-level playing field than you'll find on the East Coast, letting process take the lead over age. At least for now.

xxx

High West began as little more than a distillpub (a brewpub for whiskey) in Park City, a ski town north of Salt Lake City and host to the annual Sundance Film Festival. My first visit there was in 2012 for Sundance. My wife and college roommate had directed competing films, and I passed out a few flasks of Kings County to festivalgoers. High West was a big brand by then and had built their reputation by inhabiting the brand space that Bulleit's frontier whiskey was aiming for, but with the credibility of being launched in the West by an independent producer and doing genuinely innovative things with sourced whiskeys, including some very old whiskeys that had been acquired from the usual suspects.

High West began as a distillpub (like a brewpub for whiskey) in the resort town of Park City, Utah.

High West was especially transparent when many brands weren't, allowing whiskey fans to geek out on blends of bourbon and rye (Bourye) and blends of Scotch and bourbon (Campfire). These sourced whiskeys quickly outpaced any plans High West had to release their own whiskeys, but you could find the house-distilled products in Utah, including a silver oat white whiskey that was interesting to me.

When I finally got to visit with distiller Brendan Coyle in 2012, I was surprised at how small the original distillery is, though it is a feat of engineering, packing legitimate fermentation capacity into a restaurant basement. Much of the blending and bottling happened elsewhere, and soon High West built a custom distillery high in the mountains. One interesting thing to note: High West invested in Forsyth equipment that mimicked its hybrid pot still back in Park City—pot distillation followed by a column—whereas most bourbon and rye in the US is first column distilled followed by finishing in a doubler (a kind of pot still).

An interesting aspect of distilling at elevation is that the boiling point of alcohol, already lower than that of water, drops. Some distillers at sea level have invested in vacuum stills that reduce the pressure inside the still to vaporize alcohol at a lower temperature, with the argument that cooking the grain at a high temperature takes it further from its essential nature. I've seen it locally in New York with Greenhook Ginsmiths, which makes a remarkably good gin using a vacuum still. Now-defunct Arcane Spirits in Brooklyn used a vacuum still to make whiskey from beer as a point of differentiation. Western distillers are often at least a mile high in elevation already, which lowers the boiling point enough to qualify as a factor in these whiskeys. High West began at its Saloon in Park City at 7,000 feet. Its new facility is a little lower, but still high enough to be a consideration. What elevation does to aging whiskey is not fully understood (aging at sea level is not fully understood, and we have centuries of data on it). Stranahan's keeps its aging inventory humid with water misters and at a constant temperature. As to what this does for High West, it may be too early to say; for now, the brand is still relying on sourced whiskeys for many of its products.

If you accept the sourcing history and context, High West is reliable. Their holiday release, A Midwinter Nights Dram, is a personal favorite—a high-priced whiskey that holds up to its promise. And Campfire is a cool whiskey that deserves wider appreciation than it gets.

High West marked one of the first big acquisitions in craft distilling. Constellation bought the brand for $180 million in a bidding war with several other companies. That set off a series of acquisitions in whiskey, and High West may always be perceived as an early indicator of things to come.

One other distillery, Wyoming Whiskey, made a strong entry into the market, though with a more traditional mash bill/column-still program that would fit nicely in Kentucky. The whiskeys I've tried are well-made and clean, though it could be hard to make a strong argument for Wyoming (the brand) over so many other regional offerings. Wyoming formed a strategic partnership in 2018 with Edrington, a family of Scotch whiskies most known for Macallan.

FOUR FROM HIGH WEST

HIGH WEST AMERICAN PRAIRIE RESERVE

A light balance of corn and caramel, this whiskey is a solid base hit. A gentle whiskey that improves its source material (MGP) through blending. Subsequent releases are labeled more squarely as bourbon, but it's the same whiskey inside.

92pf	$30	C	SW	Constellation

HIGH WEST CAMPFIRE

A blend of rye, bourbon, and Scotch whiskey, this is one of the subtler uses of peat in American whiskey, but the balance is nice. One of the best arguments for American independent bottlers, this is a whiskey that may have been born of disparate geographies but belongs to the imagination of the American West. A great deal at $35, though this has become rarer and more expensive lately.

92pf	$35 ($80)	C	SW	Constellation

HIGH WEST SON OF BOURYE

A viscous rye, but flavor that is mainly by the book: sweet and soft with a little almond cookie, balanced oak, but then disappears too quickly. I'm not sure why anyone would mix bourbon with rye, since most bourbons contain rye and most ryes contain corn, but here we are.

92pf	$40 (discontinued)	C	SW	Constellation

A MIDWINTER NIGHT'S DRAM

Of all the barrel-finished whiskeys, this is one that really makes a strong argument for the practice. Worth it at shelf price, to my palate—I can't speak to some grumbling about variability, but the label's power of suggestion works well for this excellent, winter-spiced holiday warmer.

98.6pf (variable)	$125 ($250)	C	SW	Constellation

THE SPECTRUM OF AUTHENTICITY IN AMERICAN WHISKEY

UNTRANSPARENT SOURCED

These are brands that say very little about where the whiskey comes from or why it exists. These are often joke labels but sometimes big gimmick brands or brands meant to appeal to a niche audience—or brands so generic they appeal to anyone who can't be bothered to look under the hood.

- No age statement
- Vague mash bill or production specifics
- Geography of bottling is highlighted
- Misleading or tangential narrative

TOKEN STILLS

These are distillers that have built an enormous business off of sleight of hand and have built or installed a token still on-site, hoping you won't notice that the still is nowhere near large enough to ever service the demands of the brand. Most people will swear they make their own, though the math is not on their side.

- Gimmicky story
- 250+ gallon pot
- Geography is overemphasized
- Marketing heavy
- Misleading narrative

EMERGING STILLS

These are distillers that have sourced whiskey from elsewhere but are in the process of building production capacity to meet demand in-house.

- Undifferentiated whiskey
- Some transparency
- Well financed
- Founding narrative led
- Visitor-friendly location
- Promises juice soon

INDEPENDENT BOTTLERS

These are what we'd call independent bottlers after the scotch model. They are making a business out of sourcing and blending barrels, often from big distillers or small craft distillers, but with purpose and style.

- Creativity and variety
- Barrel finishes
- Barrel-proof options
- Production narratives
- Batch specific

There is a pretty clear spectrum when it comes to whiskey that pits authenticity and idiosyncrasy at one end of a spectrum with a generic product and deceptive marketing on the other. Yes, there are examples of crossover (High West, for instance, has an interesting distilling program that complements a mostly sourced/blending program), but they are rare. In this business, you are out to make either perfect whiskey or a quick buck, and those end goals generally lead to wildly different places.

HERITAGE DISTILLERS

These are the big guys that make their own whiskeys and much of what goes into other people's bottles, made in facilities that have been around. There's a level of craft and integrity to the process and they are proud to talk about it on tours. But they are also big businesses, which often favors a very few stakeholders and leaves others out to dry.

- 36-inch column or greater
- Typical mash bills
- Standard cooperage
- Multiple expressions

COLUMN CRAFT

These are distillers that are sourcing grains from local farms but are running pretty typical mash bill whiskey through a small to medium column still, and aging mostly in standard cooperage.

- Small column stills
- Typical mash bills
- Standard cooperage
- Barrel finishes common

POT STILL

Perfectionist distillers that are sourcing quality ingredients, distilling on small pot stills, aging in a variety of cooperage types, and focus on sensory evaluation.

- Grain to glass
- Obsessive sourcing
- Pot stills
- Variety of products
- Relentlessly creative

OBSESSIVE CRAFT

These distillers seek to control every aspect of production, doing their own floor malting, open fermentation, using heirloom grains, handmade stills, and are run by generally maverick, idiosyncratic distillers who answer to themselves.

- Farming own grains
- Direct-fired pot stills
- Floor malting
- Unusual or heritage stills

St. George Spirits inhabits an old airplane hanger at a defunct naval base in Alameda with sweeping views of San Francisco Bay.

11

BREWER'S MALT WHISKEYS

Most of the barley grown in the United States comes from Idaho (33 percent), Montana (20 percent), and North Dakota (26 percent). So, it may not be a surprise that the distillers in the population centers of the Pacific Northwest have been drawn to barley-based whiskeys. There is a cultural precedent here too. Craft beer thrived on the West Coast long before smaller brewers found traction on the East Coast. If America was settled east to west, then cities like San Francisco, Portland, and Seattle became a terminus for restless, searching souls, piling up here where the sun sets over the ocean and the aristocracy and traditions of the East Coast receded into darkness.

In the same way, craft spirits have been quicker to catch on here, and in fact this region can claim some of the oldest nontraditional distillers or the first "micro" distillers by the most conventional definitions before craft distillery became the accepted term. Distillers like Charbay, St. George, and Clear Creek were pioneers triangulating between the wine business that flourished here, craft beer that revolutionized a staid industry, and Old World brandy production. Many of these early distillers opened by making unaged fruit brandies but found a more enduring and receptive audience for their whiskeys, often barley based and more in the tradition of Irish and Scotch, and other world whiskeys derived from barley and malted barley.

Before we go any further, an explanation of what is meant by "malt" is warranted. Anyone who was ever a child on Halloween knows what a malted milk ball is, or perhaps has ordered a malted milkshake. The word "malt" refers to the process of germinating a seed, awakening the enzymes that convert stored starch into energy for a plant to grow, and it can be used by brewers and distillers to break down the starch in grain to simpler sugars (which yeast will then use to make alcohol). Any grain can be malted, which is setting the conditions for seeds to sprout but stopping just before a seed splits open. Worldwide, malted barley is the most popular malted grain, and indeed the word "malt" usually is understood to mean malted barley exclusively. Malted milk, made with malt flour, was once perceived as a health food, and so found its way into ice cream and candy to make it more palatable, and then became an item of nostalgia.

Malt is the most prized ingredient in world whiskeys. Single-malt scotch is well known; it refers to whiskeys made from 100 percent malted barley at a single distillery. Malt whiskey in the United States is made from 51 percent malted barley aged in new barrels but is a very niche item not commonly made. Malt liquor is artificially strengthened beer, something else entirely, and often sold in 40-ounce bottles. The nomenclature gets a little complicated.

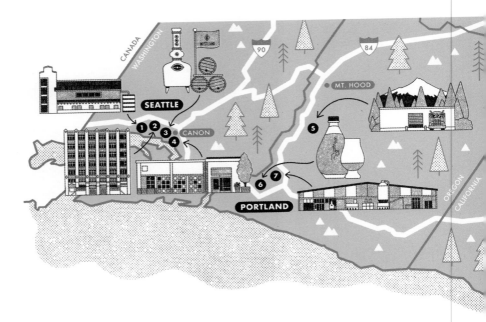

WEST COAST WHISKEY

Distillers of the West Coast have gravitated to barley malt whiskeys, but generally take a creative and determined approach to whiskey making, letting ingredients, idiosyncrasy, and variety guide their products. While the East Coast is tradition-bound, the West has long embraced entrepreneurship and innovation as well as a deeper appreciation for the natural environment—all of which informs the whiskeys of the coast.

But worldwide, malt whiskeys are the standard for the highest class of whiskey, and many Scotch, Irish, Japanese, and other world whiskeys are based on this style. A whiskey from Sweden or Australia will mostly likely be malt based, but malt whiskey in the US was mostly unknown until a group of distillers in the West set about finding a path for American single malt. The story of West Coast distilling and American single malt is one of roads that run close together, converging at times and diverging at others. And with former brewers taking the lead in opening many of the West Coast distilleries, it's no surprise that malt would take center stage.

xxx

Portland is a hub of craft everything comestible, to a cartoonish degree that has been lampooned enough. The notion that a hobbyist could open

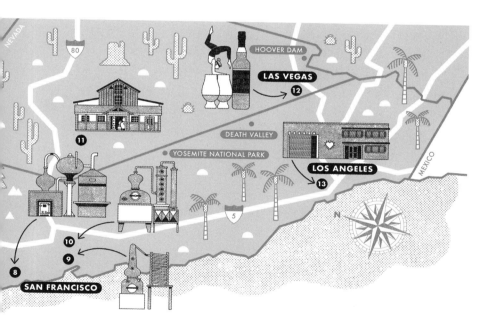

1. WOODINVILLE WHISKEY	6. FREELAND SPIRITS	10. ST. GEORGE SPIRITS
2. COPPERWORKS	7. HOUSE SPIRITS/ WESTWARD	11. FREY RANCH
3. WESTLAND		12. LOST SPIRITS
4. OOLA	8. CHARBAY	13. GREENBAR DISTILLERY
5. CLEAR CREEK/HOOD RIVER	9. OLD POTRERO/ HOTALING & CO.	

a pickle business with a website and a social media presence is no longer laughable—indeed, it's the standard template for scaling a small food or beverage business. Portland has small businesses in ample supply, and yes, there are some that can be overly precious, but what was once easy to mock has become a baseline part of urban life in a youthful city with food trucks, creative restaurants, artisan shops, and a vibrant nightlife.

Portland in the early aughts, like Brooklyn, was a place where a creative foodie could open a coffee roastery, or a chocolate factory, or a beef jerky brand with some secondhand equipment and a website. Before online transactions were common, this seemed hubristic and solipsistic, but also made for good coffee, chocolate, and jerky. Some businesses took off, some sold out, some failed. That artisan mania has been tempered with time and experience: Running a business is hard and only the committed and lucky will succeed. And even then, a lovingly well-made product is rarely a way to get rich quick, as the very things that make it excellent often make it rarefied, expensive, and hard to scale.

Portland has a surplus of this type of business, which makes it an emporium of artisanal wonders. It's also a charming city that doesn't seem too big or small and feels laid-back like California but industrious too. It's also located in a stunningly beautiful part of the country, where the majesty of the mountains, roiling black rivers, and evergreen forests are never far away.

I visited in 2017 with my family, staying in Oregon City, a postcard of a town just south of Portland near the historic falls of the Willamette River and an enormous paper mill that anchors the south end of town. A municipal elevator connects the upper, more residential neighborhood with the lower portion of the town, which has the commercial shops and restaurants, filled with just the right amount of quirk for a holiday weekend in the summer.

From there I set out to visit the city's distilleries and started with its largest, House Spirits, which had just moved to a 14,000-square-foot facility. House Spirits began in 2004 when former brewer Christian Krogstad began distilling an incredible variety of spirits, often sold in 375ml bottles with a plain, matter-of-fact label typed with notes articulating the product's

Westward Whiskey is a project of House Spirits, once a creative and prolific small distiller that took its haul from selling Aviation Gin and turned exclusively to malt whiskey.

features. One of the projects, Aviation Gin, became a commercial success that was eventually sold off to Davos Brands, with Ryan Reynolds as an investor, and eventually Diageo.

That sale helped finance other interests, including an aquavit and what Krogstad had always wanted to make, a single-malt whiskey. Westward Whiskey is now the main project of House Spirits, produced in a 3,000-gallon Vendome pot still in the spacious new facility. Westward is a straight malt whiskey, aged in lightly charred new cooperage, which puts Westward in a category with Stranahan's, and while the latter has been successful commercially, Westward is perhaps still finding its audience,

PORTLAND'S OBSESSIVE CRAFT

WESTWARD WHISKEY

Rich caramel, heavily malty, molasses. A well-made whiskey, but in a category that doesn't like to be quite so sweet. I find it a little hard to love this whiskey, but it has lots of partisans around. American single malt should be a big tent.

90pf	$75	P	TC	Semi-independent

WESTWARD STOUT FINISHED WHISKEY

I like the concept of a beer barrel finished whiskey, but in this case, it may exacerbate certain flavor elements about the Westward malts that I'm not sure how I feel about. It's a maximalist malt, and I tend to like those. I just can't wrap my head around this one.

90pf	$90	P	TC	Semi-independent

CLEAR CREEK MCCARTHY'S WHISKEY

A totally cool whiskey making good use of peat in what might otherwise be called a young American malt. The peat gives a grown-up heft and complexity that vibe nicely with its Oregon origins, conjuring a dank, wet forest and a smoky campfire. New owners so far are being good stewards of this very singular whiskey.

85pf	$60	H	TC	Hood River Distillers

though it is the better-made whiskey. Pricing is hard for malt whiskeys, since barley is more expensive and malting adds cost versus traditional corn or rye-based whiskeys. And with so much malt whiskey available from historic and established distillers all over the world, American single malt has an uphill climb.

That climb is still a worthy endeavor. Many distillers making single malt in the US, Kings County included, believe that we can make the best malt whiskey in the world with enough time and patience. Westward was one of the leading distillers to pursue an American Single Malt designation, a new standard of identity (how the federal government classifies spirits) for American-made whiskey from malted barley. Most of the best global whiskey is made from malted barley, so it is a little surprising that US distillers don't have an equivalent category other than straight malt, which requires only 51 percent malt and a new barrel. American Single Malt, or ASM, is proposed as 100 percent malt and can use any cooperage. Westward is a stake in the ground for American Single Malt, but with most American whiskey drinkers suffering from bourbon mania, it may take time, which is generally not a problem for whiskey.

I next visited Clear Creek Distilling, then one of the most interesting distillers in the United States, and a pioneer in craft. I visited with a tour on an afternoon and had a thoughtful guide walk our small group through the space, a somewhat dismal industrial building without windows. A group of surprisingly small pot stills did the work here, in a setup that looked like five pistons on a giant internal combustion engine. The air had the sweet reek of fermented juice.

Clear Creek is most known for making magical eaux-de-vie from local pear and other fruits. A single-malt, McCarthy's, was some of the best American whiskey I've ever tasted, but it wasn't even the best on the tasting table when the tour ended, which was filled with distillates from cherry, pear, plum, and a strange elixir made from Douglas fir buds infused in brandy. The distillery was an alchemist's cabinet full of eccentric and beautiful spirits.

I say *was*, because when I visited, the distillery had just been sold as founder Steven McCarthy retired, but the new owners hadn't changed very much just yet. In the years since, they have closed the Portland distillery and moved production to their location in Hood River and continue to make many of the same spirits. While the new owners may have kept up the original varieties, it's hard not to mourn the closing of a very formative urban distillery that inspired many others.

One distillery I didn't get to visit was Freeland Spirits, which was just getting started in 2017. Pitched as an all-female brand, Freeland's production is overseen by Molly Troupe, who has created a gin and blended

Inside the former Clear Creek Distillery, one of the earliest pioneers of craft distilling in the United States, makers of McCarthy Peated Single Malt and a host of creative and traditional fruit brandies

some sourced whiskeys while actively distilling. I met Molly while visiting distilleries in Tennessee and know her to be a quiet force in the business. The company's distinctive teardrop-shaped bottles are hard to miss, and an overarching elevated aesthetic applies not just to the thoughtfully designed tasting room, distillery, and packaging, but also to what goes in the bottle.

Oregon Spirit Distillers in Bend, founded by Brad Irwin, is a stealth player in Oregon whiskey. I got to know Brad's distillery and whiskeys through Marianne Eaves, who put our distilleries in her first blind tasting project. Oregon Spirit is a little more traditional to American whiskey than some other players in Oregon, with two bourbons, a rye, and a wheat whiskey. With serious capacity, this distillery is playing to win with their own whiskeys and have been somewhat overlooked by whiskey media so far.

Over my long Fourth of July week in Oregon, I hiked above Multnomah Falls, had lunch at the Timberline Lodge (the hotel from Kubrick's *The Shining*), and explored the Columbia River Gorge. The most interesting spirit I tasted in Oregon came not from a distiller but from a winemaker, who had a barrel of brandy set up in his aging cave, whose name will be withheld for protection. My wife had wrapped shooting a TV show, and the crew had gathered for a wine tasting. The vintner distilled enough off the books every year to keep a few barrels for his own fun, and we took the occasion to sample straight from the barrel. My experience in Portland was made perfect by this illicit dram—an artisan's side hustle in deeper artisanship, not for the money but the pleasure. There is nothing silly about good food and drink, and Portland has both.

XXX

Seattle, more than any other city on the West Coast, is a great stop for whiskey. Seattle may represent the perfect confluence of creative craftsmen, business intelligence, and a supportive community that set the precise conditions for craft distillers to flourish.

My first visit to Seattle came in 2015 for the American Distilling Institute's annual trade show, and I immediately set out to visit the local distillers, starting with Copperworks, a malt-whiskey distillery well situated downtown, just across from Pike's Place Market. If you visit any distiller in Seattle, Copperworks is a good bet for convenience and the excellence of their product. Using two beautiful Forsyth pot stills, the distillery is focused on American single malt but also produces gin and vodka. Jason Parker and Micah Nutt have done quite a bit here with a well-organized and beautiful production distillery, a variety of white and brown spirits that appeal broadly, a downtown location, and one tidbit I appreciated from my visit: municipal steam as a utility. Space constraints limit the operation, and plans have been announced for an offsite expansion.

I visited again in fall 2022 on a day when wildfire smoke hazed up Seattle's downtown. Copperworks doesn't have a "flagship" whiskey, pre-ferring to issue numbered and special releases, each a different iteration using different malts, or barrel finishes. I was drawn to a proofy 2022 Craft Malt Week release, but the standard releases of 044 and 045 were great. I was perhaps least interested in the oldest whiskey, a flood-relief batch that paled next to other woodier editions. Still, Copperworks is using

WOODINVILLE WHISKEY

WOODINVILLE BOURBON

Earthy and spicy, making good use of rye, Woodinville is a great bourbon for those who want to taste beyond Kentucky, still want an excellent whiskey, but don't want to get too weird. This makes comparably priced Kentucky bourbon taste anemic by comparison.

90pf	$40	H	TC	LVMH

WOODINVILLE RYE

Cocoa and leather on the nose, and a rich, bold rye presence with notes of butterscotch and brown sugar and a short finish. But I don't count it against this great rye whiskey, which mediates nicely between the barely legal Kentucky rye and more full-flavored craft. Very solid pour.

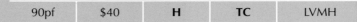

90pf	$40	H	TC	LVMH

mostly new oak for its current releases, with second-fill barrels coming for a more traditional single-malt profile. I have the feeling I'll be more drawn to these, but it's hard to argue with the integrity, creativity, and quality coming from Copperworks. It's a great meeting spot for whiskey lovers from around the world, and I've run into friends and made new ones while here.

I traveled to the Seattle suburb of Woodinville for my next visit, a hub of winemaking for the grape-growing region east of Seattle. Woodinville Whiskey doesn't quite fit the mold of brewer's-malt whiskeys, as they specialize in bourbon and rye. Founders Orlin Sorensen and Brett Carlile were entrepreneurial and looking to start a business and found whiskey. They begin in a small location near many of the production facilities for Seattle's wine region. They hired the tireless Dave Pickerell to teach them distilling and settled on a few differentiating aspects to their production, which has run on increasingly larger Kothe hybrid stills, with eight plates for single-pass distillation. Corn and rye are grown at a dedicated farm, which also houses the barrel-aging and bottling facility, east of Seattle by a few hours' drive. Roller mills create a less processed grain in the mashing phase, but fermentation happens in 9,000-gallon steel tanks (so many of them, there isn't room for much else at the distillery). I would argue Woodinville treads a nice line between Kentucky bourbon and craft whiskey. If you are looking for true craft whiskey that doesn't stray too far from tradition, this is a good option, and I wouldn't be surprised if Woodinville bests Kentucky in upcoming tastings. They've arrived with

Woodinville Whiskey Company is in wine country near Seattle but has focused on very classic, well-distilled bourbon and rye.

well-aged whiskey and a scale that allows volume but also in ways that industrial distillers just don't have.

Their bourbon and rye are quite nice, aged five-plus years per Brett, who toured me around the distillery. Barrel-strength versions are also good. With only two mash bills, a high-rye bourbon and a 100-percent rye whiskey, they have been playing around with barrel finishes. I tried a port-finish (lightly treated), manzanilla (sweet orange), and Pedro Ximénez (PX) finished bourbon, though I preferred the unfinished versions.

As craft distilleries go, Woodinville is large and well-funded (LVMH bought them as the only American distillery in their lineup), the kind of place where branded black fleeces and vests are commonly worn for pride. I remember tasting through more experimental whiskeys back in 2015, but they are later stage now and most of the creativity and play is coming from finishes. They do have an unbeatable price at $40 retail ($55 in Washington, the highest state liquor taxes in the US). And there are some interesting quirks of their production, though mostly this is in the model of big, ambitious hybrid-still distillers like Laws Whiskey House, Cedar Ridge, and others that are looking to do regional but classic whiskeys at a fair price. Nothing wrong with that.

I dropped in at OOLA, an odd and scrappy player on the Seattle scene. I visited in 2015 when a steampunk-inspired still—maybe built from an old boiler—gave the impression of a distillery cobbled together with discarded parts from another era. Maybe too much of the impression, as it worked more as a set piece than a practical production still. A move in 2020 to a more spacious setting, and more legitimate equipment, helped OOLA focus, perhaps, but there's still the charm of a business that is clearly being improvised all the way along. Its flagship bourbon is house distilled for now, but earlier iterations weren't always, and owner Kirby Kallas-Lewis wasn't particularly dogmatic about sourcing or not sourcing (in fact, I tried a great whiskey called Three Shores that was a mix of house bourbon, Canadian rye, and Scotch whisky). More niche than most, but still well established in Seattle, OOLA represents a sort of riff on whiskey that reflects its founder's artistic background and offers a quirky alternative to the better-financed and more entrenched players.

Canon is one of the preeminent whiskey library–styled bars in the United States.

Seattle's bar scene does a good job of supporting its local distillers, but the temple to whiskey is Canon, the whiskey-library bar that remains standout nationally for its wide collection in a beautiful room. It's a fine place to enjoy a dram. However, keep your mind open, for there is plenty more to visit, including the new Here Today Brewery that is run by a former Kings County distiller, Chris Elford, who offered me a smoked-malt session beer that was pretty wild. I dropped in just before the public opening and a few months before its James Beard nomination—another feather in the cap for Elford, who has built a few bars in Seattle, including Navy Strength and Trade Winds Tavern.

Still, the best stop in Seattle for the whiskey-minded is most likely Westland, a sizable distiller of American single malt and the leading force behind the category in both legal advocacy and cultural appreciation. Westland does a few weird things, as a distiller, beginning with a mash bill that includes a variety of malt types. People often confuse the "single malt" designation as being from one type of malted barley, but the single refers to malt whiskey from a single distillery. Westland uses up to five types of malt, including roasted malts. They use both new and used cooperage and both American Standard Barrels and other types of European casks. They have explored different types of oak, Garryana (Oregon white oak) and many varietals of barley. The results are always excellent and interesting.

An unusual aspect of the Pacific Northwest whiskeys is that they mostly hold proof as they age. Unlike the East Coast, where proof goes up, or Scotland, where proof goes down, the PNW splits the middle (or sees a very slight decrease).

Westland does have a flagship whiskey, which is an oak-forward malt in the wheelhouse of Stranahan's or Westward, but from there, the product line is all special releases (much like Copperworks). I prefer some of their lighter whiskeys, as port-finish, new-barrel malt whiskey can get a little heavy handed and covers over any grain characteristics that were carefully built in the first place.

Westland's blending team is much like our own at Kings County—obsessive and highly dedicated to making the most of the stock. Westland was purchased soon after its first whiskeys came out (announced in 2016) by Rémy Cointreau, whose other whiskey is the creative and fascinating Bruichladdich on Islay in Scotland. As corporate parents go, Rémy may

Westland's variables are varieties of malted barley and a range of nontraditional cooperage.

Of all those from American distillers, Westland's whiskeys arguably are most inspired from Scotch whisky production.

be good stewards for Westland, and there are lots of affinities among these two great distillers. Whether or not American palates go for either of them, time will tell. For this distiller, I wouldn't pass on a chance to try any bottle of Westland, and their Peat Week is one of the drop-dead finest American whiskeys ever released, a feat it manages to keep up year over year. If you like peat, this whiskey will deliver.

XXX

Craft distilling truly began in the San Francisco Bay Area, and that is ironically where we'll visit the last of the great distillers in this book. I visited on Halloween weekend in 2022, when Northern California had the bluster and gray skies of an East Coast fall day. Across town, Elon Musk was having his first day as owner of Twitter, but I was happy to be in the epicenter of the old-school farm-to-table ethos, something that California does better than anywhere.

Anchor Steam, a malty brown lager founded in late-1800s San Francisco, began a second act when Fritz Maytag (a scion of the appliance makers) bought the bewery and established his place in beer's renaissance, beginning in 1965. He also later built a distillery in 1994 to make Old Potrero rye, distilled from 100-percent malted rye and aged in used or new barrels depending on how old your bottle. For a rye drinker, this should be a staple of a complete collection; there aren't many all-rye distillers outside of the Northeast. Maytag sold the brewery in 2010, and it stopped production in 2023. The distillery passed to Hotaling in 2019 and has been closed to the public for some time, but a history of production on an iconic pot still with an air-cooled worm is a good indication that this is a serious malt whiskey, even if the malted grain here is rye.

Across the bay, St. George Spirits began in 1982, and is generally thought of as the first craft distiller in the US (though Germain Robin and Charbay started at roughly the same time and might disagree). St. George was founded by Jorg Rupf, a German who had worked in the ministry of culture there and moved to Berkeley to do postdoctoral research on arts funding. When presented with the pleasures of California, Rupf never left. He started St. George to focus on German-style eaux-de-vies, or fruit brandies. They were a niche distiller for many years, supporting the wine trade with a pear brandy and other fruit distillates. Lance Winters, an engineer and brewer who loved whiskey, found Rupf and began distilling for St. George. Winters helped grow the distillery beyond fruit brandies, and together they launched Hangar One Vodka. Rupf sold that brand and promptly retired, handing over the rest of the business to Winters, who runs it to this day with Dave Smith.

After its first two decades, St. George moved to a 65,000-square-foot hangar on Alameda Island in San Francisco Bay. It is unquestionably the most beautifully situated distillery in the United States, and the arrangement of the stills, tanks, and barrels in the light-filled space is a dream environment to conjure the best spirits. Winters has always been interested in whiskey, and St. George makes a small amount each year, often aged in a variety of cooperages and with differing mash bills, but most often malt whiskey. After the sale of vodka, Winters turned his attention to gin,

SEATTLE SINGLE MALTS

COPPERWORKS #46

Malt, simple syrup, cocoa, and stone fruit define a softer, barrel-forward American single malt. A middle-of-the-road whiskey for anyone curious for the category.

Variable	$70	P	TC	Independent

COPPERWORKS KENTUCKY RELIEF

A nice pour with sweet notes of brown sugar and malt, banana, and toffee. I expected a little more heft for the proof; maybe these Kentucky barrels had nothing left to give. Still, whiskey for a good cause, and a fun comparison to Copperworks' new barrel standard release.

98pf	$90	P	TC	Independent

WESTLAND AMERICAN SINGLE MALT

A confident whiskey from a newer craft distiller. Complex, rich malt whiskey that makes good use of old wood. Notes of hay, citrus peel, raisin, and a dry finish that put this in a category with fine Scotch whiskies more than American single malts.

92pf	$70	H	TC	Rémy

WESTLAND GARRYANA

This whiskey is partly aged in Garry oak barrels, an oak species native to Oregon (distinct from Quercus alba, the white oak used for most American whiskey barrels). Though not a drastic departure from the flagship, there is a little more baking spice and a warmer body from a little higher proof. A lovely whiskey that proves Westland's restless creativity and sense of perfection.

100pf	$150	H	TC	Rémy

WESTLAND PEAT WEEK

Nothing closer in American whiskey to an old Laphroaig, but with more texture and depth. A very cool American whiskey without peer.

100pf	$100	H	TC	Rémy

and these remain the core of St. George's production. They make Terroir Gin, which he describes as quintessentially Californian in nose and flavor. Other spirits I sampled, including a chili and bell pepper vodka, a basil vodka, and a Californian Agricole-style rum, were all totally singular and great (the rum is weird, full disclosure).

But for whiskeys, St. George does its own style. St. George is batched, so year over year, the flagship whiskey will vary based on age and cooperage. The latest is a very balanced malt whiskey. I also tried their 40th Anniversary Edition, a rich, spicy malt whiskey that spoke to the very best of American and European tradition, with spirit dating back to their first experiments in whiskey in the 1990s. Another crazy spirit: rye whiskey from rye grown on the upper slopes of Mt. Shasta, a microclimate that created a strange and funky fermentation that Winters assumed would fail in aging but made a very clean and rich rye in the end, with spearmint and baking spice. Still, my favorite of the whole whiskey portfolio may have been the youngest, called Baller, a light malt whiskey with notes of pear, lychee, and vanilla. Designed as a whiskey for highballs at a local Japanese restaurant where the staff often congregate, the whiskey may be aimed at cocktails, but I found it perfectly sippable, signaling a direction in American whiskey that is an ideal rebuttal to the barrel-proof, oak-bomb bourbons that seem to dominate a certain subset of the online hivemind.

Lance is a contrarian and an enthusiast, and his obsession with distilling seemingly hasn't flagged in more than twenty years. It's rare to find a distillery where the location, the product, the facility, and the minds behind the brand are all so remarkably excellent. Still, there is a lot of production capacity, and St. George could devote more of their attention to whiskey and we would all be better for it. With great power comes great responsibility, as they say.

After my St. George visit, I drove two hours north to Ukiah, California, in wine and weed country of Mendocino County. Charbay Distillery exists in a series of garage bays in an unmarked industrial park, an inconspicuous setting for one of the true pioneers in craft spirits, but also one of the most fascinating stills and distillery programs in all American whiskey.

A test still at St. George is a symbol of the creative energy that goes into its spirits. Whiskeys are only a portfolio full of liqueurs, gins, fruit brandies, and category-bending concoctions.

Charbay is the work of the Karakasevic family, distillers going back thirteen generations from the former Yugoslavia. I met with Marko, who runs the family business with his wife, Jenni. Charbay is first and foremost a brandy distillery, and they run a Charentais still, an alembic-style still not seen very frequently outside of Cognac. The gas-fired pot is connected to a worm tub through a pre-heater (see illustration on page 249). The design, which looks like a couple dollops of copper soft serve, is very old, even if the still itself is not. Like many things that come from European tradition, they don't change what works.

I sat down with Marko and immediately sampled the oldest American spirit I've ever tried: a 27-year-old grape brandy distilled in 1983 from Folle Blanche grapes grown in Mendocino County. It was a lovely spirit, very clean and perfect. I was here for the whiskeys, and we started tasting straight from the barrels. Marko outsources mashing and fermentation to a local brewer, Bear Republic. Sometimes he distills their beer, sometimes he distills brews specifically made to distill. I first tried a bourbon mash of 51 percent corn, 49 percent barley, already a signal we were in strange territory. Marko liked the spirit too much to dilute it to 125, so it went in the barrel at distillation strength, precluding the bourbon designation. The alembic still gives a lot of the Charbay whiskeys a family note, a kind of funky, meaty character that is really unlike any other American whiskey. While this might have been bourbon adjacent, it was a very cool, odd whiskey, landing more squarely between American malt and bourbon than maybe anything I've tried, with an almost-savory twist I attribute to their brandy still.

We moved on to another row of barrels, distillate from salvaged beer made at a brewery being sold off for parts. Stout, barley wine, and ale mixed together to make a malt whiskey, aged in a variety of cooperages. Charbay is known for hopped whiskeys, something I tend to turn away from in concept, but nothing on my visit seemed out of place, and a distilled stout was even stranger, like a few drops of chicory coffee in a malt whiskey (with a brandy twist).

As the session wore on, Marko's eccentricities came out, maybe most highlighted by a lengthy rant against brisket (overcooked and gelatinous!). For all the time with distillers I spent, very few talked about food, and none with views as fervently held as Marko's. I also got a little taste of the family dynamics. Marko has been the sole distiller, sometimes running the still for 24-hour sessions to clear a tanker before the fermentation went bad. But being the thirteenth in line carries pressures, as does being a small business.

Those eccentricities are very apparent in the whiskeys, brandies, and a peculiar decade-old rum, and a tequila Marko imports from friends in Durango, Mexico. Even the flavored vodkas are a cut above the market, with green tea, Meyer lemon, and blood orange elevating a low-stakes moneymaker. By the end, the table was littered with open bottles, and rather than any single impression of a whiskey, I was left with an indelible impression of a maker.

The distillers at St. George and Charbay embody what has made craft distilling such a formidable movement in the United States, but also why craft whiskey has taken so much time to catch on. They refuse to abide by tradition (53-gallon barrels are here, but so are hogsheads and puncheons, and rarely new, white oak from the usual cooperages). Bourbon is a product to invert or subvert, or an afterthought.

Charbay's charentais still is one of only a handful operating in the United States, and is perhaps the one that has been most devoted to whiskey production.

CALIFORNIA'S EXACTING DISTILLERS

OLD POTRERO RYE

What was once one of the only US sources for rye aged in a used barrel has been rebranded and reformulated with a more conventional, oak-forward new barrel aging for its flagship rye. Heavy malted rye, marshmallow, cinnamon. The older bottles would be a find, but the recent changes aren't for me.

97pf	$65	P 6 yr	TC	Hotaling & Co.

WAYWARD WHISKEY

A brilliant distiller in Santa Cruz, Sean Venus's whiskey doesn't get much beyond California. Not to be confused with Westland or Westward, Wayward is a malt whiskey with notes of melon and toffee, fresh fruit and dates, and a touch of black pepper on the finish. A true California whiskey.

92pf	$55	P	TC	Independent

ST. GEORGE SINGLE MALT

Bright, rich, and viscous, this is very well made malt whiskey that's perfectly suited to the Golden State. The rare American malt that sits between sweet and dry, this has a nice grain-forward base that is perfectly layered with caramel and a touch of cocoa.

86pf	$110	H	TC	Independent

It's a completely different approach from the commercial world of column-distilled, cheap distillates made by the tanker truck, yet very rewarding for those bold enough to venture beyond the well-traveled roads of bourbon and rye. The West Coast, true to form, is full of innovative free thinkers, and it shows in the whiskeys in this chapter. Yet for all this talent, most are known only to a handful of drinkers. The volumes for whiskey are low, as most independent businesses are forced to turn

ST. GEORGE BALLER WHISKEY

Melon, lychee, and peach sorbet with a soft, creamy richness, with a wisp of smoke, this is a delicate malt whiskey, light and balanced, a tricky feat that St. George has done nicely.

94pf	$50	H	TC	Independent

CHARBAY DOUBLED AND TWISTED

Charbay's whiskey projects are definitely at the fringe of American whiskey. Using a Charentais still and wash brewed by local breweries delivered in tankers, this whiskey defies any categorization, but there is a beautiful malt base that runs deep, with a skunky, flinty, slightly hoppy pot-still funk that secures its place as a great and totally singular whiskey.

90pf	$50	Charentais Pot	TC	Independent

CHARBAY R5

Funkier, richer, with a wisp of smoke on the finish, this whiskey is unlike anything else in the US. A happy, hoppy accident in distilled beer taken to the extreme, this whiskey conjures the scrubby pine forests of Mendocino County, where hops and its psychoactive cousin, cannabis, both thrive.

99pf	$65	Charentais Pot	TC	Independent

to gin or vodkas built on purchased spirit to keep the lights on. These whiskeys are loss leaders, I'd argue, selling for much less than their worth, as palates haven't quite caught on to their game. And who knows if they ever will, as we're forty years in for Charbay and St. George (and thirty for Potrero). The reward isn't dollars or volume but the whiskey itself. And while every distiller may advocate for that as the standard, few distillers live it so unabashedly as these Bay Area pioneers.

Lost Spirits in 2018, Downtown Los Angeles, California

12

THE END OF WHISKEY

It makes sense to end this journey in Los Angeles, where I have done most of the writing of this book, and where I've lived part-time since 2013. It's not a great whiskey city, not even a very good drinking city in my experience, but a good place for endings, especially narratives about America, where the historic Route 66 drops into the Pacific Ocean and the exuberance and decadence of American culture turns back on itself to produce our highest and lowest forms of entertainment. Our whiskey journey stops here, with a sunset over Santa Monica Pier and the vast sea beyond.

Los Angeles of course is a one-industry town, and that industry is fantasy. The best of Los Angeles embraces this fantasy, whether that is architecture, entertainment, or even whiskey. There are other cities that trade in fantasies. Las Vegas comes to mind, but that is a very specific fantasy, and if you don't exactly share it, the artifice of the city feels thin. Los Angeles is a city for the protagonist to conjure their best narrative, and then luxuriate in it.

For whiskey watering holes, there's not much to recommend, though everyone should enjoy the bliss of a Manhattan on the terrace at the Chateau Marmont. There are whiskey bars, as in any city, including the original outpost of Seven Grand and its Jackalope back room. Two great locations I got to know as whiskey bars are Tom Bergin's and the Whiskey Lounge, operated in a hidden attic and basement, respectively, but both have closed. The Thirsty Crow on Sunset is a fine enough whiskey dive, but hardly a landmark. This is, after all, a city on the edge of the desert and closer to Jalisco than Kentucky, both as the crow flies and spiritually.

Despite the dearth of watering holes, Los Angeles has a small distilling scene, the best of which focuses on the botanical richness of a city and region where anything will grow, year-round, with the right attention.

Greenbar is probably the largest and most visible, with a California poppy liqueur as a flagship, and a host of certified organic gins and vodkas (there remain few organic spirits in broad distribution).

XXX

I dwell on Los Angeles and its knack for artifice not to provide color to a list of whiskey bars or distillers, but because the best distillery tour I ever experienced was in an otherwise nondescript building in the warehouse district of downtown LA. And to discuss two kinds of whiskey that exist beyond the styles covered so far: rapid-aged whiskey, a sort of cheat on time; and non-alcoholic whiskey, the sort of contradiction in terms that cheats in a different way. Two important concepts at the fringe of whiskey, and worth a small bit of exploration here at the end.

I visited Lost Spirits, the brainchild of distiller Bryan Davis, in downtown Los Angeles on New Year's Eve 2017 with brewer Mike Lockwood, who was working for the great Craftsman Ales brewery in Pasadena at the time. We entered through a red door adorned with circus imagery and were ushered into a room lined with green plants to wait for our guide. After a review of various ground rules, we headed into an antechamber filled with twinkling lights to sample some of their spirits and learn their process. From there, a boat ride in a long tank of condenser water led to the distillery itself, where two hand-built stills spit vapor from a dragon's mouth into a spirit safe. The distillery produced rum on-site, but it was the next room, where the rum and a sourced whiskey underwent its most significant transformation, in a "reactor" that mimics aspects of the aging process.

Here was a detour on science and chemical signatures that I'll discuss later, but if I give Davis credit for anything, it's posing great questions while telling a compelling story. After stopping in a workshop room and learning about the American chestnut blight and its impact on whiskey cooperage, another boat ride led to an "Island of Dr. Moreau" themed encampment, where we tasted whiskeys and rums and talked with the founder himself. Davis presents more credibly as a mad scientist than an academic one, but it's in this context that his work shines most brightly—indeed his whiskeys and rum are the most refined rapid-aged spirits I've tried.

The entrance to Lost Spirits's Los Angeles iteration was on an unremarkable industrial block in Downtown's Arts District.

I'm not giving much away in describing my 2017 visit, because the tour has already been reimagined and reinvented as a performance in Las Vegas (an immersive environment with several stages for burlesque acts, contortionists, and dancers that just happens to also include a distillery). Perhaps true to form, Lost Spirits is currently lost; its Los Angeles factory closed while the Vegas residency has expanded, signaling where it may find its eventual footing. Davis's interest is not necessarily conventional spirits production but experiential marketing—not just his whiskeys, but a whole new way of looking at spirits.

Or is it? Rapid aging has been around as long as people have understood the virtues of aging spirits. Even Jack Daniel's Lincoln County process could be construed as a boost to the aging process, leaching the new-make whiskey through maple charcoal, which, among other virtues, makes Jack Daniel's whiskey taste more mature at a younger age.

And yet with the craft boom, rapid aging entered the American whiskey conversation with a full-throated battle cry, arguing that technology could solve this age-old conundrum once and for all. Spirits makers know that temperature and pressure are related factors in aging, as well as wood, which ages right along with the whiskey in a somewhat less-discussed aspect of maturation. Steam pipes along the floor of the Woodford Reserve's oldest rickhouses are clues that heat-cycling in maturation has been around at least a century. But go on any Kentucky tour and you'll hear that the best whiskey comes from the bottom of the warehouse, where temperatures are more even (requiring longer aging). Cooperage is often pre-aged, with staves being air-dried for up to twenty-four months for the best barrels, and many European spirits depend on barrels that have already been in production for years, as either Kentucky bourbon or some other type of barrel. Cognac reuses until the barrels can no longer hold

Lost Spirits in Las Vegas is now less of a distillery and more of a performance, and its signature spirits are now rums, not whiskeys.

spirit, and then some spirit is transferred to demi-johns: glass containers shrouded in wicker or burlap to keep out the light where the spirit is held in a state of suspended animation, awaiting the maker's call.

What of the science behind Davis's claims? Any hobby distiller will know that infusion of oak is the majority of what happens in aging by flavor, and it's easy to come close to aged whiskey with oak chips in a tank. Still, that nagging remainder is what makes rapid aging a perplexing proposition. Davis won't precisely describe his process, but light is a part of it. Degradation of wood is part of what makes maturation difficult to replicate with, for instance, small barrels or wood chips. It's not just that the spirit needs to age, but so too does the cooperage. Like seasoning, the amount of oak also plays a role. Adding just the right amount while not overwhelming the whiskey is exactly the work a conventional distiller will do, and rapid aging faces all the same sensory challenges of finding consistency with conventional aging—something Davis has achieved with well-regarded spirits.

Around the same time, and more visibly, Cleveland Whiskey entered the arena with its own rapid-aging technology. Its founder, Tom Lix, promoted his process, which depended on wood infusion through pressurization, in bottles that slyly touted the city name on the label, perhaps trading on Cleveland's reputation as a manufacturing comeback city. President Obama visited Lix in 2015, clearly playing his visit as a political charade with his main antagonist, Mitch McConnell, of Kentucky. The stunt didn't change the game for Cleveland, which hasn't made much of an impact outside of Ohio, except earning scorn from whiskey purists online. The Cleveland that I tried blind back in 2012 against Knob Creek and other robust, well-aged bourbons was a little on the nose, but by no means the embarrassment to whiskey that is sometimes described in online commentary. It's a decent fake. And a product without an audience when nine-year bourbon could be had at the same price back in 2012, when Cleveland launched. Now that same bourbon is selling for sixty dollars a bottle, Cleveland has more of a place for its spirits. However, my hunch is that most people will find plenty to buy in the forty-dollar range before any rapid-aged bourbon.

Terressentia began in 2006 with a process to improve flavor without relying on the traditional methods of barrel aging or filtration. The company purchased a historic distillery in Owensboro, Kentucky, and began bourbon production with an eye toward employing its trademarked TerraPURE system to rapid-age its whiskey. The market wasn't interested in rapid-aged whiskey, but contract whiskey was a good side hustle. Pivoting away from their rapid aging roots, the distillery was rechristened with a historical name, Green River, and focused on traditional whiskey production and the house brand. It has since been acquired by Bardstown Bourbon Company.

Perhaps the most brazen of the rapid agers is the so-called molecular whiskey sold as Glyph, produced by a company called Endless West. The makers of this spirit also tout having replicated chemical signatures. They framed the company as a tech company, rather than a distillery or a manufacturer, presuming, perhaps, that a Silicon Valley approach to whiskey might have some appeal (admittedly the company emerged when tech generally had a more favorable view from consumers).

Endless West just raised $60 million in capital, hoping that other companies might be interested in the technology, which appears to be chemical analysis and chemical addition to traditionally produced neutral ethanol. Artificial flavoring through chemical analysis is not a new business, not even very new to whiskey, but the tech spin appears to have some traction, at least with journalists if not actual consumers. The argument for lab-derived spirits is also tied to sustainability, but whiskey production accounts for .38 percent of all corn grown in the US. If one's concern is the environment, tackling corn subsidies and fuel-ethanol regulations might have some credible impact. And despite the storytelling, in practice Endless West is essentially flavoring commodity neutral alcohol—like all rapid agers—which is still derived from grain and fermentation in the normal way, so that argument breaks down even further. Wood for barrels can be forested sustainably, and barrels get reused many times for other spirits. Most wood for whiskey barrels lasts decades before it is destroyed, in contrast to so many other uses for wood.

But setting aside all the marketing, let's discuss the science. Replicating a chemical signature is not the ultimate test of a spirit. The true test would

MOLECULAR WHISKEYS

GLYPH 85H

A pleasing amount of spice, this is more like a spiced rum than a whiskey, but in that regard, it conjures a Christmas toddy. A balanced, even lovely spirit, but no one would confuse this for whiskey.

86pf	$40	C	SW	Independent

GLYPH SPICE

A more spice-forward dram, I think meant to evoke an American whiskey more than the flagship 85H, but it goes a little too far. Sacchariny fruity notes lie over a bed of heavy mulling spice that hammers hard for 43 proof. They were closer with the first one.

86pf	$40	C	SW	Independent

CLEVELAND BLACK RESERVE BOURBON

As rapid aging goes, this is perhaps the most credible in the landscape of American whiskey. It's not that far off from the oak profile of a decade-old bourbon. There is a bright corn tone that is quite nice, even with a slightly short finish. You could sneak this in a blind line up and fool some people (myself included), but why would you when it's priced about the same as legitimately aged Knob Creek?

100pf	$35	C	SW	Independent

LOST SPIRITS ABOMINATION

A pretty stunning heavily peated whiskey. The label says finished with Riesling-seasoned staves, though I'd be hard-pressed to pull those notes out. There's a sweetness that usually betrays impatience, but whether dessert wine or simply youth, it doesn't actually take away from the whiskey. This is a cool whiskey regardless (and because of) its rapid-aging backstory. It may become a collector's whiskey, as the distiller has pivoted to other focuses.

108pf	$50 (discontinued)	P	SW	Independent

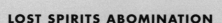

NON-ALCOHOLIC WHISKEYS

LYRE'S AMERICAN MALT

The thinnest of the non-alcoholic whiskeys I found. Honey and citrus notes over a warm malty layer. Maybe useful as an Irish whiskey alternative, but that's being a little generous to Lyre's (and perhaps unkind to Irish whiskey).

0pf	$30			Independent

RITUAL ZERO

Caramel and maple are strong here, without too much spice. It's definitely sweet, a kind of plummy, pomegranate note. A well-built, balanced drink, but maybe not much of a whiskey substitute.

	0pf	$35			Independent

KENTUCKY 74

The heft of bourbon and a lot of complex flavors, though also in the realm of a flat root beer. There's caramel, spice, ginger, and a strong cherry note that make for something I'd drink with seltzer.

0pf	$35			Independent

MONDAY ZERO ALCOHOL WHISKEY

The best of the non-alcoholic alternatives, but you'd still be forgiven for thinking this was a liquefied Yankee Candle. Here is a lot of caramel, a spicy peppery backbone, and a cola corn syrup note that isn't that far off from bourbon. For a bourbon alternative in cocktails, this is a good bet, but let's be clear—its similarity to bourbon is abstract and you'd be right to say it has very little in common with an aged whiskey.

0pf	$45			Independent

be showing that the average person can't discern the difference between a traditionally produced and a lab-synthesized spirit. To my knowledge, no producer has staked their chemical-signature product on a double-blind panel of average Joes, and no independent panel of judges has tried. Think of it as the "Turing Test" of whiskey. When is the artifice indistinguishable from the work of mother nature? By this measure, molecular whiskey hasn't been proven.

Is flavor even that important? It's an interesting thought experiment to suppose that a rapid ager could achieve a spirit that tasted identical to 21-year Kentucky bourbon or 30-year-old Scotch. Would anyone even want that? My experience as both a consumer and a distiller is that people like the truth of a fine old thing as much as they care about flavor. There are so many ways to get different flavors out of whiskey, but no other way than patience to get time into a whiskey—a fact that is well understood and appreciated by most drinkers as a fundamental factor in the pleasure of whiskey.

Glyph, as a whiskey, doesn't taste like Pappy Van Winkle or even a bourbon. Perhaps its closest analog is an oak-forward Irish whiskey. Which brings me back to Bryan Davis. Davis at least understands the consumer of spirits and offers a product and a story that meet the whiskey drinker where they are.

That's why Davis's positioning as a mad scientist and a fantasist suited his Los Angeles dream factory and works even better as Las Vegas performance art. He's selling alchemy and a narrative that upends a lot of received wisdom—all of which lands squarely but only when guided through his funhouse and concluding with his whiskeys, which are absolutely the evolution of that spatial and cognitive journey. Other purveyors seem to be putting a tech costume on old-fashioned flavor-house food science. But let's not call it something new, much less revolutionary.

XXX

Last and least, in terms of potency, I'm including a brief discussion of no-alcohol whiskey. Here is where the conundrum of replicating the flavor of fine old whiskey really comes up against a truly useful agenda: a no-alcohol beverage for someone who likes whiskey and wants the conviviality of alcohol but doesn't want to drink and doesn't want to fuss about it. To me, this is a legitimate challenge and a worthy one. For all the reasons to like alcohol, there are just as many reasons to avoid it but preserve the original intent: geniality, hospitality, open conversation, acclimation to a new circumstance, forging relationships. These are all worthy pursuits for human interaction that benefit from—but shouldn't require—alcohol. The social rituals are real, and there's a need for alcohol alternatives beyond the near beer that my dad drank for years.

While beer and even wine can be satisfactorily de-boozed, spiritous liquors pose a challenge. Perhaps the easiest spirit to get close to is gin, as it is the original flavored vodka, and juniper is an odd but familiar flavor that doesn't find much purpose in other food and beverage applications. Seedlip arrived and demonstrated the opportunity in the space, but hasn't attempted a whiskey alternative, perhaps knowing that meeting that challenge is especially daunting.

I'll mention four here that are ambitious and well-distributed. Lyre's American Malt is a nice, lighter-profile whiskey alternative. It's got vanilla and oaky notes that come close to the flavor but lack the punch of whiskey. Ritual Zero Proof has a little more heft but more berry fruit and sweetness that take it further from whiskey for me. Kentucky 74 has a little more oomph, dialing up the bitterness and cola notes for a more complex spirit. Monday's zero alcohol whiskey is the closest of the group, with a nice balance of sugar, spice, bitter, and fruit. It's also the one that tastes most like a Yankee Candle, but sometimes bourbon does too. At $40 a bottle, it's the most expensive but also the most complex.

I could see myself drinking this in our tasting room, as I'm often asked to host groups while needing to stay sober, and it's not worth an explanation of why I'm not joining in. But in practice, I would rather turn to a non-alcoholic beer. That may be a cop-out, but this is a concept that probably has a long trajectory of innovation and development ahead of it. Still, I have high hopes for the idea, even tinkered a little myself. But it's a very hard feat to pull off, I can say from experience.

THE MORNING AFTER

Having tasted through almost two hundred whiskeys and many more that didn't make the cut, what did we learn? While there are any number of critics, competitions, and tasting panels meant to offer consumer guidance, very few have focused on distillers over brands; few have placed large distillers on an even playing field with smaller distillers; and none have the ambition to consider the totality of whiskey at a time. The Reddtors, TikTokers, and Instagrammers create a lot of cacophony that is rarely objective or independent. So where did we land? Here is what I notice.

Some legacy players have let their guard down. Maker's Mark, once a benchmark, has aimed at a wider audience with a cheaper formulation and a lower price while resting on old laurels, hoping no one would notice. Knob Creek, from the same company, remains remarkably the same, despite packaging iterations and age statement changes. New distillers like Bardstown Bourbon Co. and Wilderness Trail have arrived to carve a new kind of premium whiskey that may have been ceded by the larger brands, who have put forward their own more expensive bottles in new packaging that rarely deliver better whiskeys. Craft players in Kentucky have brought more authenticity and truly small-batch production to an industry that had lost some of the credibility upon which it depended. Maverick distillers, first in Texas and then in the West and, yes, even the Northeast, are finding a toehold in a new landscape of American whiskey that is more diverse, more flavorful, and probably more like whiskey used to be before it became homogenous, corporate, and predictable.

As the bourbon market has shown its first indications of slowing down after years of growth and talk of a bubble preoccupies distillers and consumers alike, it's worth reflecting on this moment, fertile, full of promise and variety, but one that feels like it may be coming to an end. Worthy small distillers are closing and larger brands are retrenching. Whiskey is commerce, after all. The whiskey of today is changing constantly. New whiskeys arrive,bottles reformulate; flavor drifts; good whiskeys are discontinued. Anyone tasting through whiskeys of the past knows that change is the only constant, despite all the storytelling to the contrary.

I like a lot of whiskeys, and the multiplicity of this moment might be more important than any single favorites. I like to look at the whole landscape, how it changes over time, and how in a few years, today's reality will look different. So I think it's best to mark that we are drinking at a moment in time, one that will never be replicated, with beautiful whiskeys that will certainly be gone tomorrow. This is the aspect of whiskey I most appreciate, and the one that reminds me we have only today. Our best bottles should be vehicles for connection and conviviality, because tomorrow is another day, another set of circumstances, and everything changes. Today we have beautiful whiskeys to enjoy, to savor, to consecrate our joys and commiserate our sorrows. Tomorrow everything will be different, and then different again.

Harlan, Kentucky, is not far from the Wilderness Road that brought whiskey to Kentucky, but is more known for coal mining and union disputes than for whiskey, aged or illicit.

EPILOGUE

COMING HOME

After a long journey, there is no satisfaction like coming home. On a spring day late in the making of this book, I got a message from my sister that her best friend Laura had died of cancer at thirty-nine. It was not unexpected but disorienting and destabilizing. Suddenly, I was on my way home.

Since I had last been there, my hometown has gone "wet," meaning the city has voted to allow alcohol sales both in restaurants and at retail. My little-league teammate Leo Miller has opened the first liquor store in Harlan since Prohibition. Across town, a brewery has opened on the courthouse square, a culture shock for a city and county that had been bone dry for decades. Harlan is clearly joining the modern era. But the county has lost residents steadily over recent decades, and the town is far emptier than when I knew it. Despite that loss, the brewery was a lively place on a Friday night, and it was good to commune with old friends. The Louisville Orchestra happened to be in town, and Harlan seemed especially cosmopolitan compared to my memory.

The following day, I traveled over the mountain into Virginia. Laura's family lives along the Clinch River in an ancient farmhouse surrounded by chickens, dogs, and cats (and any number of wilder creatures up the hillside). After I moved away, the Harris farm ended up being a gathering place for my family. We'd lost our home as my parents split up and everyone spread out throughout the country. The farmhouse, a two-story, stripped-down colonial house overlooking a modest green valley, is a postcard from the American imagination, and it came to symbolize home to me, making the present loss even more devastating. We spent many Thanksgivings and Christmases in the house, markers of time through my early adulthood. Laura's parents are both great cooks, which made those visits even more memorable.

I hadn't been back since 2016, right after my dad died. And I remembered the same displaced feeling of being home, a home that was slipping away or maybe even wasn't really mine to begin with, but one that I craved so much that I set about starting my own family shortly after that visit, making this return especially bittersweet.

The adage "Home is where the heart is" actually has it backwards. The heart has no volition in the matter. A true home pulls on the heart until it knows no other. Homes are incubators of hearts, and over time the repetition of loving builds into a sense of home. Laura's family are all fierce-hearted, a quality not genetic in my family, but one I nonetheless recognize is the best of all traits. Home, as a place, is a complicated and consequential thing.

Reckoning with home, remembering good memories grown vague through the compounding of time, is a way of understanding how I got into whiskey in the first place. Whiskey reminds me of an abstract but very real pull—a yearning for a place, a memory, a feeling of being surrounded by warm hearts and good food, and a comfort from another time. Being here, along the ancient Wilderness Road into the interior of the nation and the birthplace of country music, is to be near a nerve close to the heart of a mythic America, somewhere both universal and highly personal at the same time. Here is where early distillers crafted corn liquor in hollow log stills, forging the early whiskey that would evolve into bourbon, more American than apple pie, more comfort than a hand-sewn patchwork quilt.

If whiskey does this for anyone else, I hope it is a great blessing. Sharing my whiskey is like an invitation into my home, and so many others on this journey through whiskey have shared their whiskeys, their distilleries, and sometimes their homes with me. Drinking is best as a shared experience, made even richer when communing with someone who knows the drink better than anyone else.

ACKNOWLEDGMENTS

I'm indebted to the distillers in the pages of this book. Not just the distillers, but also the blenders and warehouse workers, tasting-room hosts, the salespeople, the brand ambassadors, and all the people who contribute to the ecosystem of a distillery. Drinking whiskey with anyone is an intimate experience, not to be taken lightly or for granted, but a glass with a fellow distiller is an especially sublime experience. And my gratitude to the makers in these pages knows no bounds.

There are too many to name, but let me mention the following people who helped this book into existence: Rob Arnold, Steve Beam, Dan Beimborn, Darek Bell, Alan Bishop, John "J.B." Brittle, Brett Carlile, Chuck Cowdery, Brendan Coyle, Bryan Davis, Marianne Eaves, Ralph and Gable Erenzo, Dan Garrison, Heather Greene, Dr. Pat Heist, Wes Henderson, Jared Himstedt, Paul Hletko, Eric Jett, Kirby Kallas-Lewis, Marko Karakasevic, Allen Katz, Tom Koerner, Max Kristula-Green, Drew Kulsveen, James Kunz, Alan Laws, Todd Leopold, Jason Levinson, Timothy Luscher, David Meier, Meagan and Patrick Miller, Fred Minnick, Reid Mitenbuler, Chris Montana, Sherrie Moore, Royce Neeley, Ale Ochoa, Stephen Paul, Ty Phelps, Tom Potter, Noah Rothbaum, Jimmy Russell, Daric Schlesselman, Dave Schmier, Michael Sebastien, Dave Smith, Chip Tate, Molly Troupe, Thad Vogler, Fawn Weaver, Christopher Briar Williams, Jamie Windon, Lance Winters, Erik Wolfe, and David Wondrich.

A special thanks to those currently or formerly at Kings County Distillery, whose perspective on whiskey helped inform mine and to whom I am indebted—in particular those who helped in some way on this book: Nicole Austin, Jen Blair, Ryan Ciuchta, Brandon Collins, Grace Dunn, Gaby Eisenman, Chris Elford, Devin Ershow, Cary Ann Fuller, David Haskell, Jess Kantor-Kowal, Mike Lockwood, Andrew Lohfeld, David Nichols, Sebastian Oja, and Nathan Reinke.

To those I didn't specifically name but whose evangelism helps support the whiskey in these pages, thank you. Their labor is our great enjoyment, and if you ever get the chance to say thank you in person, which I hope you do, please send them my regards.